DEEP SECRETS

DEEP SECRETS

BOYS' FRIENDSHIPS

AND THE CRISIS OF CONNECTION

Niobe Way

HARVARD UNIVERSITY PRESS
Cambridge, Massachusetts, and London, England
2011

Library of Congress Cataloging-in-Publication Data

Way, Niobe
  Deep secrets : boys' friendships and the crisis of connection / Niobe Way.
      p. cm.
  Includes bibliographical references and index.
  ISBN 978-0-674-04664-1 (alk. paper)
   1. Male friendship. 2. Emotions in adolescence. 3. Emotions in children.
I. Title.
  BF575.F66W39 2011
  155.5'32—dc22   2010047702

To Raphael, Justin, and Lucan

my home boys

What we think about ourselves and our possibilities
determines what we aspire to become.

 —Robert Frank, American economist

CONTENTS

1. The Hidden Landscape of Boys' Friendships   1
2. Investigating Boys, Friendships, and Human Nature   37

Part I: Friendships during Early and Middle Adolescence
3. "Sometimes You Need to Spill Your Heart Out to Somebody"   91
4. Boys with Feelings   117
5. Nick and George   143

Part II: Friendships during Late Adolescence
6. "When You Grow Up, Your Heart Dies"   183
7. As Boys Become Men   209
8. Fernando and Danny   229
9. The Crisis of Connection   262

Notes 283   Acknowledgments 315   Index 319

THE HIDDEN LANDSCAPE
OF BOYS' FRIENDSHIPS

It is the middle of June and the New York City heat is on full blast, making it even hotter in the empty high school classroom where 15-year-old Justin[1] and his interviewer José sit in the late afternoon. Justin, whose mother is Puerto Rican and whose father is Irish and Italian American, is being interviewed for my school-based research project on boys' social and emotional development. There is neither an air conditioner nor a fan in the classroom, so Justin, in his baggy jeans and t-shirt, pulls out a notebook from his backpack and starts to fan himself as he listens to José begin the interview protocol. This meeting is the second of four annual interviews. The first set of questions is about Justin's friends in general. He responds by discussing his network of peers in school. Turning to the topic of close friendships, he says:

> [My best friend and I] love each other . . . that's it . . . you have this thing that is deep, so deep, it's within you, you can't explain it. It's just a thing that you know that that person is that person . . . and that is all that should be important in our friendship . . . I guess in life, sometimes two people can really, really understand each other and really have a trust, respect, and love for each other. It just happens, it's human nature.

Listening to boys, particularly those in early and middle adolescence, speak about their male friendships is like reading an old-fashioned romance novel in which the female protagonist is describing her passionate feelings for her man. At the edge of manhood, when pressures to conform to gender expectations intensify,[2] boys speak about their male friends with abandon, referring to them as people whom they love and to their feelings as, to put it in Justin's words, "this thing that is deep, so deep, it's within you, you can't explain it." They talk in great detail and with tremendous affect about their best friends, with whom they share their deepest secrets and without whom they would, according to 15-year-old Malcolm, "feel lost."

Boys also underscore how important the sharing of thoughts and feelings are in these friendships for their psychological well-being. George at 16 years old says that close friends are important because, "I mean, if you just have your mother and your parents [to talk to], then you're just gonna have all these ideas bottled up and you're just gonna go wacko because you can't express yourself even more." Chen at 15 years old says that he needs a close friend so "you have someone to talk to, like you have problems with something, you go talk to him. You know, if you keep it all the stuff to yourself, you go crazy. Try to take it out on someone else." Kai says bluntly at the age of 14: "you need a friend or else, you would be depressed, you won't be happy, you would try to kill yourself, 'cause then you'll be all alone and no one to talk to."

Set against a culture that perceives boys and men to be activity oriented, emotionally illiterate, and interested only in independence, these responses seem shocking. The image of the lone cowboy, the cultural icon of masculinity and the symbol of independence and thus of maturity in the West, suggests that what boys want and need most are opportunities for competition and autonomy. Yet the vast majority of the hundreds of boys whom my research team and I have interviewed from early to late adolescence suggest that their closest friendships share the plot of

Love Story more than the plot of *Lord of the Flies*. Boys valued their male friendships greatly and saw them as essential components to their health, not because their friends were worthy opponents in the competition for manhood but because they were able to share their thoughts and feelings—their deepest secrets—with these friends.

F. G. Bonser, a psychologist working at the beginning of the twentieth century, called intimate friendships "the most potent in the development of man as a member of society."[3] William Bukowski, a developmental psychologist working at the end of the twentieth century, refers to close friendships as the "most enduring form of relationship across the life span."[4] Yet looking at the vast quantity of articles and books on boys, adolescence, and human development, one rarely sees a discussion of these intimate relationships. Reflecting a culture that values romantic relationships more than friendships and in which only females are thought to desire intimate friendships and have feelings more generally, the current scholarship on boys, friendships, and adolescence misses a major theme. Scholars pay almost no attention to what Justin describes with such love and affection and what has been considered critical for healthy development for over a century: emotionally intimate male friendships.

When male friendships are discussed in scholarly or popular literature, they are often relegated to the superficial category of "buddies" and described as "loose collections that offer very little sharing or emotional support."[5] Male friends are framed as back-slapping pals more interested in playing, competing, and boasting about various types of conquests than in talking together or sharing the details of their inner lives. These relationships are, in essence, defined by their simplicity rather than by their complexity, emotional nuance, and depth. In our twenty-first-century American culture, in which vulnerable emotions and same-sex intimacy are perceived as girlish and gay[6], heterosexual boys are described as uninterested in having intimate male friendships, and the stereotype that boys are "only interested in one thing" is perpetuated.

When I began writing this book, friends and colleagues remarked, somewhat smugly, that it would be a short book as there is not much to say when it comes to boys' friendships. While some were willing to admit that friendships such as Justin's are possible, and most remembered having had them when they were younger, they thought they were rare among teenage boys, who—they were quick to point out—mostly have sex or sports on the brain. Kenneth Rubin a developmental psychologist who studies children's friendships, writes:

> Girls' interactions satisfy social or communal needs or focus on achieving closeness and connection through the sharing of thoughts, emotions, and understanding. Girls, in other words, like to talk about their happy times, and their miseries about the people they know and their feelings about them. . . . Boys' interactions conversely serve to promote and solidify individualist or agentic needs for action, control, excitement, personal achievement or one-upmanship and so on. Boys tend to come together in competitive hierarchies, each determined through participating in activities that challenge the individual to prove his mettle in comparison to his peers.[7]

He adds that teenage boys, in particular, may find it easier to be on intimate terms with their parents than with their closest buddy given the lack of comfort most boys feel when it comes to intimacy.[8] The gender stereotypes that he reiterates run deep in American culture. Clinical psychologist William Pollack describes the "mask of masculinity" that boys wear that reinforces a code of conduct he calls the "boy code"—a code that equates being emotionally stoic, invulnerable, physically tough, and independent with being male. If boys and young men do not follow this "boy code," according to Pollack, they are at best picked on and at worst tortured.[9] We have seen evidence of the harmful consequences of this boy code in the recent spate of suicides of boys and young men who were harassed by their peers for acting "gay" or "girlish." Addressing an older group of adolescent boys, sociologist Michael Kimmel notes in *Guyland* that young men between the ages of 16 and 26 adhere to the same "boy code" but he calls it a "guy code." "The Guy Code, and the Boy Code, before it, demands that boys and young men shut down emotionally, that they suppress compassion and inflate ambition. And it extracts compliance with coercion and fear."[10] These scholars argue, in essence, that boys are socialized from a very young age to be emotionally stoic, aggressive, and seemingly invulnerable and that "as a result, boys feel effeminate not only if they express emotions, but even if they feel them."[11] Our "hyper" masculine American culture—a culture in which heterosexual men do not hold hands and boys do not share beds unless they are from the same family—frames boys and men as unable to have and thus as uninterested in having intimate male friendships.

Even the fundamental capacity for males to have rich and emotionally satisfying lives is questioned by scholars. Psychologist Stephen Frosh summarizes this view: "Boys (and men) are [perceived as] emotionally inarticulate, lacking the capacity to 'name' and therefore even to experience feelings and emotions, and particularly to engage in sustained and reflective conversation about their feelings for and relationships with others."[12] In their best-selling book *Raising Cain*, the authors conclude:

> The majority of boys are not prepared to manage the complexities of a loving relationship because they've been shortchanged on the basic skills of emotional literacy: empathy, conscience, the vocabulary for meaningful emotional expression, and the idea that emotional interdependence is an asset—not a liability.[13]

The extent to which these "emotionally illiterate" assumptions about boys (and men) characterize the social science literature is evident in the fact that while friendships have been the topic of research for over a century, only a handful of studies have focused on boys' close friendships in particular.

While these representations of boys are considered true for all boys, ethnic minority and poor and working class boys, particularly those who are Black and Latino, are assumed to be even less likely than their White peers to have emotionally expressive male friendships, given their supposed "culture"[14] of aggression and violence. Such boys are stereotyped as being "hyper" masculine[15] and thus unlikely to have friendships that entail much vulnerability. Images of rappers like 50 Cent and Lil' Wayne are emblematic of this stereotype. The only ethnic minority or poor and working class boys who are exempt from these stereotypes are Asian boys. Yet these boys have to contend with an entirely different set of damaging stereotypes that feminize their bodies and their academic achievements. David Eng, an English professor, writes about the psychologically debilitating effect of the feminization of Asian men[16]—a stereotype that is so pervasive and insidious that a popularized image of a Chinese kung fu hero is a rotund and soft panda bear. One could not imagine the use of such an image of a White, Black, or Latino kung fu hero. In a context where being Asian means being perceived as inherently more female and, as a recent men's magazine article suggested, gay, Asian boys struggle to assert their masculinity and, for those who are straight, their heterosexuality.[17] Ironically, however, this feminization does not grant Asian males the emotional latitude of females. Asian males, as with their non-Asian peers, are also stereotyped as unemotional and inexpressive.[18] While some scholars attribute this emotional stoicism to "Asian culture," others see it as a combination of both ethnic and gender norms and assume implicitly that Asian boys are just as emotionally illiterate as their Black, Latino, and White working, middle, and upper class peers, but for different reasons.

The odd refusal in scholarship or in popular culture to recognize the social and emotional skills of boys and their intimate friendships more generally is underscored when we look outside of the modern, American landscape. Honeymoons in the nineteenth century involved bringing best friends and family along for the trip.[19] Anthropologist Peter Nardi, who has conducted research on friendships among non-American men, concludes: "when examining men's friendships from the perspective of other cultures, it is the American style that seems strange. . . . In short, contemporary American mainstream masculinity is rather unique in its suppression of displays of affection and of close and intimate friendships between adult men."[20] He notes the extent to which male friendships are formalized in many countries and provides the example of southern Ghana, where same-sex best friends go through a marriage ceremony similar to that performed for husbands and wives. In Cameroon, adults pressure their children to find a best friend, much in the same way that American parents pressure their adult children to find a romantic partner.[21] In China, at least until the late 1990s, and in other Eastern and Middle Eastern countries, heterosexual men, especially those from rural areas, hold hands with their friends and regularly rely on them for emotional support. The Lakotas, a Native American tribe, have a long tradition of emotionally intimate friendships; "the emphasis for Indian men was a close emotional bond."[22] The assumption behind these practices is that a best friend is more important for one's emotional well-being than even one's spouse, as it is with a best friend that one can be most vulnerable.[23] It is only in modern America and in countries that are heavily influenced by American culture that boys' emotional and social skills and their intimate same-sex friendships are ignored or dismissed as female, childlike, or gay.

Yet for over 20 years, my studies of the social and emotional development of boys have shown us that boys are both having and wanting intimate male friendships. When Kevin is asked what he likes about his close friends, he says: "The energy. The energy. There is so much love between all of us. All my friends just love each other so much." While scholars such as William Pollack and Michael Kimmel accurately portray the gender straitjackets that boys face, they overlook the ways in which boys regularly challenge or resist these straitjackets, particularly in the context of their close male friendships. This omission prevents us, as I will argue throughout the book, from understanding boys more fully and thus effectively addressing their needs. Teenage boys, particularly during early and middle adolescence—feeling the hormonal changes in their own bodies and thus their own physical vulnerability—speak about their male friendships with such passion that colleagues have inquired, "How did you get the boys to speak like that?" My research team and I did not "get them" to speak like that. We simply asked them about their friendships and this is what they told us.

Over a century of social science research, including our own,[24] has underscored the significance of friendships for all aspects of well-being. Close friendships provide a sense of self-worth, validation, and connectedness to the larger world and significantly enhance psychological, physical, and academic well-being.[25] Adolescents without close friendships are at risk of depression, suicide, dropping out, disengagement from school, early pregnancy, drug use, and gang membership.[26] Research has even suggested that the effects of the quality of friendships on psychological adjustment may be stronger for boys than for girls.[27] Psychologist Cynthia Erdley and her colleagues find that the association between loneliness and friendship quality—levels of intimacy, companionship, validation, and guidance—is only significant for boys.[28] While not finding gender differences, my studies in the United States and in China indicate that emotional support from close friends during adolescence is more predictive of psychological and academic adjustment than support from parents.[29] Furthermore, boys who report high levels of intimacy and support in their friendships are more likely to indicate that they are academically engaged (i.e., do their homework) than those who report low levels of support.[30]

In an experimental design, social psychologists at the University of Virginia found that perceptions of task difficulty were deeply shaped by the proximity of a friend.[31] The researchers

asked college students to stand at the base of a hill while carry-
ing a weighted backpack and estimate the steepness of the hill.
Some participants stood next to close friends whom they had
known a long time, some stood next to friends they had not
known for long, some stood next to strangers, and the others
stood alone during the exercise. The participants who stood with
close friends gave significantly lower estimates of the steepness
of the hill than those who stood alone, next to strangers, or to
newly formed friends. The longer the close friends had known
each other, the less steep the hill appeared to the participants involved in the study. In other words, the world was perceived as
less difficult when standing next to a close friend than when
standing next to someone who was less close or no one at all.

Among adult men and women, research also indicates that
those who have close friendships or strong social support networks are less prone to depression and more likely to thrive in all
areas of their lives than their more isolated peers. Having friendships among adults has been found to be more predictive of psychological and physical health than having spouses or extended
family members.[32] In a six-year study of 736 middle-aged men,
attachment to a single person did not appear to lower the risk of
heart attack and fatal coronary heart disease, whereas having
close friendships did.[33] Smoking was the only risk factor com-
parable in strength to lack of friendship support. Health researchers find that people with strong friendships are less likely
than others to get colds and other common illnesses, which they
hypothesize may be due to having lower stress levels, and that
people with fewer friends are at higher risk of death.[34]

In their book *The Spirit Level*, epidemiologist Richard Wilkinson and Kate Pickett conclude that the two most important factors that determine the health and well-being of people living in
developed nations are social status and friendships: "a lack of
friends and low social status are among the most important
sources of chronic stress affecting the health of populations in
rich countries today."[35] Along with other social scientists, they

emphasize that the quality of social relations, including the extent of trust within a community, can mean the difference between life and death. In his book on the heat wave in Chicago in 1995 that killed approximately 700 people, Eric Klinenberg, a sociologist, reported that those who were most at risk for death were those in neighborhoods with weak social networks and much evidence of distrust (e.g., not opening the window or going outside during the heat wave despite the lack of air conditioning). Those from the most socially connected neighborhoods, in contrast, and those individuals who had strong social networks, regardless of their social class or age, were most likely to survive.[36] A *New York Times* reporter summarizing the research on the links between health and friendships concludes: "friendships are an undervalued resource. The consistent message from the research is that friends make your life better."[37] And, as we see from Klinenberg's research, they also save lives.

My research has revealed not only the significance of friendships but also that a study of friendship is more than simply a study of friendship. Listening to boys speak about their friendships throughout adolescence provides a window into the ways boys both receive and respond to their cultural context. Their interviews suggest that socialization is not only a passive process by which children accommodate or adhere to the conventions, expectations, stereotypes, and constraints of their micro (e.g., family) and macro (e.g., American) cultures. They also actively participate, resist, and challenge those cultures.[38] While boys may accommodate, for example, to conventions of emotional stoicism and autonomy in their peer relations, they may also resist these conventions by having emotionally intimate male friendships. Boys' interviews about their close friendships reveal the agentic nature of human development and the limitations of listening with only one ear.[39]

My studies, furthermore, reveal a disconnection between the cultural construction of boyhood and boys' lived experiences. The general lack of interest in the scholarly and popular culture regarding the dynamics of close friendships among males combined with boys' passion for these relationships, their emotional acuity, and the significance they give them suggests that our expectations and stereotypes of boys are preventing us from seeing boys—their social and emotional desires and capacities—in broad daylight. The consequence of such disconnection and blindness is evident in the statistics suggesting a "boy crisis"[40] as well as the rising rates of suicide among middle-aged people.[41] Boys' problems, at the very root, are not related to their biology or psychology but to a culture that refuses to see boys (and men, girls, and women) as more than a set of gender and, in the case of boys of color, racial stereotypes. Given the nature of these stereotypes, the very social and emotional skills that are necessary for boys to thrive[42] are not fostered.

MY FRIENDSHIP STUDIES

I began to recognize the importance for boys of their close friendships as a high school counselor in the late 1980s. While I expected to hear stories about girls, peers, school, and parents, I did not anticipate the extent to which boys wanted to talk about their close male friendships in particular. Boys did indeed talk about what I expected, but they also spent a great deal of time talking about who betrayed whom, who was a new close friend, who could and could not be trusted with their "deep secrets." I took these unexpected "findings" into my research and began, as a developmental psychologist, to explore boys' experience of friendships and how these friendships changed from early to late adolescence. My research, which has taken place over the past 20 years, has suggested two overarching sets of themes. The first set indicates that boys, especially during early and middle adolescence, have or want emotionally intimate male friendships that entail shared secrets and feelings. These shared secrets and feelings are, furthermore, the primary reason why they consider their friendships close and what they enjoy most about their male friendships. Included in this first set is the pattern that boys explicitly link "talking" and the "sharing of secrets" in these relationships to their mental health, claiming that they would go "wacko" without having "someone to talk to." The second set of themes is that as these boys become men, they grow more fearful of betrayal by and distrustful of their male peers and less willing to have emotionally intimate male friendships. They also begin to speak increasingly of feeling lonely and depressed. While they continue to desire intimate friendships, they feel they can no longer "find" the type of trustworthy, close friend they had when they were younger. As will become evident throughout the book, these themes were not heard from a small group of boys within my studies; they were heard by at least three-fourths of the boys (depending on the study) we interviewed from early to late adolescence. Black, Latino, Asian American, and White boys spoke about having and wanting intimate male friendships and then gradually losing these relationships and their trust in their male peers. The consequences of this loss, as the boys reveal, are dramatic.

Secrets and Vulnerability

When asked what he likes most about his friendship, Mark says in his freshman year: "[My best friend] could just tell me anything and I could tell him anything. Like I always know everything about him. We always chill, like we don't hide secrets from each other. We tell each other our problems." Albert, in his junior year, says to his interviewer, "I would like a friend that if I got anything to say to him or like any problems or anything, I'll tell him and he'll tell me his problems." Boys' stories of intimate male friendships were not revealed exclusively by those who were isolated in school, but also came from popular boys who looked cool in their stylishly hip-hop, low-riding pants and baseball caps or hoods drawn low over their brows. Boys who have been portrayed as more interested in engaging in sports and, in the case of urban teens, with killing each other than in sharing their thoughts and feelings and having intimate friendships, spoke about "deep depth" friendships that "you would feel lost without."

Felix says in his sophomore year when asked what he likes about his best friend:

> Regardless of what happens, he will be there. There is nothing we don't do or say, there is nothing I can do or say that would make us less close than we are . . . yes, he is the only person that I know that I am never going to NOT have a relationship with, understand? Yes, it's not going to ever change between us . . . we love each other, we agree how we feel. If we don't like it we are going to change it right now . . . I will always catch myself thinking about the level me and him are on. It always seems to escalate.

Benjamin also makes explicit his sense of vulnerability in explaining what he likes about his best friend: "Mmmm, most everything. His kindness. Everything. I know, I know he, you know, he cares for people, ME, you know." William, a sophomore, says that he trusts his friends because "I know none of my friends would do anything to hurt me. . . . These are people I could depend on or call my friends because we've been through thick and thin together. We've had arguments, we are still friends." The boys in my studies repeatedly express their vulnerabilities and their firm beliefs that their closest male friends will care for them in the deepest of ways.

I am not the only scholar to note such patterns of male intimacy. In a survey study of friendships of 2,035 teenagers (756 boys) conducted in 1904, researchers concluded that intimate, "secret sharing" friendships are common among both boys and girls. G. Stanley Hall, the psychologist who coined the concept of adolescence in the late nineteenth century, said that during early adolescence "confidences are shared with those of equal age and withheld from parents, *especially by boys,* to an extent probably little suspected by parents."[43] Harry Stack Sullivan, an

American psychiatrist who focused exclusively on boys' development, wrote during the middle of the twentieth century:

> The beginning of preadolescence is . . . spectacularly marked, in my
> scheme of development, by the appearance of a new type of interest
> in another person. . . . it is a specific new type of interest in a partic-
> ular member of the same sex who becomes a chum or a close friend.
> This change represents the beginning of something very like full-
> blown, psychiatrically defined love. In other words, the other fellow
> takes on a perfectly novel relationship with the person concerned: he
> becomes of practically equal importance in all fields of value. Noth-
> ing remotely like that has ever appeared before.[44]

Sullivan wrote extensively about the importance of "chumships"
for developing a sense of self-worth, for interpersonal understanding, and for future romantic relationships. He emphasized
both the prevalence of these relationships and their significance
for boys' future well-being.

Other scholars have also noted the extent to which boys speak
in emotionally vulnerable ways with their peers and have close
friendships that entail much talk and self-disclosure.[45] In a book
about masculinities and British adolescent boys, psychologist
Stephen Frosh states in a footnote that it was remarkable the extent to which the boys in his studies spoke on the phone with
each other, often in conversations that lasted for hours.[46] Although he does not give such behavior much weight in his book,
it clearly contradicts the stereotype that "boys don't talk." While
clinical psychologist William Pollack devotes minimal attention
to boys' friendships in his best-selling books on boys, he offers
evidence of the type of intimacy that the boys in my studies describe. The mostly suburban middle and upper class White boys
in his books discuss "needing" someone to talk to, relying on
their friends to share their secrets, "expressing" their feelings
with their closest friends, and telling each other "everything."
Pierre, a 17-year-old boy from a suburb in the Northwest, says

about his best friends: "Eric and I communicate really well. And I have another close friend, Kurt, who I went to elementary school with. I can really, really, feel open with him. We know each other's lives very intimately just because we have known each other since we were in kindergarten, and we can really talk freely and openly."[47] James, a 16-year-old suburban teenager, says, "Always make sure there's someone in your life you can fall back on, so in hard times, you'll have a shoulder to cry on, and have as many friends as you possibly can." Graham, a 17-year-old suburban teenager, says:

> If I'm I'm [sic] ever really upset I talk to my best friend Colin. It's so important to have a best friend. One of my good friends doesn't have one and just shuts down if you ask him how things are going with his girlfriend. . . . Just last week, one of my friends [who is on the football team] came up to me and was so upset about something that he started crying. . . . He's very upset. I just tried to be a good listener.[48]

Expressing the same level of emotional sensitivity that the boys in my studies did, Pierre, James, and Graham suggest that boys from a wide range of racial and socioeconomic backgrounds experience friendships in similar ways.

Like Pollack, journalist Malina Saval in her book *The Secret Lives of Boys* does not focus on friendships in particular. However, her case studies of boys from across the United States reveal the importance of these relationships in boys' lives. For example, Preston, a White boy from a wealthy family from a Northeastern city, speaks about the close friendship he has with an older teenage boy who has been hired by Preston's family to serve as his "big brother." After spending time together on numerous family trips, their relationship blossoms into a meaningful friendship for both boys. Preston refers to his "best friend" as someone with whom he can share everything, including "deeper stuff."[49] Clinical psychologist Michael Thompson and his colleagues indicate that sharing secrets forms a core part of close friendships—even among boys.[50] Reflecting a culture that does not believe that boys are emotionally articulate, Thompson expresses surprise, in a parenthetical sentence, at boys' conversations about friends: "I am always pleasantly surprised when boys, who often have a tough time articulating their inner lives, are suddenly eloquent when describing the emotional qualities of their friendships."[51] The fact that clinicians and journalists have noted the intimacy in and the emotional quality of boys' descriptions of their friendships as well as the friendships themselves but continue to diminish or ignore their significance speaks to the extent to which we are stuck in a set of gender stereotypes. We simply don't believe that boys, especially during adolescence, could be having emotionally intimate male friendships.

Researchers have also found that boys are as acutely attuned as girls to the emotional complexities in their friendships; have equivalent levels of intimate knowledge about their best friends; are as likely to share each other's emotional state when with their friends; and are exceptionally articulate about their emotional lives with their male friends.[52] Psychologist Margarita Azmitia and her students find in their studies of adolescents that boys are as likely as girls to self-disclose in their friendships; define intimacy in same-sex friendships similarly; and are equally likely to have such friendships at some point during adolescence.[53] Yet boys continue to be portrayed in books, articles, and popular culture as uninterested in having or unable to have the types of intimate friendships that are so typical among girls.

Time and again when I tell parents of teenage boys what I have learned from my own research as well as others, they talk about their sons who have (or have had) a close male friend on whom they rely for emotional support. They often comment, with some amusement and surprise, on the frequency of their sons' phone or computer contact with their best friend "even though they just spent the entire school day together." One parent recalled finding a letter written by her 11-year-old son to his best friend expressing love for him "that even words could not express." Although by the age of 18 her son had become emotionally hardened and no longer claimed to have a male best friend, at the tender age of 11 he had spoken with unmitigated affection about his feelings for his best friend. Teachers of adolescent boys also testify to the importance of close friendships for their male and female students and observe that boys are often more consumed with the tensions within their friendships than with their schoolwork or even with their girlfriends or parents. After hearing a professional presentation at a conference on boys' development and the masculine stance that boys take with their peers, a teacher at a private middle school told me that the boys in her school did not fit this description: "My boys are all over each other, they hang on each other and they openly express feelings of love and affection for each other." After examining the clinical and empirical research literature and after listening to parents, teachers, and the boys in my studies for close to two decades, the question arises of how many of the boys do, in fact, fit the gender stereotypic description, at least when it comes to their close male friendships.

One of my sharpest memories of my youngest brother is of an occasion when he was 15; he was sitting in the backyard of my parents' house (while I was listening through the window) earnestly discussing with his two close friends from the junior varsity basketball team why what one of them had said had hurt the other boy's feelings. For almost an hour, this group of three boys—two of whom had girlfriends—sat in the sun together to process their feelings of vulnerability and hurt. My brother attempted to play the moderator between the other two, and they eventually came to a resolution, but not until all three boys had expressed their feelings about what had occurred. These moments, according to my brother 14 years later, were common among his male friends during the early years of high school.

Once I became attuned to the possibility of intimacy between boys, I began to hear it everywhere. Driving home from a soccer game in Boston, one of my best friends hears her 14-year-old son and his best friend, Paul, talking in the back seat of the car. She doesn't hear the entire conversation, but she does hear the best friend, with whom her son speaks daily on the phone or on the Internet, say in a soft but assertive voice, "we don't talk anymore." When she asks her son later what they were talking about, he claims that his best friend was "getting hormonal" on him, implicitly feminizing his friend's statement and dismissing the importance of the conversation. When boys are asked by their mothers to be explicit about the intimacy in their friendships, they are likely to downplay it for fear that it will be perceived as abnormal. While her son's response to her question reveals the attitudes of the culture, Paul's remark to my best friend's son indicates that they had a friendship in which "talk" and sharing secrets were core components.

And then, just as Paul notes, something happens as boys enter late adolescence . . .

Loss, Distrust, and Desire

As boys enter middle to late adolescence, they do, in fact, begin to talk less. Starting at around the age of 15 or 16, they begin to sound like gender stereotypes. They start using phrases such as "no homo" immediately following any intimate disclosure about their friends, and they tell us that they don't have time for their male friends, even though their desire for these relationships remains. They also start to dismiss the significance of the loss. Right at the moment in development when the suicide rate among boys in the United States increases to four times the rate of girls (versus two times the rate of girls in early adolescence), boys become less emotionally articulate, speak about losing their closest male friends, and become increasingly distrustful of their male peers. Rather than simply "advancing" during late adolescence, as most of the developmental psychology textbooks teach us, teenage boys also experience a dramatic loss that appears to have long-term consequences.

When Justin, as a senior, is asked how his friendships have changed since he was a freshman, he says:

> I don't know, maybe, not a lot, but I guess that best friends become close friends. So that's basically the only thing that changed. It's like best friends become close friends, close friends become general friends and then general friends become acquaintances. So they just . . . If there's distance whether it's, I don't know, natural or whatever. You can say that but it just happens that way.

Naturalizing something that is not natural, and which Justin knows is not natural, as evidenced by his response during his sophomore year that intimate friendships are a part of "human nature," Justin explains the loss that so many of the boys in my studies have described.

Jason had a close male friend in his freshman year with whom he shared all his secrets and believed friendships were important because "(then) you are not lonely . . . you need someone to turn to when things are bad." Three years later, when asked if he has any close friends, he says no and immediately adds that while he has nothing against gay people, he himself is not gay. Other late adolescent boys responded similarly. As boys become men, having close male friendships becomes linked to sexuality. Boys who had had close friendships in early adolescence claimed not to be "gay" when asked the same questions about friendships during late adolescence. Jason, however, adds at the end of the interview that he "wouldn't mind" having a close male friendship like the one he had when he was younger.

Joseph says in his freshman and sophomore years that he has been close to his best friend for 10 years. The following year, he no longer has a best friend because "you can't trust nobody these days." When the interviewer asks why he feels this way, he tells him that he has experienced a series of betrayals over the past year. Experiences of betrayal did not register lightly for the boys in my studies. Already discouraged by mainstream American culture from having intimate male friendships, boys become particularly reluctant when they experience betrayal.

Guillermo, who sounds similar to Joseph if a bit less angry, says in his junior year:

> [I: Do you have a close or best friend this year?] Not really. I think myself. The friend I had, I lost it . . . That was the only person that I could trust and we talked about everything. When I was down, he used to help me feel better. The same I did to him. So I feel pretty lonely and sometimes depressed . . . because I don't have no one to go out with, no one to speak on the phone, no one to tell my secrets, no one for me to solve my problems. [I: Why don't you think you have someone?] Because I think that it will never be the same, you know, I think that when you have a real friend and you lost it, I don't think you find another one like him. That's the point of view I have . . . I tried to look for a person, you know, but it's not that easy.

Guillermo discusses the loss of his close male friends but remains emotionally attuned. The content of boys' stories indicated a loss, but the form of their stories—or the language itself—often suggested that the boys remain skilled at mapping the relational world.

Victor says in his junior year that he doesn't have a best friend this year but he would like one:

> I wouldn't say . . . I don't say I would 'cause I feel that a friend is going to be there for you and they'll support you and stuff like that. Whether they're good or bad times, you can share with them, you would share your feelings with them, your true feelings . . . that's why I don't think I have any real close friends. I mean, things can travel around in a school and things would go around, and the story would change from person to person. Yeah, basically I hate it, I hate it, 'cause you know I wouldn't mind talking to somebody my age that I can relate to 'em on a different basis.

Like Guillermo, Victor longs to find the type of intimate male friend he had earlier, but fears of betrayal prevent him from continuing to pursue the possibility.

Occasionally boys did not directly express their yearning for intimate male friendships, but the tone of their voices suggested that they felt poorly about the loss of their formerly close friendships. Eric speaks extensively in his junior year about his losses since middle school. In middle school, he claims, he had a "crew of boys" with whom he used to spend all of his time. "It was like the four of us in eighth grade. We hung out all the time. It would be the four of us all the time. . . . I don't see them anymore. I don't even talk to them anymore." When asked why he doesn't see them, Eric says in a very quiet voice, as if to suggest that he doesn't quite believe what he is about to say, that they transferred to different schools and the boys who remain in his school live too far away for him to see them. When asked about having a best friend, he says, "No, I don't have any best friends. I was best friends with Keith last year. We don't even talk anymore. . . . I don't care." Like the little boy Pierre in Maurice Sendak's story of the boy who didn't care, boys who claimed not to care during late adolescence suggested that they cared deeply. While boys occasionally gave explicit reasons for such losses such as a change of classrooms, schools, or even neighborhoods, the fact that the losses occurred right at the age when the suicide rate among boys increases so dramatically, suggests that there is another story going on.

The "other" story seems to be in part explained by the boys who explicitly linked their losses to maturity. Mohammed, who tells his best friend all of his secrets during his freshman and sophomore years, says in his junior year: "But I don't know. Recently . . . you know I kind of changed something. Not that much, but you know I feel like there's no need to—I could keep [my feelings] to myself. You know, I'm mature enough." Interpreting a desire to share feelings as a sign of immaturity, Mohammed shuts down. He also begins, in this same year, to speak for the first time in his interview of feeling depressed and isolated. He understands that there are consequences of becoming "mature."

In their groundbreaking work on adolescent girls, Lyn Mikel Brown and Carol Gilligan note a similar pattern of loss among girls, but at an earlier age.[54] Girls during late childhood (ages 8–11), they find, are able to speak freely and honestly in their relationships. Yet on the brink of adolescence (ages 12 or 13), girls often lose their courage and become increasingly disconnected from their real thoughts and feelings. While developmental psychologists focus on the leaps in cognitive abilities (e.g., the ability to use abstract reasoning) during adolescence, Brown and Gilligan note a significant loss in girls' development. They find that girls who once were outspoken warriors become lost in a world of "I don't know" and "forget" what they used to know about themselves and their relational worlds. Gilligan describes this "developmental impasse":

> [During adolescence] If girls say what is on their minds or in their hearts, if they speak freely and reveal what they see and hear and know through experience, they are in danger of losing their relationships, but if they do not say what they are feeling and thinking, they will lose relationships and be out of connection with other people. Either way, they will lose relationships and be all alone.[55]

Girls enter the world of womanhood—a world that encourages the sacrificing of one's own needs to the needs of others—and lose their willingness to speak freely in their relationships. My studies suggest that boys, too, experience a loss during adolescence—but in late adolescence. Boys enter their teenage years with a tremendous desire and capacity to engage in close and intimate friendships with other boys, despite the cultural dictates that discourage such behavior. Yet as they enter manhood, they begin to lose their way. Their emotionally sensitive and astute voices become fearful and wary. Words such as "love" and "happy," so pervasive in their interviews during early and middle adolescence, give way to expressions of anger and frustration or simply of not caring any longer. They also speak of having to disconnect from their peers and family in the name of being "independent" and "mature" and of feeling lonely.

The loss of friendships during adolescence is evident in other studies of adolescents as well. In Michael Thompson's book *Best Friends, Worst Enemies,* he describes the friendships of Hal and Jack, who were best friends "right through the spring of their sophomore year" and then grew apart beginning in their junior year.[56] As seniors they run into each other, and Jack later confides to Thompson that he is "dying" to tell Hal, "You've been in my mind. I just wrote an essay about us in my English class. I wish I could read it to you now." The essay, shown to Thompson, expresses their former closeness and the deep desire Jack has to reconnect to his former best friend, Hal. According to Thompson, the two young men split apart because of "Jack's athletic career, his bond with teammates, and the acclaim he was getting in high school."[57] Just like the boys in my studies, however, these reasons appear to be capturing the surface story rather than what is happening underneath.

Research on men's friendships has also suggested a loss during adolescence.[58] Psychologist Stuart Miller concludes:

> Most men, particularly if they think about it, if they let themselves feel their personal trust about it, will admit they are disappointed in their friendships with other men . . . Since most men don't let themselves think or feel about friends, this immense collective and personal disappointment is usually concealed, sloughed over, shrugged away. . . . Men [however] secretly cherish the memories.[59]

Scholars investigating men's lives more generally also find that men remember having intimate friendships during early and middle adolescence and then losing such friendship. The story of loss is explicit in their narratives, as is the story of desire.[60]

In research on the social nature of the brain among 9- to 17-year-olds, researchers at the National Institute of Mental Health find that the activity in certain emotional and social areas of

., the insular cortex) decreases during adolescence
n though it increases for girls.[61] According to these
: "Among males, findings of an age-related decrease
[during ... olescence] in insula activation may suggest a reduced
level of affective engagement, and particularly for somatic-
related emotional responses in males through adolescence."[62]
The cause of this decrease in insula activation, however, may lie
with the cultural context for boys during adolescence, when being emotional is frowned upon. Even though boys between the
ages of 9 and 14 have insular activity rates that are, in fact,
higher than girls, the decline in this activity during adolescence is
likely affected by the context of gender stereotypes. Culture, as
so many neuroscientists and social scientists have noted, affects
the workings of the brain just as the structure of the brain affects
behavior.[63]

Yet the story of the lack of intimate friendships among males
and their attempts at emotional stoicism and autonomy is not
new. We have heard it many times before. Boys and men are not
able to be nor interested in being—for various reasons that range
from nature to patriarchal "nurture"—as emotional and relational as girls and women and thus have a harder time finding
close male friendships. The story that is overlooked is that boys
do, in fact, have intimate male friendships and continue to desire
such friendships into late adolescence and, according to the research on adults, even into old age. Even though boys experience
a decline in their willingness to trust and engage intimately with
male friends during adolescence, their desires for such intimacy
do not diminish over time.

THE THICK CULTURE

Why have we not noticed this pattern of friendships among
boys? Thick culture explanations or interpretations help us answer that question. My understanding of this construct comes, in
part, from Clifford Geertz's constructs of "thin and thick interpretations."[64] I extend his framework, however, to include not

only interpretations but also the investigation of interpretations. Such investigations expose the fact that while thin culture interpretations or those that remain on the surface are often offered to explain troublesome patterns: they prevent us, as I will show throughout this book, from getting to the root of these problems. Thick culture interpretations explicitly reject thin culture ones based on the grounds that the culture itself is invisible in such interpretations, and thus they fail to adequately explain the problems.

In Geertz's view, thin interpretations note or describe an act (i.e., winking an eye), whereas thick interpretations reveal the symbolic meaning of an act.[65] In my construction, thin culture explanations or interpretations (I use these terms interchangeably) are the easy and frequently repeated stereotypic, clichéd, and static frameworks that are commonly offered to explain why, for example, boys don't have intimate male friendships during late adolescence or why there is a "boy crisis." Thick culture analyses, in contrast, examine the stereotypes and clichés themselves and the processes that lead to such static cultural frameworks— which often have little to do with what actually occurs—in the first place.

Thin culture interpretations of why boys don't have friendships during late adolescence include that boys don't have time for friends and that they are more interested in having a girlfriend (i.e., sex) than in having a male friend. These interpretations remain on the surface and don't explain why boys and young men in the nineteenth century, in contrast to the early part of the twenty-first century, continued to have close male friendships throughout their lives. Furthermore, they don't explain why couples took their best friends on their honeymoons in the nineteenth century but not in the twenty-first century. Thin culture interpretations of the "boy crisis" in education indicate that the crisis is caused by a lack of male teachers, male role models, a lack of recess time, and a lack of male-oriented reading activities in schools. They fail to provide the reasons for such gaps and why there is no need for male-oriented reading activities for boys in most of the world. Exploring the reasons for these patterns leads us into the thick of it.

Thick culture explanations for the loss of intimate friendships focus on conventions of masculinity and the implicit homophobia and sexism that discourage such friendships among boys and men in the first place. They also draw attention to the ways in which these conventions and the gender straitjackets associated with them have grown more rigid as we become more socially progressive, revealing a powerful backlash to women's and gay rights. In addition, they examine the larger sociological pattern of a decline in social connectedness[66] and empathy that most assuredly makes it difficult for boys to stay connected to each other. And finally, thick culture explanations examine our resistance to hearing what boys are saying about their friendships and point to our cultural equation of emotional vulnerability with being gay and girlish as the primary culprit. Our resistance, in other words, reflects our fear of making our boys into girls or gay. Thus, rather than challenging such stereotypes, we ignore critical components of boys' experiences.

Thick culture analyses of the "boy crisis" in education draw attention to the fact that we don't have many male teachers because we have made teaching children a feminine activity; we don't have enough male role models because men are encouraged via conventions of masculinity to disconnect from themselves and others and thus make poor role models; and we don't have enough recess time for boys (or girls) because we make a mind/body split in education, like we do in the larger culture, and think that education should only treat the mind. We disconnect from our knowledge that we can't treat the mind without treating the body. Thick culture analyses of the "boy crisis" also point to the fact that we have made reading a "feminine" rather than a "human" activity,[67] that being uneducated is idealized in our political system, and that we have gendered basic human capacities and desires and thus prevented boys from getting what they need. Thick culture analyses focus on what boys are telling us they need rather than on stereotypic descriptions of boys coming from scholars and other experts whose descriptions may capture a part of boys' experience but not the whole.

Thick culture analyses explore why, at this moment in time, with this particular group of people, and at this particular age, do we see patterns such as the loss of friendships during late adolescence or the "boy crisis." Such analyses probe why we aren't able to see the hand in front of our face; why we haven't noticed that boys are indeed having emotionally intimate male friendships during adolescence; and that there is not a "boy crisis" but a human crisis of connection as indicated by the decline in social connectedness and empathy.[68] Thick culture analyses examine why we remain stuck in thin culture interpretations of the loss of friendships and the boy crisis as well as of numerous other societal challenges (e.g., the achievement gap, divorce, suicide). Entering into the thick of it means understanding that we are living in a scientific culture in which we trust only what we expect to see (i.e., based on a hypothesis), which is not necessarily consistent with what we actually see or feel. Thus, it is not surprising that we do not see the intimate patterns in boys' friendships or recognize that what boys have in their friendships (e.g., competition) may not be the same thing as what they want, and while boys may report lower levels of intimacy in their friendships than girls, they still have emotionally intimate male friendships.

Thick culture explanations reveal, furthermore, that our blindness to boys' friendships as well as to why they lose their close friendships is due to the fact that we live in a culture that does not place much value on friendships.[69] As Judith Harris in her book *The Nurture Assumption* claims, our cultural "obsession" with the influence of parents on children—due in large part to Freud's early theories of parental influence and to our desire to think that the power is in our hands—has made us poor listeners, unable to recognize the fundamental role that peers and friendships play in girls' and boys' lives.[70] Due to our culture's devaluing of friendships, we have also become less likely to have them. Sociologists from the University of Arizona and Duke University have found in their nationwide studies that the likelihood of American adults having close friendships has declined significantly over the past two decades. While in 1985 the modal number of confidantes for American adults was three, the modal number of confidantes in 2004 was zero, "with almost half of the population (43.6) now reporting that they discuss important matters with either no one or with only one other person."[71] Furthermore, the proportion of adults reporting that they talk to a friend about "important" or "personal" matters has dropped from 80 percent in 1985 to 57.2 percent in 2004, and the percentage of adults who report having no close friends at all has increased from 36 percent in 1985 to 53.4 percent by 2004.[72] If the larger culture does not value friendships, the chances that boys' friendships will be seen and appreciated for their significance as well as fostered during late adolescence are highly unlikely.

Thick culture explanations of why we are having a hard time hearing what boys are saying and doing in their friendships draw attention to the fact that we do not, furthermore, believe that our emotions and relationships are shaped by culture. In her book *Pink Brain, Blue Brain,* Lise Eliot, a neuroscientist, makes the point eloquently. Drawing from years of research, Eliot concludes "infant brains are so malleable that small differences at birth become amplified over time, as parents, teachers, peers, and the culture at large unwittingly reinforce gender stereotypes . . . Girls are not naturally more empathic than boys, they are just allowed to express their feelings more."[73] Eliot draws attention to the ways in which we make our stereotypes about girls, boys, emotions, and relationships into what is *naturally* rather than what ought *not* to be culturally. She concludes that "boys are empathetic and can learn to be even more so if we don't exaggerate stereotypes and try to focus on their emotional development as much as on their athletic and academic skills."[74]

Frans de Waal, a world-renowned primatologist, makes a related point in his book *The Age of Empathy*. Rather than focusing on gender differences per se, de Waal simply sets out to show that empathy and the emotional and social skills that are evident among the boys in my studies are fundamentally human (and nonhuman primate) qualities. De Waal reveals through extensive research that we have told ourselves a story of human nature that is not true. We are not simply a selfish and competitive species; we are also deeply empathic, social, and relational, and such capacities are at the root of why we have thrived for so long as a species.[75] What Eliot's book does explicitly, de Waal's book does implicitly by underscoring the ways we have naturalized our stereotypes and made our conceptions of man into literal interpretations of men.

Staying in the thick of it leads us to understand that we live in a culture where core human capacities such as emotional expression, responsiveness, empathy, and needs such as intimate friendships are given a sex (i.e., girl) and a sexuality (i.e., gay). As a sixth-grade boy in one of my studies put it: "what is difficult is like men showing their emotions because people might think of them as another way if they show their emotions. That's why men try to, you know, try to hold it in and stuff . . . I think that's negative . . . because it's feelings and everybody has feelings and stuff."[76] In his book about men's friendships, Stuart Miller notes how often his colleagues told him that his topic sounded like it was about homosexuality. Miller writes: "I couldn't believe [their] reactions. Surely the great tradition of male friendship, celebrated in the West by Homer and Aristotle and Cicero, by Montaigne and Shakespeare and Pope, was what people would think of when I said 'male friendship.'"[77] Yet even those who study boys and men draw a link between emotional expression, vulnerability, and sexual orientation.

Sitting in a conference room with my graduate students at New York University, I tell a story of a boy who, at seven, told me that he thought he was good at understanding his best friends' feelings. The students, all of whom are sensitive to issues of homophobia and other vestiges of patriarchy, begin to smile knowingly. I ask them why and they say that perhaps this boy was beginning to experience same-sex attractions. Were I not so acutely aware of my American culture that equates "feelings" between boys as evidence of sexual orientation, I would have been surprised by their reaction. Experiences like these happen frequently. A few months ago a friend told me that she thinks her brother's oldest son is gay. When I asked for reasons, she quickly responded: "He takes his friendships with other boys so seriously and is so distraught when they betray him." Rather than seeing this behavior as evidence of his emotional depth and maturity, my friend sees it as a sign of the boy's sexual orientation.

Yet the equation of emotions and intimacy with a sex and a sexual orientation is historically new and culturally specific. Historian Stephanie Coontz notes that in earlier centuries:

> No one thought it "unwomanly" to be hardheaded in business or "unmanly" to weep. But as economic production moved outside the household, the work activities and emotional responsibilities of men and women began to diverge. Men increasingly labored in impersonal institutions that required that feelings be kept under wraps. And the work that wives did at home focused less on producing goods than on providing a haven for husbands and children.[78]

Making a similar distinction between the nineteenth- and twentieth-century notions of masculinity, sociologist Karen Hansen concludes in her chapter on intimate friendships among men in antebellum New England:

> There is great difficulty in studying same-sex relationships in a heterosexist and homophobic society [in the late twentieth century] because of the tendency to distort innocent relations, to read consummated sexual activity into passionate innuendos, or because of an inability to put aside twentieth-century biases in order to be sensitive to a pre-Freudian epoch.[79]

Hansen and others have noted that the introduction of the word "homosexual" in the late nineteenth century and the resulting division between heterosexuals and homosexuals, as well as the

Freudian compulsion during the twentieth century to sexualize all human behavior, have made it virtually impossible to talk about or even listen to stories of intimate, nonsexual relationships without assuming sexual desire is at the root.

Letters between young men during the nineteenth century suggest that their friendships were often vulnerable and intimate. It was acceptable among both middle and working class men to show affection and be emotionally intimate with other man (even sharing a bed), particularly before they were married.[80] According to historian E. A. Rotundo, who investigated male friendships in the middle class from 1800 to 1900:

> When Daniel Webster [a senator from Massachusetts] was eighteen years old, he called his best friend "the only friend of my heart, the partner of my joys, grief, and affections, the only participator of my most secret thoughts." And four years later in 1804, young Daniel asked another close friend: "What is this world worth without the enjoyment of friendship, and the cultivation of the social feelings of the heart?" He answered his own question later in the same letter when he told his friend: "My heart is now so full of matters and things impatient to be whispered into the ear of a trusty friend, that I think I could pour them into yours till it ran over."[81]

These scholars reject the modern impulse to turn emotional vulnerability with other men into a sign of sexuality. Hansen argues about the nineteenth century:

> Manhood was not threatened by physical [or emotional] intimacy because the word homosexual was not in the nineteenth century vocabulary. Individuals did not self-consciously worry about their behavior. They did not fear same-sex relationships. In addition, the culture as a whole did not stigmatize the behavior.[82]

It was with the introduction of the term "homosexual" as well as the increased awareness, introduced by Freud and his followers, of the sexual undertones of behavior, that the expression of emotions between men was framed as suggestive of homosexuality.

The diminished gender segregation during the twentieth century may have also, ironically, exacerbated the problem by creating a structure in which men, particularly those who identify as heterosexual, feel even more compelled to adhere to gender stereotypes so that their heterosexuality is not questioned. In an "integrated" culture, where women and gay people mingle with men and straight people but where few straight men want to be perceived as gay, heterosexual men likely feel increasingly anxious regarding their sexual status. Thus, they may adhere to gender stereotypes with even more ferocity than previous generations to prove that they are straight.

In parts of China and India that are highly gender segregated as well as intolerant of homosexuality, one often sees evidence of what appears to be nonsexual male intimacy (e.g., holding hands, sleeping in the same bed) among boys and men. Walter Williams notes that in cultures that "do not divide up people into 'homosexuals' and 'heterosexuals,' there is remarkable freedom from worry among males that others will perceive them to be members of a distinct 'homosexual' category."[83] Yet this pattern speaks to the problem and not to the solution. Sexual oppression and gender segregation are obviously not strategies for fostering boys' and men's emotional capacities and their friendships more specifically. Psychologist Howard Stevenson argues that adherence to extreme forms of masculinity among Black males may be a necessary survival strategy in a racist context but is not one that leads to long-term liberation.[84] Similarly, adherence to rigid gender stereotypes may feel necessary among American, heterosexual males in a homophobic and sexist context, but it will not lead to long-term happiness and well-being.[85]

Yet the astonishing fact is that, despite the larger cultural patterns of devaluing friendships and of equating intimate friendships with sex and sexuality, American adolescent boys in the late twentieth century and early part of the twenty-first century *are* having the same kind of male friendships that nineteenth-century young men had: intimate, emotional, and vulnerable. As in the cultures before and around them, they know what is required of them to be a boy and become a man—they know what the conventions of masculinity ask of them—but they continue to openly discuss their sadness, their joys, and their hurt when friends betray them. These boys' resistance to gender stereotypes is especially remarkable given that they express these feelings during a developmental period—early and middle adolescence—when homophobia is at a peak.[86] Just as Harry Stack Sullivan found, boys such as Justin and Felix do, in fact, have male chums whom they love, and they are willing to tell us that directly. If we stay in the thick of it—if we listen to boys carefully and place them in their historical, political, and social contexts—we will hear what lies at the core of boys' struggles and what boys want and need to thrive.

OVERVIEW

Drawing from my longitudinal research studies of boys conducted at different times over the past 20 years, this book focuses on boys' friendships from early to late adolescence—the secrets and feelings they share during the early years of adolescence and the loss and distrust, coupled with desire for intimacy, that they experience in their male friendships as they become men. The book reveals not only the secrets boys share with each other but also the secret in the larger culture, that is, the intimacy in boys' friendships and the strong desires for such relationships as boys grow older. The fact that boys have close male friendships and then lose them or at least lose their trust in other boys is a cultural secret but is, according to the boys' interviews, no secret to the boys themselves.

The book also explores the ways the cultural context shapes boys' friendships. The influence of context, regardless of the level of analysis, can be perceived in the diversity of responses. If all boys, for example, responded to our questions in the same way, it would be difficult to *see* the context that shapes boys' relationships. In my studies, the boys did not all sound the same. Thus, I am able to explore the root of the diversity as well as the similarity of their responses. While most boys spoke at great length about their feelings for their friends and their fears of being hurt by their male peers, others had a harder time expressing themselves and retreated to an attitude of coolness and distance. Some boys experienced a dramatic loss in their friendships or in their ability to trust their male peers during adolescence, or both, whereas others maintained their closest friendships throughout adolescence even if the quality of the intimacy or the trust declined over time.

The variation across boys can be explained by a combination of factors, including their families and their schools, as well as by stereotypes about ethnicity, race, socioeconomic status, sexual orientation, and immigrant status. Black and Latino boys, for example, faced different gender-based challenges from the Asian American or White boys, and these translated, at times, into different patterns of friendships. While differences were not evident at the broadest level (e.g., boys across ethnicities and races had emotionally intimate friendships and began to struggle in these relationships as they grew older), there were differences in the details. This book explores the differences and the commonalities across boys, with the patterns reminding us that while the immediate contexts (e.g., family, peers, school) make a difference, so do the expectations, stereotypes, and conventions found in the larger American context.

Finally, this book reveals the ways boys' friendships are not just relevant to an understanding of boys' friendships. The boys in my studies offer empirical proof for the recent paradigm shift occurring among natural and social scientists who argue, from their own empirical data, that what makes us human is our empathic, intersubjective, and deeply social capacities—our capacity, in other words, to have emotionally intimate relationships.[87] They reveal that empathy and having and wanting intimate friendships is not simply a female or a gay story but a deeply human story. It is only our culture, according to numerous scholars, that distorts these fundamentally human capacities.[88]

The boys in my studies are ethnically, racially, and socioeconomically diverse but include primarily ethnic and racial minority youth from poor and working class families who live in cities in the Northeast of the United States. I focus primarily on poor and working class urban boys of color because they not only continue to be overlooked in the scholarship on boys, friendships, and human development in general (except in a few areas such as in studies of violence and gangs) but also represent a growing percentage of the teenage population under the age of 20. Currently, 80 percent of the American population lives in urban areas, 43 percent of young people under 20 are ethnic minorities, and approximately 70 percent are from poor, working class, or lower-middle class families.[89] By 2020, ethnic minority teenagers will likely be the majority of all teenagers under 20. Thus, the boys in this book represent boys in the United States more accurately than the White, middle class and upper class boys who fill the pages of the best-selling books on boys. White, middle class and upper class families represent, according to the U.S. Census data of 2008, less than 30 percent of the population. Yet it is remarkable how similar the boys in my studies sound to boys in other studies who come from very different racial and socioeconomic backgrounds.[90] Boys across the ethnic, racial, socioeconomic, and historical spectrum are revealing their feelings, sharing their secrets, and having and wanting intimate male friendships.

This book is structured as follows. Chapter 2 provides an overview from multiple disciplines of the relevant scholarship on boys, friendships, masculinities, and the nature of human beings that have most closely shaped my own studies. This chapter also provides a description of the studies of friendships I have been conducting for close to two decades. Part I (Chapters 3–5) focuses on the themes of love and vulnerability in boys' friendships—the deep secrets—detected primarily during early and middle adolescence. Part II (Chapters 6–8) focuses on themes of loss and distrust detected primarily during late adolescence and describes the reasons for these losses and why they may differ across contexts.

Chapter 9 explores why growing up for the boys in my studies entails loss with long-term consequences. Understanding the reasons for this loss and how it reflects a larger loss in community, in friendships, and in empathy[91] in America during the twentieth century and the beginning of the twenty-first century is critical to finding a way to address this increased isolation. Just as we have been increasingly "bowling alone,"[92] so have teenagers become increasingly isolated and alienated. And, according to the social and natural sciences, this pattern is not natural.[93]

Boys' stories suggest that we need to foster our relational and emotional capacities so that boys, girls, women, and men can continue to thrive in all areas of their lives. Rather than defining maturity as the growth of self-sufficiency, autonomy, and independence, the boys suggest that it should also focus on having quality relationships with same-sex and opposite-sex peers. As long as we continue to define maturity as the opposite of relationships, name a human crisis of connection as a "boy crisis," and continue to offer thin culture interpretations of thick culture problems, we will continue to suffer the losses that appear to be "natural" but are, in fact, deeply cultural.

The urgency of this book stems from what feminist and critical race scholars have long argued: in order to challenge harmful stereotypes and open up the confines of gender and racial stereotypes so that development does not continue to be a process of disconnection and dissociation, we need to create alternative images and spaces.[94] Such "safe spaces" connote places where people can avoid becoming another "statistic" or stereotype in the stream of the dominant culture. Yet to create such spaces, we need to listen closely to the actual range of experiences among boys (and girls) and hear how they are resisting stereotypes that tell them that, for example, to speak like a human is to speak like a girl, a gay person, or a child. The importance of charting the development of friendships among boys lies with its ability to offer a new vision of what is possible in the lives of boys and men and thus also, of course, girls and women.

CHAPTER 2

INVESTIGATING BOYS,

FRIENDSHIPS, AND

HUMAN NATURE

My informal study of boys' friendships began with my second to youngest brother. Five years my junior, Lucan as a young boy had a best friend, John, with whom he spent every waking hour, playing, laughing, and talking. One day, my mother caught the two of them cutting up her much loved childhood rag doll and took both boys to task. Looking sheepish, John went home, and he never returned. For weeks, Lucan would cross the street to John's house to see if he was there, only to be told by John's parents that he did not want to play. Lucan talked endlessly about why his best friend might have felt so inconsolably betrayed, but try as he might, he never figured it out. I remember distinctly the agony this break caused my brother. Even at his current age of 41, Lucan, a happily married man, does not like to talk about the sensitive topic of the boy who broke his heart.

As a doctoral student in counseling psychology at the Graduate School of Education at Harvard University during the late 1980s, I spent hours counseling students at a local urban public high school. Each week, I would listen to teenagers talk about their struggles and attempts to cope with heartbreaks and betrayals. The most obvious discovery of my counseling years was that friendships were critical components of girls' *and* boys' lives. The adolescents spent hour upon hour talking to me about the joys, fears, pain, pleasure, and anger they experienced in their close same-sex friendships. I was familiar with the benefits and challenges of these relationships among girls. Girls' friendships, and the conflicts they had with each other, even seemed clichéd. I knew from my own experience and learned from the girls I counseled that they loved their friends and also fought with them, at times, over the most minor incidents. What I did not know was that my brother's experience was common: boys, as well as girls, had intimate same-sex friendships and felt betrayed by seemingly insignificant events.

These experiences as a counselor led me to wonder why the articles and books I was reading in my graduate school classes rarely discussed these critical relationships. Why was the passion and intensity that boys conveyed when speaking about their friendships ignored in the scholarly literature? When scholars did discuss friendships, the focus was on girls or on cognitive models of perspective taking more generally. The only exception was in the work of psychiatrist Harry Stack Sullivan, who wrote about his young male patients and their "chumships."[1] Yet his theory of chumships was based on a very small segment of the population. I could find few investigations of the intimacy that existed among the boys with whom I counseled or interacted regularly. The desire to systematically investigate patterns of friendships and to bring the voices of poor and working class youth more generally into our theories of adolescent development[2] led me to transfer out of the counseling program and into the doctoral program in human development at Harvard.

As a doctoral student in human development, I learned from the works of Erik Erikson about the growth of autonomy and independence during adolescence and how adolescents need a firm sense of self or identity before they can successfully enter into intimate and sexual relationships. I learned from other developmental psychologists that while peers, especially same-sex peers, are increasingly important during adolescence, they are often a negative social pressure encouraging a range of high-risk behaviors.[3] Harry Stack Sullivan wrote extensively about the importance of "chumships," or close same-sex friends, that he considered appropriate only for children between the ages of 9 and 12. Adolescents, he believed, shifted their attention to "lustful" relationships. The developmental literature suggested, in sum, that peers during adolescence were either bystanders in the growth toward autonomy, necessary only as a precursor to romantic relationships, or a negative influence altogether. Emotionally intimate male friendships were assumed to be absent during adolescence.

I also learned as a graduate student that the problem in the developmental psychology literature was not limited to content or to a population. It lay also with a method of investigation. Survey method, which was and continues to be the dominant form of investigation for adolescent researchers, focuses on assessing the frequency of an event or experience (e.g., how often do you . . . ?) and does not capture the nuances or meaning of that event or experience. Interview methods that allow adolescents to freely respond to a set of questions offer more opportunity for understanding meaning than do survey methods. And when such interviews are combined with formal or informal observations of youth, the opportunity for understanding meaning is enhanced as observation helps researchers make sense of interviews and draw attention to the context of a process or experience. Yet semi-structured interview methods are often not considered "empirically rigorous" as there are no statistical techniques (i.e., numbers based analysis) for determining meaning and nuance. The framework for "good science" is stuck in a one-note dialogue where numbers rule and words are suspect. Thus, entire areas of investigation (e.g., the experience of friendships) that have critical importance for the understanding of human development are overlooked as they require methods that rely on words rather than numbers.

In response to these theoretical and empirical limitations, I began, as a graduate student and eventually as a Professor in Developmental Psychology, my formal investigation of friendships among adolescents. I learned from my counseling years that if I wanted to understand the experience of friendships, I could not simply ask teenagers about their friendships. I needed to ask them about many parts of their worlds and explore how their friendships fit into their lives more generally. Thus, my investigations of friendships have always explored a broader set of questions regarding how adolescents experience their worlds (e.g., families, peers, schools, neighborhoods, identities). From adolescents' descriptions of their worlds,[4] I sought to see where they placed their friendships. Was it a topic discussed regardless of the question or was it only discussed when questions were asked specifically about friendships? What I discovered was that friendships, just as my counseling years had taught me, were at the core of what boys and girls wanted to talk about regardless of the questions asked in the interviews.

When I asked about their identities, families, peers, schools, and neighborhoods. teenagers spoke extensively about their friendships. Boys and girls spoke about who betrayed whom among their peers, who was able to keep secrets, who was able to "just have fun" and not take things too seriously, or get serious when seriousness was called for, who was their "best friend," who could be trusted to back them up in a fight or keep their family secret, who could help them with homework or help them get a girl or a boy, or who stole their girlfriend, boyfriend, or best friend. Friendships dominated their interviews from freshman to senior year in high school, only diminishing toward late adolescence as they grew increasingly worried about their futures. While scholars have written about the importance of friendships for adolescents, they have not told us that friendships, particularly emotionally intimate ones, consume boys' and girls' lives.

Deep Secrets describes the findings from my formal studies of adolescent boys and their friendships from early to late adolescence. I do not, however, simply present the data as such a purely empirical and atheoretical presentation does not allow us to see how their responses contribute to a larger conversation. The limitations of such raw empiricism, a problem throughout the social sciences,[5] become evident in the following analogy of a kitchen stove. If we examined the stove empirically to see why it gets hot at a particular moment in time without applying a framework to understand the stove itself as well as the change in temperature, we might perceive the stove and the heat of the stove as simply a physical system that has internal temperatures that change depending on various events such as the opening and closing of its door and the turning of a knob to the left or right. But in this approach, the kitchen stove is simply a *box;* it isn't being studied *as a kitchen stove.* Only when we place the box and the temperature change within a meaningful context—such as that the box is changing temperature in response to a father preparing dinner for his daughter in their home—do we begin to see the box as what it really is, a kitchen stove, and the temperature change as a product of the preparation of food for dinner.[6] Any empirical analysis, in other words, needs to be integrated into a framework that allows us to see beyond the immediate object of interest and better understand the patterns of change of that object (i.e., why the stove got hot). Thus, for my studies of boys' friendships, I draw from theory and research in the social and natural sciences to reveal the meaning and significance of boys' friendships and why they change over time.

THE FRAMEWORK

On the most general level, my study draws from ecological theories of human development that emphasize the intersections between individuals and the micro and macro contexts in which they are embedded.[7] While families and peers form a part of the micro context of development, stereotypes about gender, sexuality, race, ethnicity, and social class form a large part of the macro context of development, and it is within and in response to these social, political, and historical contexts that boys form and maintain their friendships.[8] My work, more specifically, draws from theory and research that focuses on boys, friendships, masculinities, and human nature. These literatures reveal both the thin culture interpretations of boys' experiences as well as the thick culture ones. The literature on human nature from which I draw in this book includes the work of social scientists who underscore the ways humans are both receivers of culture and responsive to culture as agents. Humans do not simply passively accept or accommodate to the messages of their culture; they also resist cultural conventions and create meanings that enhance their own well-being.[9] I also draw on work from natural and social scientists that reveals that our friendships, social networks, and abilities to cooperate, empathize, and feel other people's feelings not only make us human but have greatly fostered our ontogeny and phylogeny.[10] Our emotional and social skills are, in essence, the root of our survival as individuals and as a species.

While the scholarly work on boys, friendships, masculinities, and human nature should be a well-integrated one, it is, in fact, at least five distinct literatures that rarely draw on each other except in the most superficial ways. Scholars investigating boys' development often apply theories of masculinity to their analyses, but do not draw much insight from the work on friendships or from the broader work on human nature. The research on friendships is almost exclusively empirical with no theoretical base and pays little attention to the culture or context in which friendships occur.[11] The literature on masculinity is heavily theoretical and mostly focuses on adult men and how masculinities vary by social, economic, and political context. It rarely focuses on friendships and argues implicitly against a universal concept of human nature. The scholarship on resistance and accommodation as a fundamental human process is both theoretical and empirical but overlooks, for the most part, the experiences of boys and men in particular. The work on human nature that emphasizes its social and emotional components typically ignores the experience of children and adolescents and rarely addresses the processes by which culture or context shape these social and emotional skills. Integrating these strands of scholarly work is necessary to offer a thick culture interpretation of the patterns detected in the boys' interviews and to reveal the significance of boys' friendships for our conceptualization of boys, adolescence, and human nature. Thus, for the remainder of this chapter, I will briefly review and critique the relevant components of these literatures.

THE STUDY OF BOYS

In response to a perceived "boy crisis," an onslaught of books about boys has appeared over the past decade. We have seen books aiming to help parents raise "healthy" boys, help boys in school, help boys succeed, or simply understand boys. The problem, as it is often stated, is that boys are in trouble and we need to find ways to help them thrive. The facts often cited include the following: boys have higher rates than girls of attention deficit hyperactivity disorder, suicide, and school dropout, and lower rates of going to and staying in college.[12] Boys also continue to lag behind girls in reading and writing scores (although they continue to score higher than girls on math)[13] and are more often sent to the office at school for bad behavior. They are also more violent and aggressive than girls and report higher rates of bullying and also of being bullied by other boys.[14] Leading scholars note that homicide rates among U.S. youth have risen by more than 130 percent and suicide rates by almost 140 percent over the past 50 years, with boys aged 15–19 being four times more likely to kill themselves than girls (although girls are significantly more likely to *attempt* suicide than boys).[15] While there is much debate regarding the extent to which this "boy crisis" is more of a crisis for poor and ethnic minority boys,[16] or whether the "crisis" is simply "hype spread by antifeminist factions" in response to advancement by girls and women, books focused on the "boy crisis" dominate the shelves in bookstores across the United

States. Page upon page has been written about how boys are suffering at the hands of patriarchy, feminism, parents, teachers, or simply their own devices.

These books can be loosely divided into four groups, with each group overlapping to some degree. The first group, written primarily by clinicians and therapists, focuses almost exclusively on White middle and upper income boys (those who go to and can afford therapy) and aims to explore the negative impact of the conventions of masculinity on boys' development. The second group, also written by clinicians and focused on White middle and upper class boys, focuses on boys' biology and argues that mainstream culture (including feminism and women in general) has distorted boys' true nature. The third group focuses on the "boy crisis" in school in particular and addresses why boys are struggling. These authors often allude to either or both of the first two groups of books to justify their proposals to solve the boy crisis. The fourth group focuses on boys from diverse cultures and contexts and aims to understand the complexities of their experiences.

In the first category, one finds the best-selling *Real Boys,* by William Pollack; Dan Kindlon and Michael Thompson's *Raising Cain: Protecting the Emotional Life of Boys;* and Michael Kimmel's *Guyland,* all of which focus on the negative impact of a "too narrow definition of masculinity"[17] on the social, emotional, and academic well-being of boys. These authors draw from theoretical works on masculinity for their discussions of the conventions of masculinity that negatively affect all aspects of boys' lives. The central argument of these books is that the "boy code" or "guy code"—a code of behavior that emphasizes emotional stoicism, physical toughness, sexual promiscuity, and extreme forms of independence—is bad for boys. Adhering to the "boy code" leads boys to become emotionally illiterate, lonely, academically underachieving, and inclined to engage in high-risk behavior. Drawing from theories of gender intensification,[18] these authors underscore the felt pressure that boys experience to adhere to these codes of behavior and the suffering that boys experience as a result of such adherence. Parents, peers, the media, and other socializing elements, they argue, put tremendous pressure on boys to accommodate to these codes or gender stereotypes, and this felt pressure, as well as the enactment of gender stereotypes, is considered bad for boys' mental and physical health. These books reveal, in essence, the ways boys suffer at the hands of a macho culture that forces them to be figures of a masculine imagination rather than human beings with a range of beliefs, *feelings,* and thoughts about their worlds. They conclude by offering a range of solutions to address boys' problems—solutions that focus primarily on parents, mentors, and teachers.

While these authors offer a thick culture intepretation—they get at the underlying processes shaping boys' behaviors—and reveal the ways boys do, in fact, suffer as a result of a patriarchy that forces them to become someone whom they are not, they overlook or give short shrift to two important elements' in boys' lives: friendships and the processes by which boys resist conventions of masculinity. The tables of contents in these books make it apparent that close friends are not considered important in boys' lives, or at least not as significant as parents, girlfriends, sex, and sports. The role of close friendships is not given adequate attention in and of itself, nor is it seen as a critical part of how to help boys achieve emotional health. Peers, for the most part, are represented as negative elements who enforce the "boy code." Boys are portrayed, in essence, as passive recipients in the socialization of manhood, and peers are portrayed as the enforcer of cultural norms and ideals. This portrayal tells part of the story of boyhood but not the whole. Boys, as seen in my studies and other studies, regularly resist conventions of masculinity; and peers, particularly close male friends, often provide support for such resistance.[19] By ignoring close friendships, these authors miss a significant part of boys' experiences and thus fail to see a potential source of support for boys' social and emotional needs.

The argument in the second set of books is very different argument from those in the first one. Authors such as Michael Gurian (*A Fine Young Man*; *The Wonder of Boys*) or Leonard Sax (*Boys Adrift*) argue that the ultimate aim is not to challenge the patriarchal structure that creates the gender divide such that boys don't feel and girls don't think but to change the culture that believes that boys' toughness and emotional stoicism is socially constructed.[20] Rather than seeing typical boy behavior as a product of culture, Gurian and others maintain that it is a product of biology: "Understanding adolescent male development in the deepest way possible depends to a great extent on understanding adolescent male biology."[21] Boys, they believe, are biologically hardwired to have an emotional disadvantage when compared with their female peers. Their surging testosterone makes them more aggressive, sex obsessed, and fidgety. Girls and women, they claim, are more biologically equipped for emotional connectedness. The "solutions" these authors offer focus on changing schools and parents to more effectively respond to boys' "natural" deficits in the areas of compassion, empathy, and other relational skills and to foster "safe" environments that permit "boys to be boys" in its stereotypic sense of the phrase.

These highly essentialized representation of boys' lives provide a thin culture interpretation for boys' struggles by downplaying the existence of culture and relying on "findings" from neuroscience in an irresponsible way.[22] Lise Eliot, a neuroscientist who reviewed the existing research on biological gender differences in her book *Pink Brain, Blue Brain,* concludes that we have greatly exaggerated the extent to which boys and girls are different from each other, particularly with respect to empathy and other emotional and social skills. She reveals, in fact, that boys are more emotional at birth than girls, often being more difficult to soothe as young babies. She concludes after her thorough investigation of what we know on this topic: "The size of the [gender] gap depends on what parents emphasize and teachers teach."[23] Furthermore, if boys are are so inherently macho and testosterone driven, why are they able to speak with such eloquence and depth about their closest friendships during early and middle adolescence? Why is it that boys and men had less of a problem maintaining intimate friendships and being emotionally expressive in the nineteenth century than in the late twentieth century? Why do researchers, such as anthropologist Sarah Hrdy, find that our evolutionary grandparents were more empathic and less focused on dominance and hierarchy than we are in modern culture?[24]

Although we like to believe, as evidenced in the current fascination with all things biological or "in" the body, that our beliefs and behavior are mostly rooted in our biological makeup, scholarship has shown for decades that it is at the intersections of culture and biology that we find the most productive explanations of our attitudes and behaviors.[25] As Lionel Trilling, the renowned literary critic, reminds us: "This intense conviction of the existence of the self apart from culture is, as culture well knows, its noblest and most generous achievement."[26] In other words, our beliefs regarding the separation of self from culture or of biology from culture are a product of our culture. One can't take the culture out of our constructions of biology (or vice versa). Boys are clearly, in part, a product of their biology. Yet the ways we interpret this biology and allow or don't allow the expression of what we perceive to be biology varies across historical, political, and social contexts. This fact underscores the heavy hand of culture in boys' development and certainly boys' friendships.

The third group of books focuses on the problems boys face in school rather than on boys' development more generally and ways to solve boys' problems. Books such as *The Trouble with Boys,* by Peg Tyre, lay out the school-related problems boys have and what we should do about them.[27] They address issues such as: why 23 percent of middle class European American boys in their senior year of high school score "below basic" in reading while only 7 percent of their female counterparts score that low; or why the average high school grade point average is 3.09 for girls and 2.86 for boys; or why boys are almost twice as likely as girls to repeat a grade. Boys are also twice as likely to get suspended as girls and three times as likely to be expelled. In federal writing tests, 32 percent of girls are considered "proficient" or better while only 16 percent of boys fall into that category.[28] These authors typically take the view that families and schools are not valuing or respecting boys and are thus creating schools that are not "boy friendly." Their proposed solutions focus on interventions such as more male teachers, more recess time, and more access to "boys' books" so as to allow "boys to be boys." They also discuss absent fathers, along with absent male teachers, and thus the need for "male role models" in boys' lives. The implicit and explicit assumption is that boys have different needs from girls and thus need school and home environments that are responsive to their specific male bodies. *New York Times* columnist Nicolas Kristof shares this perspective; after expressing frustration that boys are doing poorly in various academic domains when compared to girls, Kristof concludes: "If it means nurturing boys with explosions, that's a price worth paying."[29]

The problem with these types of thin culture conclusions and with the books in this third category more generally is that culture is treated as nature and thus inevitable. While the lack of male teachers and absent fathers is clearly a problem for boys and men and girls and women, the question that gets at the "thick" of the matter is *why* are there so few male teachers in elementary or secondary schools? Why are almost a quarter of middle class White boys not reading *at grade level* during high school in the United States? Why do boys in countries such as Germany and Norway read books about a range of topics, whereas boys in the United States only read "boys' books"? Why has the "boy crisis" only emerged in the late twentieth century and early part of the twenty-first century and been particularly evident in the United States, in comparison to other Western industrialized countries? The answers to these questions lie, at least in part, with our constructions of masculinity which make few heterosexual men want to be elementary school teachers and make reading and writing, even doing well in school, into *feminine* activities.[30]

A wildly successful ad campaign by Diesel Jeans that recently won the Grand Prix for outdoor advertising at the Cannes Lions International Advertising Festival focused on telling young people to "Be Stupid," which for the purposes of the ad meant engaging in risky and irresponsible behavior (including buying their expensive jeans). One particular ad had a young man riding a bicycle on a cobblestone street with a woman wearing five-inch heels and very little clothing, precariously balanced on the handlebars. The message, clearly aimed at young men, was clear. Have fun! Who cares if anyone gets hurt! The 10 to 15-foot ads had statements such as "Smart may have the brains but Stupid has the balls." The phrase "BE STUPID" in very large letters appeared in subway cars and on street corners and was plastered on the sides of buildings in cities throughout the United States. The ad campaign, and the fact that it won major advertising awards, is a chilling reminder that we live in a culture where being smart is seen as feminine and boring and being "stupid" as masculine and exciting.

The "boy crisis" is not, at the thick level of analysis, the product of not having enough male teachers, "boy books" in the classroom, or recess time at school; it is a reflection of a culture that idolizes "stupidity" and stereotypic masculine behavior and equates the most basic of human qualities (e.g., empathy) and needs (e.g., friendships) with being girlish, childish, and gay. Thus it is extremely difficult for boys and men to find and have what they need if they are to do well in and out of school. If boys and men, both gay and straight, were encouraged to develop their natural empathy and emotional depth and have emotionally intimate friendships, if they were encouraged to be "smart"—to care about the girl on the handlebar who may fall off the bicycle—rather than to become gender stereotypes, they would not disconnect from others and wreak havoc on the world. The social and health science research has confirmed this hypothesis for over three decades. It is the blunting of boys' and men's capacity for empathy, intimacy, and emotional expression that denies them the very skills and relationships they need to thrive.[31]

The fourth group of books focused on boys does, in fact, begin to touch on these relational themes and the influence of stereotypes, expectations, and conventions in boys' lives. They focus on those who come from a different strata of society than the White, middle and upper class, American boys who dominate the boys' books in the first three groups. These works respond critically to a literature that either homogenizes boys' experiences or generalizes the experience of White middle class American boys to all boys.

Sociologist C. J. Pascoe's book *Dude, You're a Fag,* for example, includes Black and White American boys from different socioeconomic strata and concludes that masculinity looks different across race and ethnicity, with the blending of racial and masculine stereotypes being more tightly woven for Black than for White boys.[32] Journalist Malina Saval in her book *The Secret Lives of Boys* explores the experiences of gay, straight, White, Black, and Hispanic youth and notes that boys' emotional lives are significantly more nuanced than the stereotype suggests.[33] Sociologist Pedro Noguera's book *The Trouble with Black Boys* focuses on the challenges and social contradictions facing Black young men living in the United States and argues that the stereotypes that Black boys are "too aggressive, too loud, too violent, too dumb, too hard to control, too streetwise, and too focused on sports . . . have the effect of fostering the very behaviors and attitudes we find problematic and objectionable."[34] By maintaining gender and racial stereotypes, Noguera argues, we encourage their becoming reality. Ann Ferguson makes a similar point in her book *Bad Boys,* in which she reveals the negative consequences for African American boys of being labeled as "bound for jail" rather than bound for college.[35] In contrast to the books in the third group, the books in this fourth group offer a thick culture interpretation of the "boy crisis" as they reveal the underlying processes that lead to boys' problems rather than simply restate the problems (e.g., no male teachers).

Although these four groups of books on boys are distinct in numerous ways—with some presenting a thin culture interpretation of boys' experiences and others providing a thicker one—they are also similar in two ways. First and most obvious is that they present boys as passive receivers of their biology or their culture or context (e.g., both the immediate and the larger context of negative stereotypes and gender straitjackets). Only a few provide evidence that boys resist not only gender but also racial stereotypes. Yet evidence of such resistance is abundant in middle and high schools across the country.

In a high school language arts elective course called "Oh Boy: Masculinity in Twentieth-Century Literature," taught by Celine Kagan, the students in her class produced final projects focused on some aspect of masculinity.[36] In the fall semester of 2009, an Asian American boy in his junior year conducted a final project on "boys' language" and discovered in his interviews that boys preferred to discuss their feelings with their male friends than their female friends (my research has found the same pattern). He told me that he didn't expect to find that since the stereotype of boys is that they prefer to talk about feelings with girls. The boys, he said, felt that other boys were more honest than girls and thus more "safe" to talk to. In the same class, a White boy in his junior year created as his final project a comic book whose main character (who looked like the boy himself) has two types of boy on his shoulders—one a macho football player and the other "just a normal boy." The conflict for his comic book character is which "voice" to listen to when he is upset by his parents' incessant arguing. Should he listen to the athletic boy who tells him that to speak openly with his friend about his feelings is "gay" or should he listen to the "normal" boy who tells him that it will make him feel better to talk to his friend about it.

The conflict is resolved by the comic book character speaking to his friend and feeling better. The last page of the comic book is a picture of numerous boys with the same two types of boy on their shoulders. The final project of an African American boy in the same class was a painting of a boy pushing a rock up a hill that went "nowhere"; the "rock," according to the boy, was masculinity and the hill was manhood. These projects were typical of the students in Celine's class. Boys from diverse backgrounds produced projects that openly contested gender stereotypes and revealed the deep knowledge that boys have of their predicament.

Yet as my studies and other studies suggest, resistance to gender stereotypes or conventions of masculinity is not simply heard among boys taking a high school class on "masculinity." It is heard in contexts across the world, including in my studies in China,[37] begging the question: How often do boys, in fact, adhere to conventions or stereotypes of masculinity? Are we assuming that gender stereotypic boys are in the majority when they are not? By ignoring the ways that boys resist gender stereotypes and thus do not "by nature" act "like boys," we lose sight of the cultured nature of boyhood and potential strategies to create change that better supports boys' emotional, social, and academic needs.

The second similarity these four groups of books have is that they share the assumption that while boys may want friendships, they have difficulty finding or having intimate, "secret-sharing" friendships. Dan Kindlon and Michael Thompson say about boys in *Raising Cain:* "Boys can be torn between the desire to be expressive in friendship and the gender-stereotypes expectation that they be assertive, forceful, or strong and silent. Sharing secrets with a friend doesn't fit the bill."[38] Even though Michael Gurian begins his book by describing the intimate conversations he had at age 15 with his best friend, "with whom I shared some secrets and a lot of time," he argues that "male friendship is fragile in ways female friendship is not because male friendship is often not talk dependent. It is proximity—and activity—dependent."[39] Contradicting his own experience, Gurian repeats well-worn stereotypes. William Pollack, one of the few boys' authors who discuss boys' close friendships, says that "boys find it difficult to be honest about their feelings of friendship with other guys, to openly show their compassion and empathy toward male friends, and to connect with other boys in deep and meaningful ways."[40] Although intimate friendships among boys are evident in these books, and Michael Thompson and his colleagues devote an entire book to examining boys' and girls' friendships,[41] an explicit discussion of the prevalence and meaning of emotionally intimate friendships for boys is not.

THE STUDY OF FRIENDSHIPS

The early studies on friendships in the beginning of the 20th century focused on what children perceived as a good or bad friend and the activities that they did together. They concluded that "chums" (i.e., intimate friendships) were common among girls and boys and were critical to children's well-being.[42] "Chums" or close friendships have been considered, in fact, "the most potent factors in the development of man as a member of society."[43] Following these studies, Harry Stack Sullivan incorporated the idea of "chums" into his theory of human development and argued that during preadolescence (9–12 years of age) a need for intimacy arises that he defines as "that type of situation involving two people which permits validation of all components of personal worth."[44] In response to this intimacy need, preadolescents begin to have extremely close relationships with a same-sex peer. This relationship "represents the beginning of something very much like full-blown, psychiatrically defined, love."[45] It is during this period that "a child begins to develop a real sensitivity to what matters to another person."[46] Sullivan considered these "love" relationships essential for development of self-worth and the acquisition of the social skills necessary for engagement in a future romantic relationship.[47]

Empirical research has generally supported Sullivan's theory of "chumship" and found that children's descriptions of friendships show a marked increase in references to sharing intimate thoughts and feelings between preadolescence and adolescence.[48] Intimate (e.g., self-disclosing) friendships or better quality friendships (i.e., more supportive) have, furthermore, been found to be significantly associated with lower levels of depression, higher levels of self-esteem, and higher levels of school engagement and performance.[49]

Extending Sullivan's ideas about the function of close friendships, psychologist William Furman and his colleagues draw from Weiss's theory of relationships that suggests that individuals seek specific social provisions or types of support in their relationships.[50] Close friendships, according to Furman and his colleagues, provide: affection, intimacy, a sense of reliable alliance, instrumental aid, nurturance, enhancement of self-worth, and companionship.[51] These insights have generated decades of research assessing the degree to which adolescents of different ages, genders, and more recently ethnicities and nationalities experience these dimensions of close friendships and the association of these dimensions with psychological, social, and academic well-being.[52] Findings from a range of scholars, including those who have examined the more cognitive-behavioral components of friendships have found, for example, that emotional intimacy is more important for adolescents' than for children's friendships.[53]

One of the most common findings in the friendship research has been that adolescent girls are more likely to have intimate (i.e., self-disclosing) friendships than boys, whereas boys are more likely to have "activity oriented" friendships than girls.[54] Although some research has suggested that these gender differences are specific only to White middle class adolescents—with Black working class adolescents reporting no gender differences in levels of intimacy in their friendships[55]—the dominant finding (based on studies of White, middle class, American adolescents) is that girls have more emotionally oriented friendships while boys have more status oriented friendships.[56] In other words, girls like to talk about their feelings whereas boys like to play sports and games and compete with each other. Research has been done that complicates these findings, however, with reports of equal levels of self-disclosing behavior in the friendships of boys and girls and of boys defining intimacy in similar ways as girls.[57] Yet these findings have been, for the most part, left out of the larger conversation. A recent decade-in-review piece in a well-regarded adolescent journal indicated that one of the most consistent findings from the psychological field of gender is that girls are more "relationally oriented" while boys are more "object oriented."

Studies have also suggested gender differences in the association between high-quality friendships (i.e., supportive, intimate, affectionate, satisfying, reliable, etc.) and psychological adjustment. In their study of 193 third through sixth grade students, psychologist Cynthia Erdley and her colleagues found that the association between the quality of friendships and psychological adjustment was stronger for boys than for girls.[58] Others have found similar patterns.[59] Researchers have also found that the association between friendship quality and adjustment varies by age. Psychologist Duane Buhrmester's study of friendships during adolescence, for example, indicates that the association between friendship intimacy and socio-emotional adjustment is stronger in middle than in early adolescence.[60] As intimacy in friendships becomes harder to achieve for youth reaching middle to late adolescence (as is suggested by the boys in my studies), the impact of such intimacy on adjustment may become more notable.

While this body of research has greatly informed our understanding of the significance of friendships for children and adolescents, it has numerous limitations. Two of the most obvious are related to methodology and context. With few exceptions,[61] the majority of research on friendships uses survey methodology to assess the quality, quantity, and characteristics of friendships. The focus on examining the frequency of various provisions of close friendships (i.e., the survey approach) has resulted in a field that knows little about how adolescents within and across subgroups (e.g., Black, White, boys, girls) talk about their friendships. While it may be true that boys have less intimate friendships than girls, that truth tells us little about the intimacy boys do experience in their friendships. Qualitative research such as that of Margarita Azmitia and her students has suggested that boys do have intimate, "secret-sharing" male friendships.[62] Similarly, knowing that intimate friendships are a significant correlate of adolescents' psychological or academic well-being does not tell us much about the processes by which such intimacy leads to feeling good about oneself or doing well in school. In-depth, one-to-one interviews are necessary for understanding the experience and significance of intimacy in adolescents' friendships.[63]

Strikingly, the researchers on men's friendships (versus those of children or adolescents) who often rely on one-to-one interviews as their research method report findings similar to my own and other interview studies on boys' friendships.[64] The similarity underscores the issue of research methodology. When the methodology has been similar, regardless of the sample, the findings have been similar. Psychologist Stuart Miller, who conducted interviews with over 1,000 men in the United States and Europe, has found:

The older we get the more we accept our essential friendlessness with men. Of course men remember another time when they were much younger, when they believed in true friendship, they thought they had it. . . . When they had, perhaps as late as college, at least one other man with who they were deeply connected. With a smile, we all remember.[65]

Geoffrey Greif reports a similar pattern in his qualitative research with men. Most men, he states, have "lost" friendships as they have grown older and feel a distinct yearning for the recovery of these intimate connections.[66] Even qualitative researchers who are not focusing on friendships have noted this pattern of loss among men. Daniel Levinson, with his team of psychologists, sociologists, and anthropologists who studied a cross-section of adult men over several decades, concludes: "In our interviews, friendship was largely noticeable by its absence. . . . A man may have a wide social network in which he has amicable 'friendly' relationships with many men and perhaps a few women. In general, however, most men do not have an intimate male friend of the kind that they recall fondly from boyhood or youth."[67] The reasons men have lost their friends, according to these scholars, are often the same ones cited by the boys in my studies: moving, changing schools or jobs, and, perhaps most revealing, a friend's betrayal. Greif describes men "who say that when they are wronged (or have acted poorly), they do not want to re-establish the friendship, especially when trust has been broken."[68] These patterns, detected via interviews with men, are similar to what I found with adolescent boys using similar methodologies of inquiry.

In addition to the problem of methodology, the other limitation is the acontextual nature of most of this research. Even with the heavy ecological emphasis evident in psychological research over the past two decades, an examination of the ways the environment shapes friendships is almost entirely absent from the scholarly literature. One of the only exceptions is research from those studying attachment relationships between primary caretakers and children. These theorists and researchers describe the ways early mother-child attachments influence, via the internal working model of the child, the child's ability to have close relationships with others.[69] This research is focused, however, on parents and rarely, if ever, looks beyond the family unit. Yet boys

and girls live in a world that is infused with stereotypes, expectations, and cultural conventions that shape every aspect of their
lives including their peer relationships. Thus, an exploration of
friendships should address these macro-level contexts with the
context of masculinity being one of the most important.

THE STUDY OF MASCULINITY

Beginning in the 1970s, scholars began to challenge the trait-like
conceptions of masculinity (and gender more generally) that
were pervasive in the social sciences. Scholars argued that masculinity is not an inherent personality trait but reflects cultural
stereotypes, ideals, and standards about male behavior and attitudes.[70] Joseph Pleck, a leader in the study of masculinity, and
his colleagues write that "males act in the ways they do, not because of their male role identity, or their level of masculinity or
masculine traits, but because of the conception of masculinity
they internalize from their culture."[71] These socially constructed
beliefs about males, which Pleck terms "masculinity ideologies,"
reveal power dynamics and significantly influence boys' and
men's close relationships.[72] Yet scholars investigating patterns of
masculinity—unlike most of the authors of boys' books or developmental psychologists—believe that boys and men do not
simply accommodate to these gender "scripts," stereotypes, and
ideologies. They also respond to them. According to Michael
Kimmel and Michael Messner:

> The important fact of men's lives is not that they are biological
> males, but that they become men. Our sex may be male, but our
> identity as men is developed through a complex process of interac-
> tion with the culture in which we both learn the gender scripts ap-
> propriate to our culture and attempt to modify those scripts to make
> them more palatable.[73]

The idea of a socially constructed masculinity is in direct contrast to those who emphasize the essential nature of men (e.g.,

Michael Gurian, Leonard Sax). The argument of these "essentialists" is that men are naturally more competitive, autonomy seeking and emotionally stoic. They do not question, as do the social constructionists, whether what they consider the nature of men may not, in fact, be natural.

Masculinity, as a social construction, is one that poses as the antithesis of anything that is associated with being female (i.e., emotional, physically weak, and dependent).[74] Thus the definition of manhood is what is *not* female and, beginning in the late twentieth century, what is not gay. In other words, as Michael Kimmel has pointed out, homophobia as well as misogyny are at the root of mainstream or "hegemonic" masculinity.[75] "Our culture's blueprint of manhood," as social scientists Deborah David and Robert Brannon put it in describing their typology, is the following: "(a) 'no sissy stuff'—the avoidance of all feminine [or gay] behaviors and traits; (b) 'the big wheel'—the acquisition of success and status; (c) 'the sturdy oak'—strength, confidence, and independence; and (d) 'give 'em hell'—aggression, violence, and daring."[76] Similarly, psychologists Michael Cicone and Diane Ruble lay out three core dimensions of masculine "norms" or expectations based on an analysis of dozens of empirical studies: (1) How a man handles his life (*active* and *achievement-oriented*), which includes the qualities of being independent and competitive; (2) How a man handles others *(dominant),* which includes the qualities of being aggressive, powerful, assertive, and boastful; and (3) How a man handles his emotions *(level-headed),* which includes the qualities of being unemotional and having self-control.[77] Sociologist Carolyn New describes masculine conventions as the ways Western societies systematically restrict boys "access to affectionate physical contact, especially with other boys—or such contact is sexualized and forbidden. They are discouraged from the expression of grief and upset through tears, and encouraged to suppress emotions (except anger) and to ignore physical and emotional pain."[78] In essence, being a man means not being a sterotypic woman or, in cultures such as the United States, gay person.

While most studies have focused on the meaning of masculinity among Anglo or European American men in particular, studies of other cultural groups have produced similar dimensions of masculinity.[79] Psychologist Miguel Arciniega and his colleagues, for example, find that "traditional machismo" in Mexican communities entails being aggressive, competitive, and emotionally stoic.[80] Psychologists Ramaswami Mahalingam and Sundari Balan report that "hypermasculinity" among Indian men entails being dominant, aggressive, competitive, and strong.[81] My studies of Black, Latino, Asian American, and White adolescent boys, furthermore, suggest that the dimensions of masculinity that David and Brannon described in the 1970s are still dominant today among boys and men from many different ethnic and racial communities.

Research has also found, however, cultural variations as well as within-group variation in the meaning of manhood.[82] African American men, for example, particularly those from working class families, have been found to define manhood in interdependent ways; others have noted that Latinos are more likely to endorse traditional masculinity ideology than Whites or Blacks.[83] Yet these findings do not contradict the findings that suggest commonality across racial and ethnic groups in conceptions of masculinity. As psychologists Aida Hutado and Mrinal Sinha point out, while there are differences, there are also commonalities due to the fact that the power structure determines the shape of masculinity for everyone and not simply for those who share power.[84] Thus, while African American men may be more "interdependent" in their constructions of masculinity, they remain embedded in a dominant culture that values autonomy over relationships. While boys and men may adhere to mainstream conceptions of masculinity to different degrees, the conventions of emotional stoicism, independence/autonomy, and toughness/assertiveness continue to be the dominant forms of masculinity with which most males, if not all males, have to contend.

In Michael Kimmel's "Real Guy's Top Ten List" summation of the "rules" of manly behavior in the United States, he claims "the unifying emotional subtext . . . involves never showing emotions or admitting to weakness. You must show to the world that everything is going just fine, that everything is under control, that there is nothing to be concerned about."[85] The manliest rule in the book, according to Kimmel, is emotional stoicism. These "rules" have changed very little during the twentieth century with emotional stoicism evident in the icon of John Wayne in the mid-twentieth-century and icons like rapper 50 Cent and actor Bruce Willis in the early part of the twenty-first century. Since at least the time of Plato, men have been framed as rational and thus, in our Western dualistic framework, not emotional, and women as emotional and thus not rational.[86] As the title of the 1990s best seller demonstrates: *Men Are from Mars* (i.e., cold and calculating) *and Women Are from Venus* (i.e. emotionally hot). This belief that boys don't feel (and girls don't think) is evident in the literature and also in the interviews of adolescents. When asked what might be good about being a girl, a 17-year-old boy in one of my studies said: "It might be nice to be a girl because then you wouldn't have to be emotionless."

As with all qualities or dimensions of masculinity, there is, of course, variability in the value of emotional stoicism. In some cultures, according to anthropologist Bambi Schieffelin, "men are allowed to display a greater range of emotionality and are generally more labile, while women are steadier in both everyday contexts and formal contexts."[87] Within the United States, scholars have long noted the value of emotional expression found in many Latino and Black communities and explicitly not found in many Anglo American communities.[88] Miguel Arciniega and his colleagues argue that emotional sensitivity (i.e., *caballerismo*) is part of the meaning of machismo, while psychologists Richard Majors and Janet Billson claim that those in the Black community are more interested in emotional expression than emotional restraint.[89]

Psychologists Agneta Fischer and Anthony Manstead have investigated gender differences in emotional expression among adults across 37 countries.[90] Their results suggest that gender differences in intensity, duration, and expression of emotions were greater among adults from countries that adhere to an *independent* cultural orientation than among adults from countries that adhere to a more *interdependent* one. In other words, men were more likely to be emotionally expressive in countries that emphasized "interdependence" than in those that emphasized "independence." Similarly, psychologist Reed Larson and his colleagues found gender differences in emotional states among children and adults to be stronger in the United States than in Korea—a country that is typically considered more "interdependent" than the United States.[91] These findings draw attention to the cultural context of emotional states and expressions but do not challenge the fundamental premise that there are core qualities that much of the world considers manly and they include varying degrees of emotional stoicism, physical toughness, and independence.

According to psychologist Gigliana Melzi, differences in emotional expression among children are due to the socialization practices of the parents. Children of parents who speak to their children about emotions will more likely be comfortable speaking about their emotions than children of parents who do not speak to their children about emotions. Melzi and Fernandez have found that Peruvian mothers are more emotionally expressive with their three-year-old sons than with their three-year-old daughters. They conclude that this explains, at least in part, why gender differences in emotional expression are smaller in "interdependent" countries like Peru than in "independent" ones such as the United States.[92] My research with Latino youth in New York City also suggests that such youth are more likely to use emotional language, such as words referring to happiness, sadness, anger, and passion, when describing their lives than are their non-Latino peers.[93]

Yet there is much less cultural and contextual variability when one examines emotional expression and vulnerability among non-familial boys or men. Expressing vulnerabilities and weaknesses to a non-familial male is considered effeminate or "unmasculine" behavior in many cultures and contexts, even those that adhere to more "interdependent" values.[94] Similar complexities can be seen in the American context. Recent movies such as *I Love You, Man* and the popularity of terms like "Bromance" (i.e., a close friendship between two males) in American culture may suggest that being emotionally sensitive is growing in acceptance. Yet as recent cases suggest of boys who were literally teased to death by their peers for being "fags" due to their emotionally expressive ways of acting, the expression of emotions is still fraught with danger for boys across racial, ethnic, and socioeconomic boundaries. My studies and others such as Azmitia's work suggest, however, that boys are making distinctions between peers. While boys may struggle to be emotionally expressive with their peers in general, they do not appear to struggle with such expression with their closest male friends particularly during early and middle adolescence.

In addition to the value of emotional stoicism, the value of independence and autonomy for boys and men also forms a large part of the image of manhood. The privileging of autonomy over relationships (i.e., the "male" over the "female") has been, furthermore, a cornerstone of developmental psychology, with the very meaning of "maturity" being linked to autonomy and self-sufficiency.[95] Underscoring the pervasiveness of this value, Lyn Mikel Brown and her colleagues claim in their book *Packaging Boyhood* that "in media, boys see and hear lots of messages about the importance of being independent, trusting and relying on no one but themselves. Nearly every superhero story reminds boys of the danger of being too close to someone or relying too much on relationships."[96] Rap songs that advocate a "me, myself, and I" attitude among urban, hip-hop youth remind us that the value of independence and autonomy is not simply a White middle class value; it belongs to boys and men across the United

States and in many other countries as well. For those countries and cultures that idealize James Bond, needing or wanting relationships, especially expressing such a need or desire, is not what "real men" do.

As with the concept of emotional stoicism, there is also cultural variation in the value of autonomy and independence with Blacks, Latinos, and Asians, as well as poor and working class families, often considered more "interdependent" than White or Middle Class Americans.[97] Yet the focus of almost all this work is on families and how particular ethnic groups are more "family oriented" than others. The concept of "interdependence" in the scholarly literature has rarely reached beyond this core unit to include non-familial peers. The reason for such an oversight is likely due to the cultural assumption that while boys and men may need their fathers, they do not and should not "need" other males outside of the family. Boys and men from White, Black, Latino, and Asian and poor and wealthy communities are all expected to be self-reliant and independent outside of the family. Supporting this contention, my studies of middle school boys in the United States, China, and India[98] found that the boys in China and India were more likely than those in the United States to believe that boys should be autonomous with their peers.[99] The value of autonomy is evident even in traditionally "interdependent" cultures. Furthermore, we have found no ethnic differences among the Black, Latino, White, and Asian boys in the American sample of middle school boys in the extent to which they believe that boys should be autonomous and independent in the context of their peers.[100]

Finally, the value of physical toughness and assertiveness is so tightly aligned with the other two masculinity beliefs about stoicism and autonomy that it is difficult to discuss it separately. There is no doubt, however, that toughness or the desire to be perceived as unbreakable and able to "leap tall buildings in a single bound" forms the foundation of manhood for most boys and men. Across numerous cultural contexts, they engage daily in activities to prove their physical and mental prowess. Popular culture reinforces the image at newsstands, websites, and television shows, not to mention in the music and movie industries. And as with the other ideals of masculinity, the ideal of toughness is deeply shaped by its context. Where resources and opportunities are limited, the emphasis on proving one's manhood through physical toughness may be more common than in communities where the opportunities for proving manhood are more extensive and diverse (e.g., getting a prestigious job). Furthermore, being tough and assertive is often necessary for survival for those growing up in inadequately resourced and poor communities. At the same time, while physical toughness may be less necessary in wealthier neighborhoods, emotional stoicism is always necessary in the world of gender conventions. Either way, the ideals of emotional stoicism, autonomy, and physical toughness or strength touch the lives of most, if not all, boys and men within and outside the United States.

Scholars of masculinity have not simply described the ideals or conventions of being a "real" man but have also examined the oppressive consequences of adhering to such ideals. Raewyn Connell, a central figure in the study of masculinities, notes that theorists traditionally assumed that gender roles were "well defined, that socialization went ahead harmoniously, and that sex role learning was a thoroughly good thing. Internalized sex roles contributed to social stability, mental health and the performance of necessary social function."[101] Later generations of scholars, with Connell at the helm, began to challenge such assumptions and revealed the ways that adhering to masculine conventions negatively affected boys and men's health and well-being.[102] Sociologist Carolyn New writes about this oppressive process: "the misrepresentation of men's needs and capacities becomes part of the self. . . . Even if the subject retains ideas of their greater capacities and nature, they are adversely affected by being treated as other than what they are."[103] Connell argues more specifically that the denial of men's emotional capacities prevents men from having the relationships they need and challenging the patriarchal system that reinforces gender stereotypes.[104]

Psychologist Joseph Pleck describes a process he terms "gender role strain": the consequences, he claims, of having to conform to gender role norms such as aggression and emotional inhibition.[105] Pleck acknowledges that noncompliance to such "norms" frequently occurs (hence contradicting the notion of "norms") and that such violations can have negative consequences. However, he also recognizes that many of these "norms" are inherently problematic and adhering to them can harm boys and men. To prove his point, he describes dozens of studies that have found that strong adherence to ideals of masculinity is linked to delinquency, violence, drug and alcohol use, low self-esteem, anxiety, depression, and even coronary heart disease.[106] Pleck, for example, found in his analysis of survey data from 1,880 male participants aged 15–19 that males who strongly adhered to ideals of masculinity reported: (1) more sexual partners in the last year; (2) a less intimate relationship during their last intercourse with their most recent partners; (3) a view of relationships between women and men as more adversarial; and (4) less consistent condom use with their current partners.[107]

Sociologist Kristen Springer and her colleague in their analysis of a longitudinal dataset that followed 1,000 middle-aged men from 1964 to 2004 found that men who most rigidly adhered to ideals of masculinity also reported the worst physical health.[108] According to their research, adhering to masculine ideals negatively influenced preventative care seeking, regardless of a man's prior health, family background, marital status, or other socioeconomic variables. They conclude: "It's ironic that the belief in the John Wayne, Sylvester Stallone archetype of masculinity—and the idea that real men don't get sick and don't need to see the doctor, and that real men aren't vulnerable—is actually causing men to get sick . . . these stereotypes and ideals are actually a reason why men do get sick."[109]

Researchers have consistently found that adherence to conventions of masculinity are bad for boys' and men's psycho_logical and physical health.[110] Conventions of masculinity and gender and racial stereotypes are not "neutral" contexts of development but are actively damaging ones that significantly undermine boys' and men's abilities to thrive in the world and, as I will show, boys' abilities to have the very relationships they want and need.

The limitations of this body of scholarship on masculinity or masculinities lie with its focus on adult men and, like the literature on boys more generally, the lack of attention to the ways boys and men resist conventions of masculinity. Although the theoretical literature describes the active processes by which men engage in constructions of masculinity, there exist few studies that investigate the ways boys or men, particularly those who identify as heterosexual, *both* accommodate *and* resist gender stereotypes and expectations. Furthermore, few have investigated the processes of change that occur in adherence and resistance as boys become men. The study of masculinity, for the most part, has been seen as a topic for clinical psychologists and sociologists but not developmental psychologists. And even when developmental psychologists—such as Stephen Frosh in his book *Young Masculinities*—addresses the topic, very little attention is given to the ways boys *resist* as well as accommodate to conventions of masculinity.[111]

HUMAN NATURE (1): THE STUDY OF RESISTANCE

Social scientists who have focused on Black people or on girls and women's development specifically have long been interested in the processes of resistance to cultural conventions, dictates, stereotypes, and expectations. In his book *Roll, Jordan, Roll,* Eugene D. Genovese writes about how resistance was a part of the daily lives of Black slaves: "Accommodation and resistance developed as two forms of a single process by which slaves accepted what could not be avoided and simultaneously fought [resisted] individually and as a people for moral as well as physical survival."[112] Feminist and critical race scholars, extending this framework to include an analysis of gender and race, have shown through empirical research the ways Black, White, and Latino girls and women contest or challenge gender, racial, and social class stereotypes. Scholars have argued that women (and men), in fact, "do gender"—they accommodate to gender conventions in some circumstances and they resist and challenge them in others.[113] Resistance to stereotypic beliefs about, for example, "feminine goodness" has been, furthermore, consistently linked to psychological, social, and physical well-being.[114]

The education scholar Jean Anyon argues that the socialization of girls is not a one-way process of the society imposing its values on girls but a process of girls actively responding to the "social contradictions" that culture imposes on them from a very early age.[115] She finds in her ethnographic research with fifth graders that girls both resist and accommodate to gendered expectations and ideals. She concludes:

> Most girls are not passive victims of sex role stereotypes and expectations but are active participants in their own development. Indeed, one could do an analysis of minority girls, and of boys of all races and social classes, to assess how these children react to the contradictions and pressures that confront them. I would argue that accommodation and resistance [are] an integral part of the overall processes that *all* children use to construct their social identities.[116]

Underscoring the importance of these constructs for social and developmental psychologists, Anyon argues that the processes of resistance and accommodation are not specific to a certain subgroup within the human population. Rather such processes, with one taking place in the palm of the other, are evident among all children as they develop in the context of stereotypes, "norms," and expectations.

Developmental psychologists Lyn Mikel Brown and Carol Gilligan also reveal the ways girls resist gender stereotypes as they move through childhood and into adolescence.[117] These scholars' findings, based on interviewing girls from late childhood through adolescence, point, in fact, to a developmental story of resistance. Their data indicated that as girls entered adolescence they began to "discover that their honest voices were jeopardizing their relationships, not only their personal relationships but also their connection to the culture they were entering as young women."[118] Studying hundreds of girls in both private and public schools, they find that girls aged 8–11 speak their minds freely with a remarkable honesty and transparency. They resist norms of femininity that tell them to be nice, kind, and complicit with the demands of the adult female world. Once they hit adolescence, however, they began to experience a crisis of relationship—a crisis of whether to split from what they know about the world and keep their relationships or speak what they know and lose their relationships. Either option meant taking themselves out of authentic or honest relationships with themselves and with others. As girls enter adolescence, Gilligan notes, they "show signs of a resistance not to growing up but to losing their minds."[119]

Brown and Gilligan distinguish between psychological and political resistance in the development of girls. Drawing from psychoanalytic theory, they define psychological resistance as the process by which girls "resist" knowing what they know about the world—they accommodate to gender stereotypes—whereas political resistance, speaking truth to power, is the process by which girls resist that which they know is not good for them. Girls, these scholars find, reveal signs of both psychological and political resistance, with political resistance most obvious during late childhood and psychological resistance more prevalent during adolescence. If girls' political resistance finds "no effective channel for expression, it goes underground, turning into dissociation or various forms of indirect speech and self-silencing. Hence the depression, the eating disorders, and the other manifestations of psychological distress that seemed visited on girls at adolescence."[120] In other words, if girls are not supported in their political resistance, their resistance turns inward with psychological consequences.

Psychologist Janie Ward developed a similar framework for understanding resistance in the case of Black girls in particular.[121] She too distinguishes between two types of resistance: "resistance for survival" and "resistance for liberation." The first strategy, "resistance for survival" is oriented toward quick fixes that offer short-term solutions. These strategies might make you feel better for a while, but in the long run they are counterproductive to the development of self-confidence and positive identity formation. Resistance for liberation offers solutions that serve to empower African American females through confirmation of positive self-conceptions, as well as strengthening connections to the broader Black community. Examples of "resistance for survival" include "excessive autonomy" at the expense of connectedness: early and unplanned pregnancies, substance abuse, school failure, and food addictions. For African American young men, the "cool pose" or an "oppositional identity" is an example of resistance for survival. While its aim is to enhance feelings of social competence and esteem, and convey a sense of pride, such strategies impede Black girls and boys' abilities to thrive.[122]

Examples of "resistance for liberation" include a girl doing well in math and science or openly expressing her thoughts and feelings regarding racism in the classroom or sexism at home. It may also include an African American boy achieving success in school or having intimate male friendships. These types of strategies of resistance are effective at helping young people stay connected to what they know about the world. Ward finds in her research that girls who use "resistance for liberation" strategies report lower levels of psychological distress than those who use "resistance for survival" strategies.[123] Others have also found that those who are more "macho" or take a stance of "cool pose" (i.e., "resistance for survival") are more likely to report low self-esteem.[124]

While most of the work on resistance to stereotypes has focused on girls and women, there are a few examples of research on resist-

ance, explicitly, among boys. Psychologist Judy Chu, in collaboration with Carol Gilligan, for example, has explored these topics
with young boys and adolescent boys. Their work reveals the similarity between the ways that young boys read the emotional and
relational world and how they do so during early and middle adolescence. A father in their study described young boys, including
his son, as "very sensitive, they're emotional, they seem to like
each other very much." Another father said he does not want his
son to lose "his sensitivity . . . the delight he has in his friends. . . .
It's just so sweet, the sort of excitement they feel and the warmth
they feel, even if it doesn't translate into always being, getting
along together, I think they're delighted to have that connection."[125] This work raises questions about the patterns of resistance from early childhood to late adolescence. Boys' resistance to
conventions of masculinity may not begin in early adolescence but
rather in early childhood. It is only, perhaps, with the increased
pressures to be a man during late adolesence that we find boys and
men strongly adhering to gender stereotypic patterns.

Chu's research with adolescent boys, furthermore, has suggested a pattern similar to that of the boys in my studies.[126] In
her studies of mostly White boys attending private schools, Chu
finds that they are explicit about their feelings of vulnerability
and openly acknowledge their desire for intimate friendships.
Seth, a ninth grader, says that he speaks about his "feelings"
with his close friends but not with others because he knows that
"they can throw you down anytime they want—like make fun
of you if they want to or whatever." Seth suggests (albeit cir-
cuitously) that he would very much like a male best friend with
whom to share his secrets but worries that he will be perceived
as gay if he acts on such desires. Although most of the boys in my
studies did not suggest such a fear until late adolescence, Seth
rings a familiar bell in his ability to name why and how he feels
vulnerable with his peers. James, a seventh grader in Chu's study,
is explicit about wanting a friend, "to get things off your chest
and . . . having the feeling that somebody knows what you're

going through and relating. It kind of comforts [you]." Ethan, a twelfth grader, speaks about his best friend, whom he met when he was 13 and with whom he has been extremely close for four years. Chu concludes: "Far from being emotionally deficient or relationally defunct, these boys demonstrated a breadth and depth to what they are capable of knowing and doing in their relationships. The boys also expressed a wish to have friendships in which they could feel truly known and accepted."[127] Chu's work underscores the stark contrast between the stereotype and the reality of boys' experiences.

Psychologist Deborah Tolman also finds strong evidence of boys' resistance to conventions of masculinity or gender stereotypes in her studies of boys' beliefs about romantic partners.[128] Stephen Frosh, in his examination of masculinity among working class boys in England, reveals the high levels of emotional intimacy that exist between young adolescent boys.[129] Other studies of British boys have found wide variation in the extent to which they accommodate to conventions of masculinity, with some boys adhering rigidly and others being more resistant.[130] Sociologist Gil Conchas's research on high-achieving young Black men reveals the ways they resist both gender and racial stereotypes in their determination to do well in school.[131] Psychologists Michael Reichert and Sharon Ravitch find that Jewish-identified boys resist conventions of masculinity as well.[132] And psychologist Gary Barker's work focusing on boys living on the streets in Brazil reveals how they resist a set of masculine conventions that offer few paths out of poverty.[133] All of these studies present examples of the ways boys are resisting gender and racial stereotypes, or both, in their daily lives including in their relationships with their peers.

The small body of work either directly or indirectly assessing boys' resistance to stereotypes also points to the psychological and academic benefits of such resistance. Psychologist Carlos Santos found, in a longitudinal research with 500 middle school boys, that high levels of resistance to gender stereotypes in friendships—as indicated by a standardized survey—was significantly associated with both high self-esteem and low depressive symptoms.[134] These associations between resistance and psychological well-being were significant for Latino, Black, Asian American, and White boys in grades six to eight. He also found that change over time in boys' reports of resistance was significantly associated with change over time in their reports of psychological adjustment. As the level of resistance in boys' friendships increased over time, so did their psychological adjustment. In another analysis, Santos finds that higher levels of resistance to gender stereotypes in boys' friendships are associated with higher levels of academic engagement.[135]

Missing from the work on resistance—with the exception of the work of Santos and Brown and Gilligan—is attention to the way young people's ability and willingness to resist stereotypes changes over the course of their development. As with girls who become particularly attuned to emotional nuances and cultural contradictions as they enter puberty, boys become attuned to emotional and social worlds during a time when their bodies and voices are changing dramatically, forcing them, in a sense, to stay connected to their own vulnerabilities. Remembering the explanation by my friend's son that his best friend was being "hormonal" when he said "we don't talk anymore," we can surmise that boys recognize, perhaps unconsciously, the emotional quality of their friendships and attribute it to changes in their bodies. Hormonal shifts are linked to heightened emotionality, and it may well be that puberty for boys, as for girls, fosters emotional sensitivity and vulnerability, regardless of the macho culture in which they live.

The research on resistance raises the question: Why are boys stereotyped as inherently less empathic and relational than girls when they reveal such strong themes of emotional vulnerability and acuity and have such intense desires for "deep" relationships with both girls and boys? It appears that we are naturalizing our gender stereotypes rather than seeing them for what they are—a product of a "hyper" masculine culture that does not want to recognize boys' emotional and relational capacities. Yet if we stay in the thick of it, we will recognize that the problem doesn't lie with the boys themselves (or their mothers, fathers, or teachers) but with our constructions of boyhood, manhood, and human nature more generally.

HUMAN NATURE (2): THE STUDY OF HUMAN NATURE

So what is "natural" for boys? Neuroscientists, biologists, primatologists, developmental psychologists, and evolutionary anthropologists have recently published books calling for a revision of how we conceptualize human nature and human experience. Antonio Damasio, a neuroscientist whose books include *Descartes' Error* and *The Feeling of What Happens* has written extensively of how cognition or thinking depends on the capacity to feel and have emotions. The splitting of cognition and emotion—the divide that is as common in popular and scholarly culture as the subject-object or man-woman split—is only seen, according to Damasio, in brain-damaged patients.[136] Emotions or feelings, he argues, facilitate rather than impede thinking. In other words, thinking without feeling generates incoherent thought. The relevance of his arguments to an understanding of boys' development lies in the way they reveal the problems of our stereotype that boys are, by nature, less feeling oriented or emotional than girls. Feelings, Damasio argues, are an integral component of every moment of the day. Our bodies are continually registering the "feeling of what happens." The sensitivity that we hear in the stories of boys (and girls) reflects that deeply emotional state of human existence.

Frans de Waal, a primatologist who trained as a biologist, implicitly builds on this argument in his recent book *The Age of Empathy.* De Waal argues that we need an "overhaul" of our current constructions of human nature which emphasize our aggressive and competitive "nature."[137] De Waal argues that, in contrast, we are deeply emotional, empathic, and social animals, and these emotional and social qualities are what has fostered our individual and evolutionary development. Expressing frustration with those who believe that competition is our human starting point, de Waal argues that while we are competitive, it is our social and emotional sensitivity that has allowed us to flourish; "we live in an age that celebrates the cerebral and looks down upon emotions as mushy and messy."[138] Like Damasio, de Waal views emotions as the foundation of humans' ability to think and make good decisions. Emotions, for de Waal, are in the driver's seat "after which our reasoning power tries to catch up as spin doctor, concocting plausible justifications."[139] De Waal concludes:

> We're preprogrammed to reach out. Empathy is an automated response over which we have limited control. We can suppress it, mentally block it, or fail to act on it, but except for a tiny percentage of humans—known as psychopaths, no one is emotionally immune to another's situation. . . . We involuntarily enter the bodies of those around us so that their movements and emotions echo within us as if they're our own [from the very beginning of life].[140]

The relevance of de Waal's work for the study of boys is obvious. It suggests that the distinction between male as rational, autonomous, and independent and female as emotional, relational, and interdependent makes no sense. If our starting point is that our empathic and emotional capabilities are what makes us human and fosters our ability to thrive as a species, then boys' emotional sensitivity with their friends and the loss of their friendships and their emotional capability during late adolescence takes on new meaning. It underscores the necessity of responding to this loss and not simply treating it as "natural" and necessary for maturity and growth. De Waal suggests, along with Damasio, that such a loss is, in fact, unnatural and seriously detrimental for an individual and for our species.

Evolutionary anthropologist Sarah B. Hrdy adds to this conversation by claiming that our empathic nature is a core part of our distinctly human history.[141] In her book *Mothers and Others,* she argues that our evolutionary ancestors were better at fostering such empathy via the reliance on the extended family in the raising of children. This extended family system—called alloparenting—included grandmothers, grandfathers, uncles, aunts, sisters, and cousins and fostered empathy among young children by encouraging children to take different perspectives. With the growth of the nuclear family, which includes only the parents, or only the mother, in the raising of the children, natural opportunities for fostering empathy have diminished, thus making our human community as a whole less empathic.[142] The link to the work on boys can be made by understanding that boys' stories of friendships are stories of empathy and deep emotional and social connection—the very same social and emotional connection that both Hrdy and de Waal argue is so critical for human development. Furthermore, the loss boys experience during late adolescence as the imperative of the romantic relationship takes over becomes a loss not just of friendship but of something much more profound and with much greater significance for the future.

Neuroscientist Lise Eliot, in her book *Pink Brain, Blue Brain,* contributes to what appears to be a paradigm shift in our understanding of what it means to be human.[143] Eliot draws attention to the ways the culture has greatly exaggerated the gender differences in such qualities as empathy and emotional sensitivity. She argues, from her stance as a researcher of neuroplasticity, that much of what we say about boys' and girls' "brains" is simply based on cultural stereotypes of what we think is true, based on adult experience, rather than what is actually being shown to be true via neuroscientific studies. The "hard data" suggest that the empathy difference between boys and girls "is considerably smaller in children than between men and women, telling us that social factors also contribute."[144] She finds, in fact, that infant males are the more emotional of the two sexes. "As we've seen, boys are more irritable, more easily distressed, and harder to soothe than girl babies. They startle, cry, and grimace more often at least during the newborn period, and take longer than girls to establish stable sleeping patterns."[145] Eliot also describes studies of mice that reveal "testosterone grows the one structure most strongly associated with the recognition of faces and emotional expression—the amygdala."[146] If these studies can be replicated on human samples, we may find that testosterone may be helping our "feeling brain" to thrive.

These studies focused on human nature point implicitly and explicitly to culture as the root of our gender stereotypes rather than sources in nature. The limitations of these investigations, however, are that they have yet to be applied to psychological or developmental studies of children or adolescents. Scholars are often hesitant to link "universal" theories with their more localized theories about children and adolescents. Yet the integration of my data on boys' friendships with these diverse sets of scholarly work on boys, friendships, masculinities, and human nature enables me to expose the root of the problem of the loss of friendships, the "boy crisis," and the increased isolation and alienation and decreased empathy society-wide that researchers have charted over the past 30 years.[147] To understand how this root gives rise to these problems, however, it is necessary to first listen to the boys themselves. Listening closely to the boys helps us stay in the thick of it.

MY FRIENDSHIP STUDIES

My longitudinal studies of boys have consisted of three research projects conducted at different time periods over the past 20 years. The explicit aim of my research has been to understand boys' experiences of friendships, how these experiences change during adolescence, and how both the micro context (i.e., the family and school) and the macro context (i.e., cultural norms and stereotypes) shape boys' friendships. My primary discovery in doing this work is that a study of boys or friendships is never simply a study of boys or friendships. It is also a study of humans in culture and culture in humans.

Since I began to explicitly study friendships, my students and I have conducted in-depth, one-to-one interviews with hundreds of adolescent boys—boys from middle and high schools in cities within the United States and in China—over periods of three to five years. As a developmental psychologist, I am interested in how processes or experiences change over time. Thus all of my studies have entailed following the same group of adolescents for periods of three to five years during the middle or high school years. For the purposes of this book, I focus on the 135 adolescent boys who attended high school in the United States and with whom we have interviewed for at least two years as part of three separate studies of friendships.[148] The majority (75 percent) of these boys, however, were interviewed for three years or more. I focus on these boys as they represent the age group (14–18) in which the most dramatic change in friendships is evident during adolescence. While I refer to some of my findings in my middle school studies and in my study of Chinese youth throughout the book, we have not yet collected data from them during high school and thus I am not able to compare them with my high school studies.

In each of our mixed-method studies of boys' friendships, we have had high rates of initial recruitment (over 85 percent) in the schools and adequate rates of retention over 3–5 years (over 60 percent) with particularly high rates among those who remained in the same school (over 90 percent) each year. The students identified themselves as belonging to various ethnic and racial groups, including African American, Puerto Rican, Dominican, Chinese American, and European American. Teenagers also identified, occasionally, as "mixed" ethnicity/race, and approximately 10 percent of the boys identified with other ethnicities reflecting the ethnic diversity of urban public schools. Most of the students in the schools in which we collected data were eligible for federal assistance through the free or reduced-price lunch program.

The demographics of the participants represent a significant portion of teenagers in the United States. Currently, 80 percent of the American population lives in urban areas, and of young people under the age of 20, 43 percent are ethnic or racial minorities and approximately 70 percent are from poor, working class, or lower middle class families.[149] Thus, while few books on boys' development or on friendships focus on the types of boys in my studies, they better represent boys in America than do the White, middle and upper class boys who populate the best selling books on boys and the frequently cited articles on friendships.

Freshman students in high school were recruited for my studies from mainstream high school English classes in order to assure English fluency. Boys were told that the study was about understanding many aspects of teenagers' lives. We did not tell them that our interest was primarily in friendships as boys who did not have close friends would not have been willing to participate. My undergraduate and graduate students whom I trained four to five months in interviewing techniques and I administered the semi-structured interviews. Semi-structured interviewing is a challenging task as it requires the interviewer to adhere to a protocol but also allows the interviewee the freedom to explore relevant topics that are not on the protocol. The interviewer training sessions, typically done during the fall and winter of each year in which we collected data (we conducted the interviews during the spring and summer), entailed meeting weekly and listening to the interviews that had taken place the previous week or year. I would provide feedback on the extent to which the interviewer had listened carefully to what the teenager was saying and had allowed him to talk freely while staying focused on the topics on the protocol. Ongoing supervision was essential for collecting high quality interview data. Stories of emotional vulnerability, for example, would not have been so common had the interviewers not been so thoroughly trained to listen carefully and thus create a safe space in which boys could tell us what they really feel or think rather than simply what they should feel (or not feel) or think according to cultural dictates.

The interviewers represented a range of ethnicities, races, social classes, and general life experiences, but all had experience working in some capacity with youth. I tried in the early years of my studies to match interviewee and interviewer by gender and ethnicity in the belief that this would enhance the possibility of eliciting open and honest responses from the adolescents. My early experience suggested, however, that this was not necessarily the case. Most of the boys indicated that they would feel more comfortable being interviewed by a woman and I subsequently accommodated their preference. Given the conventions of masculinity, this pattern was not surprising. The male interviewers often, unintentionally, discouraged boys from being vulnerable as they wanted to be seen by the teenagers as "cool" and thus "manly." While one could also say that the women, in contrast, encouraged vulnerable responses, these responses seemed authentic. It is easier to cover vulnerability than to fake vulnerable feelings when none exist.

Matching ethnicity or race between interviewer and interviewee was not only difficult given the ethnic diversity of our samples but also did not necessarily lead to better interviews. The quality of the interview was determined almost entirely by the extent to which the interviewer created a safe space in which the teenager could talk openly. And the ability to create such a space safe was determined by the interpersonal skills, sensitivity, and curiousity of the interviewer. When the interviewer was able to genuinely join the teenager in helping him describe his world and was truly curious about what the teenager had to say, a safe space was created and the quality of the interview was good as evidenced by the thoughtfulness of the responses. Finally, I tried to have teenagers interviewed by the same interviewer each year with the belief that such continuity would enhance the quality of the interviews, but this was only possible for about half of the youth. The only apparent difference were that those who had the same interviewer as the previous year often elaborated more in their responses than those who had a new interviewer.

The interviews were open-ended and lasted for approximately two hours each year, although the length of the interview increased over each wave of data collection, with the last wave of interviews being typically three hours long. The interviews took place at the school, during lunch periods and class periods and after school; and in a few cases at the homes of the students or at a place near the school on a weekend. The interview protocol included questions concerning self-perspectives, and relationships with parents, siblings, best friends, romantic partners, peers, and teachers. We also asked many questions about school and home life more generally. We did not ask about sexual identity in particular because we were concerned that any explicit conversation about this topic would diminish the possibility of honest responses from boys about their male friendships stemming from concerns of looking gay. Given their responses during late adolescence, our concern was real. At the same time, four boys told us they were gay or bisexual and this information was incorporated in their interviews. We did not, however, have a large enough group of self-identified gay or bisexual youth to conduct a separate analysis on the differences. Thus, we focused our analysis on the boys who did not self-identify as gay or bisexual given the likelihood that intimate male friendships are experienced differently for those who are gay or bisexual and those who are not.

Although every interview protocol in all three projects included the same standard set of initial questions, follow-up questions were open-ended in order to capture the adolescents' own way of describing their lives and relationships. To provide incentives for the boys to participate, we paid them $10 for the initial interview and $20 for each consecutive interview. However, we realized after the first year of interviews that the opportunity to miss class was a greater incentive for some of the boys. While we tried to avoid this, the participants ended up missing all types of classes so they could complete the interviews. Teachers occasionally balked at our intrusiveness and were understandably unhappy about their students' absences. To mitigate the situation and thank teachers for their cooperation, we devoted time each week to helping teachers and principals with challenging tasks or difficult students. We also created various kinds of groups for teens, such as a theater group that met regularly throughout the academic year, a workshop on how to make stained glass windows, and a class on how to play the guitar (various skills that my graduate research assistants had and could teach the teenagers). These activities were appreciated by the students and staff at the schools and allowed us to better know the students and their school.

My research team's and my own direct observations of teenagers over two decades consisted of hanging out in lunchrooms, classrooms, and staff meetings and organizing after-school activities for the students in the schools. The aim of our observations was to understand the peers and friendships of teenagers in school settings. These observations took place over the entire time in which we conducted our studies (four to five years in each school) and provide data that I draw from in interpreting the interviews. I have also been observing teenagers in roles other than that of a researcher including being a counselor for adolescents, a co-founder of a local neighborhood high school, and the director of undergraduate studies at New York University. The latter role involved supervising psychology undergraduate interns who were volunteering in high schools. These experiences of engagement with teenagers, teachers, and administrators over 20 years have deeply informed my interpretation of boys' friendships.

All interviews were tape-recorded and transcribed by a professional transcriber. Once the interviews were transcribed, the analytic process began. The process of analyzing interview data begins with creating an "interpretive community," a community of scholars whose goal is to make meaning of the interviews and to make sure that the findings do not simply reflect the tunnel of the researcher's own expectations. As an interpretive community, my students and I sought to carry out what Hans-George Gadamer has said about the interpretive process:

> When we listen to someone or read a text, we discriminate from our own standpoint, among the different possible meanings—namely, what we consider possible—and we reject that remainder which seems to us unquestionably absurd. . . . We are naturally tempted to sacrifice, in the name of "impossibility," everything that we totally fail to integrate into our system of anticipations. . . . [However], the essence of questioning is to lay bare and keep alert for possibilities.[150]

For sound and meaningful analyses, our interpretive community sought to remain receptive to interpretations that at first glance might seem "impossible," "absurd," or unexpected. We took note when we were quick to dismiss an element of an interview as unimportant or uninformative or when we were confused by an interviewee's response. We sought to recognize, question, and challenge our own expectations and assumptions. The purpose of such a process was not to rid ourselves of these expectations or pretend that they can be left behind once they have been acknowledged, but to come to the edge of our own knowledge—to ask ourselves what did we learn that, in fact, we did not know? What did we expect that did not appear in the interview? How far did the interview take us into territory not yet charted?

Women and men, mostly students from New York University, and from a vast array of countries and cultures, have formed these interpretative communities in the many different phases of the studies. These women and men, most of whom had done the interviews themselves, had had extensive experience working with and, in some cases, writing about teenagers; two were teenagers themselves from local high schools (not the high schools where we conducted the research).

In these interpretive communities, we first closely read the interviews of the teenagers independently. Then we shared our observations and interpretations in weekly meetings over the course of an academic year. The members of the interpretive community have shifted many times over the course of the last decade during which most of the analyses have taken place. However, I have remained the anchor throughout, helping to guide the group and open up possibilities for students to challenge my interpretations. The ultimate aim has been to analyze the interview data in a thorough and rigorous manner. I was not interested in simply confirming my interpretations but in coming to the limits of my own knowledge so as to more deeply understand what is going on with the boys in my studies. I have encouraged disagreement and tried to provide a safe space for even the teenage members of the research team to offer a view that might not be consistent with what I've proposed. I was interested in truly understanding friendships among teenage boys.

The students and I drew on our experiences working with teenagers, our observations of the students in the schools, and our own experiences as teenagers to analyze the interview data. While our analyses focuses on the interviews themselves, they take into account the multiple ways we came to know teenagers. Our analyses of the interviews has relied on multiple techniques for analyzing qualitative data but primarily on the "Listening Guide" created by Brown and Gilligan and their students.[151] This method underscores and draws out the complexity of "voice" and of experience by paying close attention to the language interviewees have used. It attunes the reader's ear to what is being said and to what is, perhaps, not being said. Moreover, it emphasizes the relational nature of interviewing, analyzing, and interpreting interviews and people's abilities to speak about their worlds in more than one way. The Listening Guide draws heavily from literary analysis, in that the focus is on the words and meanings that are communicated through those words in an interview. The aim is not to simply paraphrase the content of the interview but to pay close attention to both the form and content of the narrative or story in the interview. How a person tells a story becomes as important as what he or she says. Furthermore, this method is explicitly attentive to cultural contexts and assumes that adolescents cannot be separated from their contexts.

The Listening Guide involves a sequence of four readings, each focusing on a different component of the interview. The first reading focuses on how the narrator tells her or his story. For the purposes of the boys' interviews, we simply read the transcript for the story the boy was telling—the "who, what, when, where, and why of the story"—and we wrote a narrative summary for each boy. A narrative summary was a brief description of the basic story the boy was communicating (e.g., he has a best friend for four years but his best friend doesn't live in the same city, etc.). Direct quotes were often used to enhance the summary and stay as close to the data as possible. In this first reading, we also listened for and recorded contradictions or inconsistencies, as well as repeated words or images. We looked for places where there appeared to be obvious revisions. We also noted how we responded to the interview, as we were always aware of the extent to which our own reactions influenced the analysis.

In the second reading, we listened to the ways the narrators spoke about themselves. We followed what Brown and Gilligan call the "I" voice (e.g. "I said . . . I did . . . I went . . .") in the story. Without using preexisting categories, the second reading invites the reader to listen to the narrators on their own terms and trace how the adolescents see themselves—aspects of the story that may not be as evident in the explicit content of the interviews. Brown and Gilligan suggest creating "I poems" with the "I" statements in the interviews. This means tracing, in the order in which the boy speaks, the ways the "I" is used. Creating an "I poem" reveals the story underneath the overt story. By tracing the ways girls spoke about themselves (e.g., "I am not . . . I am . . . I don't know . . ."), Brown and Gilligan were able to detect the uncertainty that emerged in girls' interviews at the edge of adolescence.[152] The third and fourth readings of the Listening Guide grow out of the first two and invite the researchers to investigate further by listening specifically for voices or themes that have been noted in the first two readings. These voices are often contrapuntal and have included, in the work of Brown and Gilligan, the voices of connection and disconnection.

During our first and second readings of the boys' interviews, it became clear that they were resisting conventions of masculinity, particularly those of emotional stoicism, autonomy, and physical toughness, when they spoke about their male friendships. We *did not* begin our analytic process aiming to read for these themes. These themes of resistance jumped out at us as we read the boys' responses to our questions about friendships. Boy after boy spoke about "spilling their heart out" to and wanting to share their deepest secrets with their best friends. Thus, for the third and fourth readings, we reread all of the interviews paying attention to these themes of resistance to conventions of masculinity as well as to the themes of accommodation that were so prevalent during late adolescence. To read for these two themes, we used a pink or blue highlighter to mark each instance when a boy suggested resistance (pink) or accommodation (blue) to conventions of masculinity. Resistance was defined as responses that suggested emotional intimacy or vulnerability, a need or desire for intimacy or closeness, or a willingness to appear "weak" or in need of protection; while accommodation was defined as responses that suggested emotional stoicism, autonomy, and physical toughness. The result, after completing the third and fourth reading for each interview, was that every boy's interview had both pink and blue marks, with the interviews during early and middle adolescence having more pink marks in them while the interviews during late adolescence having more blue marks.

The interviews of each boy were independently analyzed by at least two people who after coding the interviews came together in the group to discuss their analyses. We were interested in how boys described their friendships but also in the ways the cultural context shaped these descriptions. Thus throughout our analyses we discussed how the boys' gender, social and economic status, racial and ethnic identifications, sexuality, immigrant status, and nationality, as well as their experiences of stereotyping and discrimination (part of the interview protocol) shaped their experiences of boyhood, masculinity, and friendships. These discussions were incorporated in the final analysis and are discussed in chapters 4 and 7 of this book.

SUMMARY

Applying the work on boys, friendships, masculinity, and human nature to boys' experiences of friendships, we begin to see the thick culture that explains the patterns in my data and their significance. Yet we would not be able to see the thick culture if I did not integrate the relevant elements of almost half a century of scholarship in the intepretations of the boys' interviews. Scholars such as William Pollack, Michael Kimmel, and Pedro Noguera show us the detrimental effects of the patriarchy and stereotypes, in particular, on boys' development. Margarita Azmitia reveals that boys talk about their friendships in similar ways as girls; while the studies of adult men indicate that the patterns in my studies of boys are consistent with what adult men believe about friendships. And researchers of masculinity such as Joseph Pleck and Raewyn Connell describe the conventions of masculinity, the socially constructed nature of them, and the impact such conventions have on the well-being of boys and men. Scholars who study the processes of resistance and accommodation show us that these processes are a core part of human experience and that boys do, in fact, regularly resist gender stereotypes; and those who investigate the social and emotional capacities of humans reveal such skills as critical to our survival. It is only by relying on the insights from these thick and rich bodies of scholarly work that we can *see* boys' friendships (i.e., the "box in the kitchen") for what they are and why they change. Now, let's listen to the boys.

FRIENDSHIPS DURING EARLY

AND MIDDLE ADOLESCENCE

I

CHAPTER 3

"SOMETIMES YOU NEED

TO SPILL YOUR HEART

OUT TO SOMEBODY"

I've got two best friends—Willy and Brian. Like sometimes
when me and Willy argue, me and Brian are real close. Then
when me and Brian are not doing so good, me and Willy are
real close. It's like circles of love. Sometimes, we're all close.

—14-year-old boy

My ideal best friend is a close, close friend who I could say
anything to . . . 'cause sometimes you need to spill your heart
out to somebody and if there's nobody there, then you gonna
keep it inside, then you will have anger. So you need somebody to talk to always.

—15-year-old boy

Teenage boys—the same boys
who have sex, video games, and sports on their minds and are
"activity" or "object" oriented—spoke about "circles of love,"
"spilling your heart out to somebody," "sharing deep depth secrets," and "feeling lost" without their male best friends. They
suggested a capacity for and interest in emotionally intimate
friendships that have rarely been noted. Although they did indeed talk about girls, video games, and sports, they also talked
about sharing secrets with their closest friends, knowing that
these friends will not joke around when they want to talk about
"serious" topics, and expressing themselves openly with them.

Yet in books about boys or adolescents, we never hear how "sharing deep depth secrets," is, in the eyes of many teenage boys, the best part of their male friendships. We rarely hear voices like that of Brandon, who says that having an ideal friend entails "trust and love and never breaking apart." And thus we fail to recognize how pervasive these themes of emotional intimacy are among boys. Three-fourths of the boys in my studies, particularly during the first two years of high school (i.e., early to middle adolescence), spoke about wanting to share or sharing "everything" with their closest friends and about the confidence they had that these friends would not betray them by telling their secrets to other peers or laughing at their vulnerability.

The boys were acutely attuned to the emotional nuances in their friendships and valued the intimacy greatly, often placing their friendships with boys above those with girls. They were straightforward about their "need" for close friendships and used vulnerable language to express this need. Ronan says, in his freshman year, in response to a question of what he likes about his friendships, "That I'm not alone by myself. Everybody needs somebody to, like, talk to . . . besides your parents and your family." Describing the importance of trust in his friendship, he says: "Nobody would like a friend betraying you. You would feel hurt about that and I don't want to feel hurt, so that's why trust is important." Tony, who immigrated from China at the age of three, says at the age of 14 that with his male friends he "feels safe and comfortable" because they "don't play around or joke around that much." Challenging the gender stereotype of invulnerability, boys such as Ronan and Tony explicitly acknowledge their emotional fragility.

Paul says in his sophomore year about his current best friend:

> [We are] real close . . . nothing would get like in between us and . . . like if I disagree, he'll know why I'm disagreeing. Not just because I'm disagreeing. He'll be up to my level . . . He knows what I'm

about . . . like he knows, like even sometimes when I sit at home he
knows what I'm thinking. Like we already know each other like if we
came out of the same belly.

Emphasizing the extent to which his friend *knows* him, Paul describes a boy who is so close to him that he considers him a
brother in blood as well as in spirit. Placed against a culture of
masculinity that is intolerant of same-sex intimacy, especially
between males, these patterns of closeness and vulnerability in
boys' friendships are surprising.

The boys in my studies, primarily during early and middle
adolescence, spoke of shared secrets with their friends, expressed
vulnerabilities, and placed their male friendships above those
with girls. While they valued their opposite-sex friendships, if
they indeed had any, they told us that they connected more
deeply with their male friends. Boys also repeated macho
mantras about boys not crying and not being vulnerable, drawing attention to the ways boys believe in these stereotypes even if
they do not fit them. The repetition of gender stereotypes set
against their openly vulnerable responses underscores boys' resistance to such stereotypes. The boys knew what the masculine
conventions were yet they rejected them by maintaining intimate
male friendships, at least until late adolescence.

SHARING DEEP SECRETS

Alejandro, a 15-year-old, says: "I trust my friends. Like if I have a
deep secret I don't want to tell anybody, I tell one of my friends
that I know won't tell anybody else unless I give them permission
to tell somebody else." Lucas says in his ninth grade interview
when asked if friends are important: "You can't just do everything
yourself or tell your problems to yourself. You can't, like just talk
to yourself. It's good to have someone to talk to and tell your secrets to." Secret sharing or talking intimately with best friends was

what boys had and what they wanted most in their friendships. It was how they defined a best friend. And betrayal of this confidence was the primary cause for terminating a friendship.

In his freshman year, Charles says that what he likes about his friendships is the intimacy: "I don't know. Like my friends, I like how they are. . . . They are honest, like they tell me things, like they tell me their secrets." Keith says that with his best friend he shares his most intimate "secrets" and "problems" and says that he has "a good, solid relationship" that entails "not telling secrets to others and not breaking promises." Omar says about his best friend: "Me and him can talk about real serious stuff that I wouldn't even talk to my mom about." Teenage boys from Black, Latino, Asian American, and White families had the same story to tell: they had or wanted friends whom they could trust to keep their secrets and "share [their] feelings" and who would not abandon them in times of need.

A freshman boy says: "[My best friend] could just tell me anything and I could tell him anything. Like I always know everything about him. . . . We always chill, like we don't hide secrets from each other." When asked what he likes about his friend, he replies: "If I have a problem, I can go tell him. If he has a problem, he can go tell me." Similarly, Marcus says about his best friend in his sophomore year: "We share secrets that we don't talk about in the open." When asked to explain why he felt close to his male friends, he states: "If I'm having problems at home, they'll like counsel me, I just trust them with anything, like deep secrets, anything." In his freshman year, Howie says: "We're tight. We're close, like um, like if we got any problems we tell each other . . . he's easy to talk to. Like I don't have to say too much for him to understand what I'm talking about." Eddie, a sophomore says: "It's like a bond, we keep secrets, like if there is something that's important to me like I could tell him and he won't go and make fun of it. Like if my family is having problems or something." He knows he can trust his best friend because "when we were like younger it's like a lot of things that I told him that he didn't tell anybody, like it's like a lot of things he told me that I didn't tell anybody." The mutual trust was a core part of the intimacy in boys' friendships and stemmed from both a long history together in which the boys knew each other's families and the confidence that what was shared together—even family problems—would not be revealed to others.

For Will, in his sophomore year, "a friend . . . is a person that would be your friend no matter what, who will be there through thick and thin, you know, someone to talk to about everything, you know, just basically a true friend." When Eric is asked why sharing secrets is so important in his friendships, he says: "It's that you get like a closer relationship. You feel for each other more. Like we see what we like and how we are alike and, you know, like we're close to each other, real close so nothing would get like in between us." Datong, a freshman, says simply: "Friendship is all about communication, you know . . . that makes your friendship much deeper in a way, much closer." Secrets and "talk[ing] about everything" were the foundations of boys' closest friendships.

Sharing the intimate details of one's life was not only an individual exchange but also took place in a group. Michael says:

> You know on that Christmas day we all slept in this little bed. It was little, we were like squeezing and then we were listening to this cheap radio, my friend got a cheap radio, we were turning it to like a low volume and listening to songs at like 12:30 at night till like three in the morning, we were not all listening, we were talking about secrets and then that's how I know [my best friends].

Teenage boys provided vivid descriptions of both physical and psychological intimacy among their friends. They had and actively sought out friendships in which they could literally and metaphorically talk until three in the morning.

Boys repeatedly indicated that the intimacy or sharing of secrets is what they *liked most* about their friendships. Junot, a sophomore, says: "We always tell each other everything. And um like, about something happens and I save it for [my best friend]." In his junior year, he says: "[What I like most about my best friendship] is the connection. It's like, you know how you know somebody for so long you could talk about anything and you won't even think, I mean you won't even think about how 'oh what are they thinking?' You just talk." Kevin describes in his freshman year the type of friendship he would like to have: "I could tell them everything. . . . Like if I'm like having serious problems in my family, if I could tell them like without them trying to cheat or tease me or something like that. That's it."

Such open discussion of thoughts and feelings, however, was not simply what boys did. They believed sharing secrets was an absolute necessity for their emotional health and well-being. One of the boys notes (see the beginning of this chapter) that if he isn't able to "spill his heart out" to a friend, he would experience a lot of anger. Xudong says in his freshman year in response to why friendships are important:

> *Xudong:* If you don't have friends, no, you got no one to tell secrets to.
> *Interviewer:* And so what happens then?
> *X:* Then it's like you need to keep all the secrets to yourself.
> *I:* What do you think it'd be like if you didn't have someone?
> *X:* Then it's like, I always like think bad stuff in my brain 'cause like no one's helping me and I just need to keep all the secrets to myself.

Steve says in his sophomore year:

> You need friends to talk to sometimes, you know like you have nobody to talk to, you don't have a friend, it's hard. You got to keep things bottled up inside, you might just . . . crying or whatever. Like

if a family member is beating on you or something and you can't tell a friend, you might just go out, just you know do drugs, sell drugs whatever.

Sharing their innermost thoughts was according to the boys, an essential element of staying sane.

Chen says in his junior year that he needs "someone to talk to, like you have problems with something, you go talk to him. You know, if you keep it all the stuff to yourself, you go crazy. Try to take it out on someone else." Another boy concurs saying that "without friends you will go crazy or mad or you'll be lonely all of the time, be depressed." Kai says at 14-years old: "My friendships are important 'cause you need a friend or else, you would be depressed, you won't be happy, you would try to kill yourself, 'cause then you'll be all alone and no one to talk to." Augustus, who recently lost his grandmother, asks his interviewer in his sophomore year: "What if you have no family, let's say you have no family, your family passes away. Who can you go to? Who you're gonna talk to? Might as well be dead or something. I don't mean to put it in a negative way, but I am just saying—It's like not a good feeling to be alone." Another says: "If you don't have any friends you'd be lonely, depressed, . . . you gotta talk to somebody. You can't just be by yourself all day." Absorbing the messages from their American culture about the healthy nature of "talking," these boys actively resist the other messages that equate "talking" with being girlish or gay. They recognize that in the absence of trusting relationships in which they can "share everything," there will be dire social and psychological consequences.

Sharing secrets, however, was not only necessary to avoid "going crazy"; it was also helpful for boys to learn problem-solving strategies. When Tony is asked about his best friend, he says: "I feel very happy 'cause like when I talk to him about secrets right, he mostly like helps me like answers some of my questions and stuff. And sometimes when someone tells him some secrets about me right, he mostly tells me 'cause we are like best friends." Although Tony is uncertain of his friend's reliability (e.g., "sometimes" and "mostly"), he is nonetheless appreciative of his friend's help. When Jerome is asked in his freshman year to describe his best friend he says: "He's like a brother . . . When I talk about problems, he'll tell me or give me ideas or things to do." Boys shared secrets for emotional support and for guidance on how to handle difficult situations.

The content of boys' secrets varied considerably, and the term "secrets" was often used interchangeably with "problems." "Problems" were always "secrets," but "secrets" weren't necessarily problems. Amir says in his sophomore year that he shares secrets with lots of his friends but keeps the "really, really big" secrets for his best friend: "If I have like problems at home and I can't tell anybody then I would tell my best friend but if it's just a regular secret about girls then I will tell my other friends as well." Like Amir, Andy in his sophomore year also makes distinctions between types of secrets when talking about the friends whom he doesn't trust:

> I mean I can like joke around with them and like if I'm like having trouble in my classes, like if somebody knows the subject better than me, like I'll ask them. Like yeah, it's pretty much like that, not too deep though. . . . I wouldn't tell them like my too secretest things, not too secretive . . . Yeah. Like about a girl or something. I mean that's the deepest, nothing deeper than that though.

The content of "regular" or "not too deep" secrets ranged from crushes on girls to girl-related topics. "Really, really big secrets" or "secretest things" were almost always related to conflicts with or between parents or, on rare occasions, coping with disabilities or drug abuse of a family member. Paul says that he shares secrets with his best friends "all the time" and admits that it is good to have a best friend because "sometimes, like you don't want to tell your family members 'cause it's probably about them and you just tell your friend and they'll keep a secret and help you." Chen's idea of a perfect friendship in his freshman year is one in which "you trust each other, understand about each other's family problems and discuss those problems." Family-related "problems" or "secrets" were almost always considered the "deepest" secrets of all.

Boys' concerns about being betrayed by their peers were also "deep secrets" to be shared with close friends. This fear of betrayal, in fact, consumed many of the boys' interviews, especially as they entered late adolescence. In response to this concern, boys created trust tests to make sure a friend could keep their secrets. A trust test entailed a boy making up a secret and seeing whether word of this false secret got out. If the friend did not share the boy's "secrets," the friend passed the trust test, and the boy and his friend could then become closer. Francisco explains:

> Well, like I don't know, I started off with, um, oh I don't—like I'd tell him, "oh I hate this girl, she's really stupid." So he'd be like, 'oh okay.' And then I'd see the next day if he told anyone and if he didn't then I'd go like even farther into like secrets, and it all depends on the severity of it I guess. It would just get, it would just get more and more severe until like I'd see when he would just start blurting it out so.

When Thomas is asked in his sophomore year how he knows whether he can trust his friends, he says: "With certain people you tell like maybe a lie or something to see if they're gonna go around [and tell others]. It's like a test. Like you test certain people and some of them do tell, then you don't tell that person stuff that you don't want around school." For Miguel, trust tests are an essential strategy for determining trustworthiness.

> *I:* How do you know you can trust your friends?
> *M:* Because, because I, I have this little thing that I test people.
> *I:* How do you test them?
> *M:* Because I'll tell them like a thing, like a bad thing. And I wanna see if they tell anybody, especially my girl. So I tell them a lie but then I see if they tell my girl. And some of them, some of them don't, so now I know who not to trust and who to trust.

I: So how often have you done this little uh test?

M: Well, I've been doing it all year.

I: Do these guys know that you're doing it?

M: No. The only one that knows is my girl.

I: So, your best friend passed this test.

M: Yeah.

Trust tests often needed an ally, and girlfriends were, at times, the ones who helped conduct the trust tests.

Trust tests were not, however, the only strategy of building friendships. Carl in his sophomore year describes how he and his best friend grew to trust each other:

> When we first met each other, I wanted to like—when I first noticed that me and him were hanging out a lot, I wanted it to be a carefree relationship. I wanted him to be able to come over to my house and like I made sure that he trusted me. The way I did that was by showing him that I had trust for him first and that, that way he opened up to me . . . I think like everybody should have a relationship like me and Eric 'cause if he walked in this door right now, he would have such the biggest smile on his face.

Rather than testing for trustworthiness, Carl chooses to be vulnerable with his friend, knowing that such a strategy will likely enhance the trust between them. Boys revealed a sophisticated understanding of the relational world and used the same strategies that girls use with friends to become close friends[1]—they shared secrets in hopes that such intimacy and trust will be returned.

EXPRESSING VULNERABILITY

As Felix reflects on his best friendship with Devin during his sophomore year, he says: "My best friend thinks physical pain is worse than emotional pain and I don't think that's true, 'cause physical pain could last but for so long, but when it's in the mind, it doesn't go away." Acutely attuned to the nuances of the emotional world, Felix is typical of the boys during their freshman and sophomore years. In addition to sharing secrets, boys were openly vulnerable with their closest friends (and with their male and female interviewers) and spoke explicitly about vulnerability. In his senior year, Felix says:

> I don't give—I don't give my heart out to too many people, you know, especially when it could get broken or hurt easily. I've been through too many times of that. So it's like I don't have any room—I have to recuperate from my heart broken. There's been death in my family, girlfriends, you know, guy friends. I don't have any more for my heart to get stepped on. So I've picked myself up for awhile. I'm walking. But you know, you never know when you fall down again. So I'm trying to just keep my eye out.

Felix vividly expressed the wariness that comes after a broken heart. And in this scenario, his heart is not simply broken over a girl or a family member but a "guy friend." Feelings for family members, girl friends, and "guy friends" were blended together in a seamless discussion of having his "heart stepped on."

Keith explains about his close friends in his sophomore year: "When I need help, they're there for me. When I'm hungry, they buy junk food and give it to me. When I feel lonely, they comfort me." Using the language of romance, Mike describes his best friends in sophomore year: "You could tell them anything, you could give them anything. It's like you're giving yourself to them." Justin says in his freshman year when considering whether he would like to be closer to his male friends:

> I think so. But I don't really know if they're gonna stay here for four years. So I feel like I can't get too attached 'cause then if they leave, I still get attached to them even though 'cause a friend, he, he could come and go even though I really don't want it to happen. But it could come and go. I could make new friends or whatever. So I, doesn't matter if I get attached to them or not. I don't know . . . I don't want to [become attached] because if they leave I really don't, I never really got emotional for a guy before but I don't know if I would or if I wouldn't.

Justin's struggle is palpable as he expresses both his desire for closeness and a fear that if he allows himself to feel "attached" he will get hurt (although by his sophomore year he has a best friend). He attempts to assert the masculine convention ("doesn't matter if I get attached to them or not") but then acknowledges that is not really what he feels. If we trace the voice of the "I" in Justin's response, we hear his conflict as he tries to articulate what he really feels but cannot quite spit out:

> I don't
> I feel
> I can't
>
> I still get
> I really don't
> I could
> I get
>
> I don't
> I don't
> I really don't
> I never
> I don't
>
> I would
> I wouldn't

Justin's desire for "attachment" and his fear of being abandoned is apparent, as is his uncertainty whether he can say what he feels to the interviewer. His ambivalence about directly expressing himself is suggested as he poses a question at the end of the passage to which he already knows the answer.

The vulnerability in boys' stories was often evident most often when they were asked what they liked about their friendships. A sophomore boy says that what he likes most is that "Just basically I can just tell them everything, pretty much like, they won't make fun of me, like they won't laugh or anything, like if I told them something you know, embarrassing." Similarly, Benjamin makes explicit his sense of vulnerability in explaining what he likes about his best friend:

> Mmm, most everything. His kindness. Everything. I know, I know he, you know, he cares for people, me, you know. He's not like that, you see him in the street, he's not like, he is not like that you know what I'm saying, walk by and, you know, he talks to you, even if he won't, he won't, he won't, he won't you know like just see you and just don't say anything. He'll talk to you.

Struggling to say what he knows ("I know, I know he, you know, he cares for people, *me*, you know")—feelings that are not part of the "boy code"—Benjamin describes a world where kindness, mutual recognition, and support are central.

William says in his sophomore year that he trusts his friends because: "I know none of my friends wouldn't do anything to hurt me. . . . These are people I could depend on or call my friends because we've been through thick and thin together. We've had arguments, we are still friends." The intimacy in his friendships as well as his sense of safety from emotional harm is evident in his response. Ethan also wears his vulnerability on his sleeve: "Once you have trust with your friends, then everything else is all right. 'Cause nobody would like somebody, like your friend, doing something bad back to you. You would feel hurt about that and I don't want to feel hurt. So that's why trust is important."

Describing what he likes about his best friend, David says in his sophomore year:

> I think our relationship is wonderful. Because we like, I can't explain. The feelings that I have for him if something would happen to

him, I probably won't feel right. . . . Like when he was sick and I hadn't seen him for like a week and I went to his house and I, and I asked his grandmother what was wrong with him and he was in the room like he couldn't move. So I went in there. I sat in his house for the whole day talking to him. And like the next day he got up and he felt better.

David's response suggests that he is sharply attuned to his own vulnerability (e.g., "I probably won't feel right") and to his friend's. He also knows, like so many of his peers, that "talking" (e.g., "I sat in his house for the whole day talking to him") is good for his friend's health ("and like the next day he got up and he felt better").

Being direct about his feeling of vulnerability, Paul says in his junior year:

Yeah 'cause [my best friend] is like a second person you could speak to . . . It's like see how the kids carry a little teddy bear or whatever and when they cry, they'll hold it and stuff. So when like you get up-set or something you just walk over to them and they'll loosen, they'll loosen up whatever. They'll be like yeah it's all right, even though it's not.

Paul recognizes both the safety or unconditional love that a friend provides but also the ways boys cover over and tell stories that they know are not true ("They'll be like yeah, it's all right, even though it's not").

While some boys were willing to directly express vulnerability when speaking about their closest friends, others repeated masculine conventions only to reveal their more vulnerable sides at other points in the interview. Carl says:

C: Sometimes . . . my friends are kind of harsh sometimes. Like sometimes I'll tell them [for example] my teachers recommended me for this award, and I was telling them and they was like "so what?" . . . at the moment that, you know, that hurts me, you know, I'll be like, "oh. alright so . . ." I'll be like, "shut up," you know, you just start playing and stuff . . .

> *I:* Would you ever tell your friends that like it hurts me when you say that?
>
> *C:* Yeah, like we talk about it a lot 'cause you know me and my friends we, you know, we have arguments and stuff. And when we have arguments, you know, we let each other know how we feel. We're not like afraid to tell each other.

Woven into Carl's response is his adherence ("I'll be like shut up, you know, you just start playing and stuff") as well his resistance to conventions of masculinity. Like the girls in Jean Anyon's studies,[2] the boys revealed their knowledge of the dictates of manhood (i.e., be emotionally stoic) and their willingness to reject those very same dictates when with their closest friends.

This "code switching" was also evident in Milo's interview. When the interviewer asked him to describe how it felt when he was teased by his best friend, he said: "I know he's playing so it doesn't really, it doesn't feel bad, but if I didn't know he was playing, he probably would be able to hurt somebody. He would get somebody mad enough to do something, you know." His switch from the first person (i.e., "I") to the use of "somebody" right at the moment when his vulnerability is made explicit underscores the danger or sense of risk boys feel when expressing such vulnerability. Yet the boys almost always expressed it anyway.

James says he doesn't like that his friends will "sometimes . . . see someone who looks like fat and they will like tease them maybe. But I don't tease them or anything. I like tell them not to tease that person but they keep on teasing, you know, like that." He doesn't like this "mean" behavior because, he says, it makes him "look mean" as well. Similarly, Mike also doesn't like it when his friends are mean: "Sometimes, my friends will say stuff about my other friends behind their backs, um. I don't like that. If you gonna say something, just say it to his face." His defensiveness for his friends is also heard in his response to what type of friendship he would like:

> An honest friendship 'cause I don't like nobody lying, talking about somebody else. . . . They often tell lies about my friend and that stuff ain't true. So I'll be like "why are you lying about him?" and stuff like that. They'll be like "he ain't good, he's wacked, c'mon let's go, let's leave him, let's leave him . . . He ain't got no money, he ain't got no [video] games, c'mon let's go." Stuff like that. And they be lying about it.

The fact that he sees the exclusion of his friends as a betrayal as well as a form of dishonesty speaks to his firm sense of justice along with his empathic sensibility.

Boys' expressions of vulnerability, care, and empathy were evident not only when they discussed the details of their daily lives with their closest friends but also when they spoke more abstractly about the importance of friendships. Lorenzo says in his junior year:

> Everybody needs somebody. Some people are good to hang out with because they're good friends, you know. And they will be there for you. Somebody, in other words, when you need a shoulder to cry on inside, you need a arm to punch when you are mad and things like that, you know.

When asked about the meaning of an ideal friendship, Danny says in his freshman year:

> *D:* Ideal friendship? Be like ah I could trust them, or he could trust me, or we could play together, and he wouldn't get mad at everything. And then he could trust me when I get mad [at him]. . . .
> *I:* Why do you want that kind of a friendship?
> *D:* 'Cause like, it's like having a second, second voice from yourself. Friends, you can talk to them about a lot of things that you would normally talk about only to yourself. So having a friend is like um when you're in trouble you can talk to them about things. They could help you so you don't have to worry about yourself.

Recognizing the necessity for trust in a friendship especially when there is anger, Danny wants a mutually trusting friendship that would entail less anger. The importance for Danny of such a friendship lies with the fact that he won't feel alone and have to "worry about" himself by himself. The way he aligns himself with his ideal" friend ("a second voice from yourself") as well as his open admission of wanting such a tightly woven friendship reveals his vulnerability as well his willingness to express such vulnerability.

When Steve describes in his freshman year why he thinks friendships are important, he says "because without friendships, you know, you won't get along with anybody and it's harder in life . . . it's someone to comfort you when you are feeling down, and without a friendship, then life is not worth living." An example of what he means by a friend "comforting him" includes:

> I lost um maybe I had a goldfish and I had it for a long time. I won it at the fair. I haven't had that in a long time because every time I had goldfishes, they often die fast. But I had this goldfish for a long time and it died, so I started crying and crying. I don't know why but I went to um, a friend, a sister, well actually I went to Thomas and he and I just, I was crying and he just told me to stop crying, and you know he comforted me, he talks to me, telling me about him losing a hamster.

Although Steve reveals his ability to express a sense of loss with his close friend, his hesitation to confess to the interviewer that he went to Thomas for support (i.e., "I don't know why but I went to um, a friend, a sister, well actually I went to Thomas") is a reminder of the cultural context of masculinity in which going to a male friend is not part of the "boy code."

Chen in his freshman year says that the intimacy is so strong between him and his best friend that it feels as if they have known each other in a past life. When asked to explain, he says: "Oh, um, when we talk, we keep telling each other secrets, and he trusts me and I trust him so we became that kind of friendship. . . . [My best friend] is kind of an open man. His feelings are open. And he, he knows a lot about how someone's feeling—

how they feel." In his sophomore year, he says that what he likes most about his friendship is that "you could tell him your feelings, and we could discuss together our feelings and how they are alike." Even into his junior year interview, feelings are critical to how he experiences his friendships: "My best friend feels the same way I do, we know the way each other feels." When asked how he knows that, he says:

> He just knows it. He will say just "yeah I'm sorry about that too 'cause like I'm just playing around, joking . . . And when his father went to Hong Kong to try to look for a job, his father was having a hard time and he didn't tell me. But I looked at him and I said "is something happening to your family?" He's like "yeah it is my father in Hong Kong and stuff . . ." I could tell his feelings.

During his freshman year, Carlos says about his best friend: "Like we could express our feelings or whatever. And tell each other how we feel. Like if I feel bad one day, I tell him why." He describes his best friends like brothers and uses language such as "we show each other love" to describe the bonds he feels with his closest friend. Carlos says: "I know the kid inside of him, inside of him. 'Cause I, I grew up with that kid, you understand? I know who he really is." Jin Long says that he is close to his best friend because he can "talk about stuff like deep deep. Our feelings and stuff like what we talked about today [in the interview]." Sharing secrets and being openly vulnerable with each other formed the foundation of boys' close friendships.

BOYS BEFORE GIRLS

One of the most unexpected subthemes in our interviews was the preference for talking to boys rather than girls when discussing their emotional concerns. When asked about the difference between his male and female friends, Kevin, who does not have a close friend during his freshman year, says: "I just feel, like, safer with boys [than with girls]. It's like I can trust the boys more than the girls because . . . they experience most of the same things as me pretty much. . . . like, you know arguments, family problems." Rather than pointing to the physical experiences or the similar interests that may draw boys together, Kevin points to the emotional problems.

Similarly, in tenth grade, Carlos says: "Um, yeah like with personal things I'm more comfortable talking with [guys]. Besides my mother, I'm more comfortable talking to a guy than a girl [about] . . . like you know, background problems or something like that. I mean like, family problems." He adds at a later point in the interview: "I'm not afraid to talk to the boys as I am to the girls. . . . I just have more confidence with the boys . . . With boys you can talk and you can talk like about more things than you can talk about with girls." Fernando says in his freshman year: "Well with the guys, we're more personal. With the girls, we just talk . . . we don't share real secrets . . . A real secret is something that happens at home, or you know, just something, at home." Strikingly, the boys' preferences were based on their belief that they could be more vulnerable with boys than girls.

This pattern of preference even applied to girlfriends. Malcolm says: "'Cause if you have a best friend, you know, you express yourself more and you're like, you, like, feel lost without him. So, you know, with [my girlfriend] it's really just we have a close relationship where we can express things." Farouk reveals a similar belief in his freshman year: "With my girlfriend, I could—I could talk to her like I can with my best friend but not tell her everything. It is—it is pretty close . . . however I'll tell my best friend my family problems if I have problems in my household but I won't tell her that." In his sophomore year, Farouk says in response to a question about the differences between his male and female friends:

Like I can't, I can't really explain it. I don't really know. I just can't like, I'll be, I don't feel so open to girls. Like I just block, like I just block it like a box at a certain point where I could tell them stuff.

> Like as my friends who are guys, these friends I could tell them any-
> thing. [With girls] we're not so tight together. I just can't, like I don't
> feel, I don't feel comfortable.

Even into his junior year, Farouk says he feels more comfortable
talking with boys than with girls:

> My friendships with boys are more tight. My friendships with girls
> are not so tight. Like, I can open myself to one of my boys, instead
> of a girl . . . with girls I can talk about school, clothes, trying to get
> jobs, stuff like that . . . with boys I talk to them about anything,
> school, girls, clothing, basically anything I have problems with, I tell
> my friends. Like if I have problems in my household, I tell my
> friends, like my tight friends.

While reminding us of the changing nature of boys' talk where
talk about "clothing" is no longer considered feminine in youth
culture,[3] Farouk indicates that he will only reveal his deepest secrets—his problems—to his closest male friends.

This preference for male intimacy may be rooted in boys' desires to connect to other boys right at the time their voices are
cracking and their bodies feel awkward. They may *feel* too vulnerable to *be* vulnerable with those they do not perceive as experiencing the same changes. Boys may also believe, in line with the
larger culture that bombards them with images of "mean girls,"
that girls are untrustworthy and gossipy. Keith says in his freshman year: "With the guys, I could tell secrets to. The girls, you
know, I don't trust them. I told one secret to a girl and then the
next day mostly everybody knew already . . . I was embar-
rassed." While describing why he hangs out with boys rather
than girls, Enrique says in his sophomore year:

> So girls, they're like kind of you know, like they have a certain atti-
> tude. One day, they say, one day they'll say hi to you and then an-
> other day, like, they won't pay much attention to you and they'll pay
> more attention to somebody else. And um, that's why I don't really,
> you know, say it that they're my best friends and stuff like that 'cause

one day if you say hi to me one day and being all kind and gentle with me than one day it's like, you don't really pay attention to me, what's the point of calling you my best friend?

Boys were deeply affected by perceived betrayals and spoke directly about how girls hurt their feelings.[4] From these experiences, they turned toward other boys as confidantes.

Girls were also perceived as impediments to male friendships. When Paul is asked in his junior year what he dislikes about his relationship with his best friend, he says:

> *P:* That he takes like, if he was hanging out with me, say for instance he was hanging out with me for, for the whole day and a girl steps up. He'll leave with her and leave me. That puts me down. 'Cause I was with him and he's gonna break out on me and leave with a chick.
>
> *I:* What would you like to change about the relationship you have with him?
>
> *P:* For him to stop doing it. If he's chilling with me and a girl comes to him, we all chilling, all three of us. Not him breaking out on me.

Paul's vulnerability is readily apparent as he explains that he doesn't want to be abandoned by his friend. Strikingly, Paul does not blame the girl for his friend "breaking out on" him. He understands it is his friend who is making the choice to leave him. Marcus vowed that he will never let a "girl come between me and my best friend." Kai says that with boys: "I do everything, hang out, play ball. . . . [With a girl] it could be a friend but it can't be like too close. 'Cause you and she can get in between you and one of your guy friends. And then 'cause of her you get into arguments with him and you lose both of them." In order not to be left alone, Kai chooses the guy friend and avoids getting close to girls. In an American culture in which a choice must be made, boys often choose the boy during early and middle adolescence and then the girl during late adolescence. The boys implicitly raise the question of why they must make such a choice. Why, as Paul pointed out, couldn't they all "chill together"?

MACHO MANTRAS

In the midst of boys' discussions of shared secrets and feelings, the mocking voice of masculine conventions was ever present. Sometimes this voice was direct, as when Omar said that the reason he wouldn't tell his best friend about his hurt feelings is because "that's gay." Other times, it was subtler, as when boys talked about their desire to have friends who knew when "something was not a joking matter." When asked in his freshman year if the teasing between his male peers results in hurt feelings, Justin says: "I really wouldn't know 'cause they never really say, oh you hurt my feelings, 'cause guys don't share things like that . . . to my knowledge, I guess, I don't know . . . I don't share my feelings with them because then they would think you were a wuss or something like that." Justin, who was quoted earlier saying he doesn't want to get "too attached" to a friend for fear that he will get hurt and who said it's "human nature" to love his male best friend, clearly straddles two worlds—a culture with a "boy code" in which sharing feelings is equivalent to being a "wuss" and his own experiences in which he knows boys do share and want to share their feelings with their closest friends.

Recognizing both the reality of his own experience and the demands of the "boy code," Marco says in his sophomore year that while he could cry in front of his best friend, he never has. However, when asked if his best friend has cried in front of him, he says: "Um yes. When he found out his mom was using drugs. That's the only time. I know it's healthy or whatever." Like Justin, Marco understands the contradictions as he stands outside ("I know it's healthy or whatever") and inside (e.g., he has never cried in front of his friend) the confines of masculine conventions. Similarly Nick knows the boy code but doesn't follow it. In his description of a situation in which his friend did not show up for an event, Nick says:

> I'm gonna get mad. I'm not gonna get mad because you dissed me, I'm gonna get mad 'cause I missed you, but I'll probably show it to you like I'm gonna get mad because you dissed me, but it's really I'm gonna get mad because I love you and I miss you. That's what it is.

Nick knows that anger is often a cover-up for sadness, and he is willing to state this directly. The fact that he not only acknowledges this cover-up but also admits to using it himself speaks to Nick's knowledge that he does not stand outside of his culture. He, like his male peers, participates in it even when he knows it's not how he really feels. Chris also knows the score. Raised by his grandparents, he says in his third year interview:

> I'm pretty happy, yes. I think I mean I got a few things that I'm real pissed off at in life, you know. I wasn't raised with my parents and stuff like that. But if you gonna let that get to you, you know what I'm saying, you are gonna be a messed up person. You have to get past that, like, you know what I'm saying? Your mother did what she did. You can't stop that, you can't go back in time. So if you want to sit there and cry over that, you are not gonna progress as a person. I need to progress. I need to be a man. I need to do what I gotta do.

Making the dictates of manhood explicit, Chris knows his real thoughts and feelings ("I got a few things that I'm real pissed off at in life"). Yet he also understands that to be a man he has to disconnect from what he knows (i.e., "so if you want to sit there and cry over it . . ."). The culturally constructed dilemma for these boys is how to stay connected to what they know and still "progress" toward manhood.

When Carl is asked about what he doesn't like about his best friends, he says: "I don't know . . . there's so much girlish bickering." The fact that Carl and his friend engage in "girlish bickering" reveals their resistance to conventions of masculinity. Yet Carl also believes that the "bickering" is "girlish" suggesting that he also accommodates. He lives in two conflicting worlds—one that equates having emotions with being unmanly and the other that knows the importance of open and honest expression even if it leads to arguments. Like the cartoon character created by a student taking a masculinity course in high school described in Chapter 2, Carl, Chris, and Nick have two boys on their shoulders. On their right shoulder sits a stereotypic football player—or their peers in general—who wants them to follow the boy code; on their left shoulder sits a "normal" boy—perhaps their closest male friend—who understands the value of open and honest expression and encourages them to have intimate friendships. The conflict for these boys is to decide to whom they will listen.

A few of the boys in my studies seemed more drawn into the framework of masculine conventions. In his freshman year, Ronan says that he has close friends but occasionally gets mad at his friends when they tease him and that "it embarrasses me in front of my other friends and I feel sad and I put my head down." In his sophomore year, he says that he trusts his friends to be there for him and if they ever betrayed him, that would "break my heart because I have known them for a long time." Yet in the midst of these responses, he says that he can be safe with his best friend because "my friend is not a homo, he's not gay." When asked to clarify, he says, "If I did have a gay friend and he's just a friend, you know, he pulls no move on me, then it's cool. He pulls a move, I dump him. I don't care." Ronan's discussion of a hypothetical gay friend is striking in the context of his stories of his close friends potentially breaking his heart, reminding us of the ways resistance and accommodation weave together.

Boys' awareness of the conventions of masculinity was not always explicit. Boys, for example, talked incessantly about not taking things seriously, especially with their friends who were not close, and the harassment that goes on between boys who take things "too seriously." Lyn Mikel Brown and her colleagues note that "marketers know boys desire desperately to be funny, because to be serious..., is to be "girl like" and responsible, studious or boring."[5] Diesel Jeans "Be Stupid" campaign underscores their point. Yet the boys, particularly during early and middle adolescence, did not always follow the dictate to laugh it off. Emilio tells his interviewer in his freshman year what his friendships with other boys are like:

> Um, well, with [my best friend], I, I, I, I really like talk to him on a serious level. Like we can have a serious conversation without having to always joke around, because sometimes some things are too, some things are too serious to go around joking around about—like some things like family.... [My other friends] they're usually, um, make a joke.... Even when, when I feel that it shouldn't really be a joke or a joking matter.

Emilio's stuttering (i.e., "I, I, I, I, really . . .") seems to serve as a warning that he is about to say something that goes against the dictates of manhood. When Carmelo is asked to describe his best friendship, he says:

> Well, I could talk more personal things with him, about me, myself, that I couldn't talk with the other guys. And, and I know for sure he, he will back me up.... Sometimes when I tell the other guys something, they might go, they might laugh or whatever. But when I tell him, he's like, all right.

Despite the pressure to have a sense of humor, boys sought male friends who could resist the manly laughter of derision and understand that "some things are too serious to go around joking." When asked to define trust in his friendships, Marcus says:

> Say if I was with these guys and these guys didn't get along with the other guys, I'll have his back, and he'll have my back, you know. . . . But that's not being trustful . . . 'cause maybe the next day, he might be the one that's joking and making fun of you.

Marcus seeks friends who will not only protect him in times of physical danger but will also protect him emotionally; friends, in other words, who are able to navigate the world with sensitivity and resist the expectation to joke about serious matters. Most of the boys in our studies had similar desires.

SUMMARY

Themes of shared secrets and vulnerabilities, a preference for boys over girls when it comes to sharing secrets, and macho mantras repeated but not necessarily followed suggests a revision is necessary in how we have constructed boys and their friendships. Boys do, in fact, seek out and have emotionally intimate male friendships and they know that these relationships are critical to their mental health. While they are familiar with the dictates of manhood, they do not consistently adhere to them. Despite a culture that equates intimate friendships with being gay or girlish, boys have them anyway particularly during early and middle adolescence. If we remain in the thick of it, the question then becomes what supports boys' abilities to have such friendships? How is it possible that in a "hyper" masculine culture such as the United States, boys find a way to have the very relationships they are not supposed to have as heterosexual boys?

CHAPTER 4

BOYS WITH FEELINGS

In the midst of a twenty-first-century culture that says that boys do not have the capacity or interest to be as emotionally astute or as relational as girls, the boys in my studies spoke with great passion about their intimate male friendships and the secrets and feelings they share together. Directly contesting the popular and scholarly view that the testosterone surges of puberty makes boys insensitive and activity oriented, these boys spoke with such emotional eloquence that they sounded "like girls." Other studies of middle and high school boys suggest that the boys in my studies are not unique: boys, particularly during early and middle adolescence, are having emotionally intimate male friendships and revealing their emotional and social skills in many different cultural contexts.[1] These research findings reveal that we have been perpetuating stereotypes about boys' emotional lives and relational desires (or lack thereof) that are simply not true. Furthermore, my research and others' indicate that such friendships, and resistance to conventions of masculinity more generally, are, for boys and men, significantly associated with psychological, physical, and academic wellbeing.[2]

The obvious question after listening to boys is: How are they able to have such friendships and emotional and social skills when they live in such a rigidly gendered context where the "boy code" and the "cool pose" dominate?[3] How is it possible that boys are able to discuss their intense feelings for their male friends in a culture that tells them that such talk makes them gay, feminine, or immature? How are boys able to articulate their desire for friends who will know when to be "serious" when seriousness is perceived to be girlish or gay? The answers to these questions lie in the micro (e.g., families, schools) and macro (e.g., cultural stereotypes, economic opportunities) contexts of boys' lives. As developmental psychologist Urie Bronfenbrenner so eloquently claimed over 30 years ago, the ecological context of the child—both the proximal or micro and distal or macro contexts—shapes children's development, including their friendships and their emotional expression.[4]

My studies suggest that boys are able to have emotionally intimate friendships and be so emotionally and socially skilled in the midst of a homophobic culture becasue of (1) boys' relationships with their parents; (2) the social dynamics in their schools; and (3) boys' social identities, which are linked to their ethnic and racial communities and, for some, economic or social privileges. These supports for boys are, of course, not the only ones that encourage boys to speak openly about their thoughts and feelings for and with their closest male friends and to have such astute insights into the psychological world. However, these are the supports that distinguished those boys in my studies who were most likely to be emotionally expressive and have intimate male friendships from those who were the least likely.

BOYS AND THEIR PARENTS

Mothers, and occasionally fathers, were a central source of emotional support in boys' lives and were, at times, identified by their sons as "best friends." In his junior year, Ricky says: "My best friend? I would like to say that I only have one friend—one best friend and that is my mother." His mother is the person with whom he shares his thoughts and feelings, even though he also has numerous friendships with boys from his school. He trusts his mother to keep his secrets "and be there" in times of need. Similarly, Mike says:

> I could always tell my mom anything . . . I used to be close [to my dad] . . . you know it was just like, he stopped wanting to go places and stuff . . . and since I was a kid, [my dad and I] were close. But like when I started like from 11 years old and up, it's not so close . . . Like I can talk to my mother, I could express my feelings more to her than to my father.

Although fathers, according to their sons, were willing to have "close" relationships with them when they were younger and when "going places" was sufficient for feelings of closeness, as boys grew older and sought more emotional sustenance, mothers were typically the parents to whom boys turned. This finding is not surprising in a culture where the expression of emotions is considered a female domain. Women learn early on to attune themselves to the emotional and social world and often foster such skills in their children.[5]

While boys didn't necessarily share "everything" with their mothers, not sharing, for example, their experiences of sex or of "wild" behavior, they did share their worries about school, their peers, their girlfriends, and their futures. They also commonly talked about their conflicts between themselves and their friends. Their mothers often provided them with emotional support and guidance on how to manage difficult situations and navigate their close relationships. Their mothers, in addition, commonly valued their children's friendships, according to their sons, and encouraged them to have close friendships. For Sam, both his mother and father valued their own friendships and believed that "you need someone to talk to, to share your feelings with."

George, an outgoing and confident boy, is equally close to both parents. With his mother, he talks about his school day, his conflicts with his peers, his crushes on girls, and eventually his relationship with his girlfriend. Although she "nags" him continually about finishing his schoolwork, George understands that she does so because she wants him to do well in school. He and his father fix cars every weekend and talk at length about various car shows that they watch on TV and, occasionally, attend. He also talks to his father about conflicts with his mother around schoolwork, and his father offers advice on how to respond to his mother's "nagging." While the content of their conversations differ, George feels equally close to both parents, and both parents strongly value friendships. George, as will become evident in the next chapter, was one of the more expressive boys in our sample, and his willingness and ability to speak in emotional terms about his friendships remained consistent over time.

John Bowlby and Mary Ainsworth's theory of attachment, one of the foundational theories in developmental psychology, argues that a close relationship between a primary caretaker, typically the mother, and the child is critical for the health and well-being of the child.[6] A relationship in which the child feels secure with the primary caretaker's attention and love provides the child with an "internal working model" that promotes the child's sense of self-worth and thus his or her ability to seek out and provide emotional support from and to others outside the family.[7] A child who has a primary caretaker who is not consistently available for nurturance and support, however, will become "insecurely" attached and will internalize that he or she is not worthy of support. Such a child, the theory indicates, will have a difficult time having emotionally intimate friendships, for a core part of having such mutually supportive relationships is having strong feelings of self-worth. The boys in my studies who seemed, in their discussions of their parents, the most "securely attached" to at least one parent were the ones who seemed the most intimately connected to and expressive with their best friends. As attachment theory would predict, these "securely" attached boys also seemed more self-confident.

Research has also shown that emotional expression, empathy, and the ability to trust nonfamilial peers is due, at least in part, to the family context. Psychologist Constance Flanagan finds that families who value social compassion, reciprocity, and giving the other person the benefit of the doubt are more likely to produce empathic children who have a sense of social responsibility.[8] While she does not focus on the links between familial values and close friendships in particular, given the association between social and emotional skills and high-quality friendships,[9] it is likely that these children will also have supportive friendships. Neuroscientist Lise Eliot, in her review of the literature on gender differences in social and emotional skills, concludes that "children who are raised in more emotionally intelligent homes—where parents talk about feelings and their causes—score higher on empathy tests than children from families who talk less about feelings, and the influence is every bit as strong for boys as for girls."[10] These studies suggest that boys who have emotionally supportive relationships at home—relationships that entail sharing thoughts and feelings together—and who have parents who value reciprocity and compassion will be likely to also have emotionally intimate friendships.

Survey data with a middle school sample of approximately 400 boys analyzed by psychologist Carlos Santos also supports these mother-related findings but in a more direct way than the previously cited studies. In a study of public middle school students,[11] standardized surveys were administered that assessed the extent to which boys felt emotionally supported by their mothers and fathers and the extent to which they resisted conventions of masculinity in their friendships (i.e., the extent to which boys openly expressed themselves and valued interdependence in their friendships). In his analysis, Santos found that boys who reported more supportive relationships with mothers, regardless of their race or ethnicity, were more likely to report that they resisted conventions of masculinity in their friendships than those who reported poorer relationships with their mothers. Furthermore, boys' reports of high levels of mother support in sixth grade predicted an increase in reports of resistance to conventions of masculinity in their friendships from sixth to eighth grade. In other words, those boys who reported having an *increasingly* supportive relationship with their mothers from sixth to eighth grade were also likely to report *increasingly* higher levels of resistance to conventions of masculinity in their friendships.[12]

Drawing from hundreds of interviews with mothers across the United States, Kate Lombardi, a journalist, reveals in her book *Oedipus Wrecks* the prevalence of close, emotionally expressive relationships between mothers and sons. Despite the cultural pressures for mothers to disconnect from their sons to prevent them from being the archetypical "mama's boy," Lombardi finds, mothers of young as well as teenage boys are talking to their sons about navigating their relationships and coping with painful feelings. Mothers understand, according to Lombardi, the life skills they are offering their sons by fostering their emotional and empathic capacities and recognize their sons' emotional sensitivities and vulnerabilities. Lombardi says that she realized she had the central theme of her book when she heard mothers tell her time and again that the vulnerability and emotional expressiveness of their sons made them the exceptions rather than the rule.[13] Mothers, in other words, were buying into a gender stereotype that was simply not true. Lombardi's work reveals not only the ways mothers are fostering their sons' emotional capacities but also the extent to which boys are emotionally expressive and want to talk about their feelings.[14]

Findings regarding father-son relationships have revealed a more complicated story. While much research exists on the positive outcomes associated with fathers who are involved in their sons' lives,[15] other research has suggested a more nuanced association. Santos's research revealed that although high levels of support by mothers was significantly associated with high levels of resistance to conventions of masculinity among boys, high levels of father support (using the same standardized survey of parental support) were significantly associated with low levels of resistance among boys.[16] In other words, those boys, regardless of ethnicity, who reported being strongly supported by their fathers were the *least likely* to resist masculine conventions in their friendships. This raises the question of whether the meaning of "support" is similar across parents for boys. My own as well as Santos's and Lombardi's findings suggest that mother support often entails emotional support, talking about feelings, and guidance on relationship issues. Father support, on the other hand, often entails engaging in activities together and speaking about sports together. These patterns are, once again, not surprising given the way our gender stereotypes set the tone for what is possible in our relationships. Fathers likely feel as much pressure, if not more, than their sons to be manly and not reveal their real thoughts and feelings or encourage such discussions with their sons as such behavior will put their sons at risk for being perceived as gay or girlish.[17] This may be especially true, ironically, for fathers who feel close to their sons. Santos's findings, as well as my data, suggest that gender stereotypes may play out differently across parental relationships.

BEYOND THE FAMILY

In addition to parental relationships, social dynamics at school fostered the boys' emotional and social skills and their resistance to masculine conventions in their friendships. The boys who were the most emotionally expressive and reported having particularly intimate male friendships were those who had the most social power with their peers in school. According to my years of observations of youth, social power among peers was acquired through numerous routes, including the familiar ones such as being athletic, tall, and conventionally good looking and having a good sense of humor.[18] Having these attributes resulted in greater social power, which, in turn, led to greater freedom to implicitly or explicitly challenge norms of masculinity. Boys, such as Nick, who were talented basketball players and who were conventionally good looking often spoke in particularly intimate and emotional terms about their male friendships. Felix was extremely popular, funny, and confident in his ability to attract girls as well as in his ability to express vulnerability without being perceived as a "wuss." Lyn Mikel Brown and her colleagues note a similar pattern in their book *Packaging Boyhood*: "The good news for parents is that being successful at sports not only protects a boy from being called gay but also gives him permission to do well academically, show sensitivity, and stick up for kids who are bullied."[19] The boys in my studies who succeeded in sports or appeared "manly" by their physical size, or both, did not seem to feel as much pressure as the other boys to prove their masculinity or, as the case may be, their heterosexuality.

In research about friendships between gay and straight adult men, sociologist Jamie Price finds a similar pattern.[20] Straight men who had emotionally intimate friendships with gay men— who didn't feel threatened by being close to a gay man even though they were straight—were often those from military families or had military training. In other words, those who are most resistant to conventions of masculinity (being a straight man and having a gay male friend is in and of itself resistant to gender stereotypes) were often those who had a stereotypically "masculine" history or family. Having such a history allowed these straight men, as Price argues, to engage in emotional relationships with gay men without feeling the need to prove their masculinity. This observation does not mean, of course, that all those who are actively involved in sports or in the military will have an enlightened sense of manhood. Yet being involved in stereotypically masculine activities that look the part, so to speak, diminishes the possibility that sensitive behavior, for example, will be "misinterpreted" among heterosexual men.

This complex process is the same one Jean Anyon describes as taking place among the girls in her studies who resisted gender conventions, but often only in the "hands" of accommodation.[21] She reveals the ways the two processes work together, with one only being possible, at times, when the other is evident. Boys resist conventions of masculinity in how and with whom they have friendships, but they use as their safety net the very same conventions. These kinetic processes underscore the ways the context is always shaping the possibilities of any interactions or attitudes. Straight men in the military or by straight boys in an urban high school would likely not engage in resistance to gender stereotypes if there was not a way to embed such behavior in a familiar set of masculine standards that make such behavior safer and less open for misinterpretation.

Part of "looking the part" of manhood in and out of school for the boys was also, as my observations revealed, contingent on the race, ethnicity, immigrant status, and sexual orientation of the boys themselves and the stereotypes associated with each of these social categories. In American culture, where masculinity is "raced," "classed," and "sexualized," as well as given a nationality, Black boys are considered more "masculine" than White or Chinese boys, and working class boys are perceived as more "masculine" than middle or upper class boys. Furthermore, looking American (e.g., baseball cap, untucked shirt, untied athletic shoes) is perceived as more masculine than looking like an immigrant (e.g., buttoned up shirts, tucked-in shirt, tied shoes). Similarly, looking straight (e.g., baseball cap, untucked shirt, untied athletic shoes), like looking American, is perceived as more masculine than looking gay (e.g., skinny jeans and tight shirts). The look of masculinity is part of the same embedded set of masculine conventions that equates emotional stoicism, physical toughness, autonomy, and heterosexuality with being a real man.

Within the context of my studies in urban America, the boys who had the "look" of masculinity and thus were considered the most "cool," according to their peers, were the Puerto Rican boys. These were the boys the non–Puerto Rican teens—particularly the Dominican American, Asian, and White teenagers—wanted to be. Amy C. Wilkins noted a similar phenomenon in her research with primarily White teenagers in Wisconsin. In her ethnographic research, she discovered a group that was labeled by their peers as "Wannabe Puerto Ricans" because they dressed and acted like stereotypes of Puerto Ricans.[22] The fact that there is a group of teenagers, even in Wisconsin, who want to be Puerto Rican speaks to the social clout of this particular ethnic group in various urban locations across the United States. In my studies of boys (and girls), the desire to be Puerto Rican was stated explicitly by the teenagers at times.[23] A Chinese American student in high school says: "I don't like to be Chinese . . . I don't know why. I just feel like I want to be Puerto Rican or something." While other adolescents simply implied such a desire. José says: "I'm proud of being Dominican . . . Some people like my sister, she doesn't like it . . . 'cause all her friends are Puerto Ricans . . . so that's what she wants to be too. But I am what I am and I can't change it, so I gotta stay there." Although José says he is proud of being Dominican, the fact that he describes his sister's desires and concludes that he *has to* "stay there" suggests a desire to be Puerto Rican and a desire not to be Dominican.

The Puerto Rican students in my studies know that their identity is desired by their non–Puerto Rican peers, and they often revel in this status.[24] They speak with great pride of the "Puerto Rican Parade," which takes place in Manhattan in the month of June each year and travels down Fifth Avenue—the central artery of Manhattan—literally stopping traffic across the city. Jasmine, whose mother is Dominican and father is Puerto Rican and who identifies with being Puerto Rican, provides evidence of this Puerto Rican pride:

> Well I think the Puerto Ricans are, well not stronger, but they're more like, hey this is what I am, I'm proud. 'Cause when I went to the Puerto Rican parade with my dad and my uncles and stuff, they're like very, "Yeah!" And all these flags and all this drama. But then like when I went to the Dominican parade with my mom and my grandma and stuff, they're like wave the flag and watch the

things go by. And I'm like whoa, it's so different. It's like, I can't explain it. It's like, Puerto Ricans, like, are more loud. I don't know.
More crazy.[25]

It was clear from the stories the teenagers told us in their interviews, as well as from our informal and formal observations,
that the Puerto Rican students were on the highest rung of the
social hierarchy in the urban public schools in which we collected data.

The Puerto Rican boys were also the most effusive and passionate in their interviews when talking about their male friendships, were the most likely to maintain close male friendships over
time, and were particularly emotionally expressive. In his analysis
of survey data from a study of middle school students, Santos
finds that the Puerto Rican boys, in contrast to the Dominican,
Black, White, and Chinese American boys, reported the highest
levels of resistance to conventions of masculinity in their friendships.[26] Non–Puerto Rican boys even noted the quality of the
emotional insights provided by their Puerto Rican peers. Carl,
who is African American, says:

> I appreciate the overall understanding of people that my Puerto Ri-
> can friends have. They have a different understanding and interpre-
> tation of life than a lot of other people would, especially at our ages,
> and I really respect them about that. I love that I can always go and
> talk and bring like people's behavior patterns. We can bring it to
> each other's attention and identify it and that's what I love about my
> Puerto Rican friends. We totally understand well, we would like to
> believe that we understand a lot more about people in the world than
> everybody else.

Carl's response reveals that not only are his Puerto Rican peers
astute observers of the relational world but that he is as well.

This high level of resistance is likely due to the social clout of
the Puerto Rican student which was, in part, rooted in an urban
culture that prefers brown over white or black skin. This

preference is reflected in the response of the Dominican girl who said that being Puerto Rican is desirable because it is "between" Black and White.[27] Puerto Ricans were idealized because of their "between" skin tone and hair, which is neither stereotypically Black nor White, and their "cool" language (Spanish versus Chinese), music, and style (hip and urban). The Dominican and Chinese American teenagers in my studies did not want to be White or Black, as Whiteness was associated with nerdiness and oppression and Blackness was associated with violence and being a victim of oppression. Although these images are polar opposites across and within race, students wanted neither extreme. They wanted to be, as the Dominican girl indicated, "in between." Students identified with those who were on top and not on the fringe.[28]

The Dominican and Chinese American teenagers, all of whom were either first or second generation immigrants, also wanted to be Puerto Rican because of their U.S. citizenship, which meant, according to the students themselves, that they were more "American." A young Puerto Rican girl describes such anti-immigrant biases in the classroom:

> One time, right like there was this girl named Jackie. She is Dominican and you know how they always saying that Dominicans are immigrants. So one day in Spanish class the teacher said that all the Dominicans in the class have to do something. And Jackie was in the class and she's like come with me, come with me. And I said "Jackie I'm not coming with you, 'cause you're still an immigrant." And um she got all mad and there was a whole big fight because of that, forget it. . . . We just stopped talking.[29]

These teenagers resisted Whiteness as the ideal but they also accommodated to mainstream beliefs about immigration and Blackness. The exceptions to this pattern were the Black and White youth. Black boys wanted to be Black without the negative stereotypes, and White boys wanted to be Black or Puerto

Rican to acquire the stereotypic "coolness" that is associated with these ethnic groups.[30]

Other reasons for such high levels of resistance to gender stereotypes among the Puerto Rican boys were likely due to a pan-ethnic culture that has a long tradition of valuing emotional expression even among boys and men. From the literature of Gabriel Garcia Marquez and Junot Diaz and the poetry of Pablo Neruda to the music of Luis Miguel or Enrique Iglesias, it is obvious that many Spanish-speaking cultures of South and Central America, the Caribbean, and Spain value emotional expression.

Yet Latino boys and men are also stereotyped as being macho. Walk into any media outlet and you will find numerous images of Latino gangsters or gangster-like Latino men. A Black man in America is stereotyped as "hyper" masculine just as being Latino is stereotyped as macho. Scholars of Latin culture define machismo as involving "physical strength, sexual attractiveness, virtue, and potency" as well as a strong sense of familial responsibility.[31] Virtue and familial responsibility, however, are rarely underscored in the popular conceptions of being Latino, whereas the more sexist elements regarding strength and control are emphasized.[32] Yet while Latin men suffer from such negative stereotyping, the stereotype may also provide a cover of sorts for emotionally expressive Latino boys growing up in a homophobic American culture. Just like sports, the military, or rap music, the stereotype of being macho may protect Latinos from having their heterosexuality challenged. Yet, like the cover provided by the stereotype of "hyper" masculinity for Black males, this cover a likely provides only the possibility of survival rather than long-term liberation.[33]

Nonetheless, perhaps, as various colleagues have suggested to me, being emotionally sensitive is not, in fact, a sign of "resistance" for Latino boys at all but simply a form of accommodation to the norms of their Latino culture. In America, however, intimate friendships and the expression of vulnerable emotions more generally are what girls and gay boys do—not what heterosexual boys do, regardless of their ethnic, racial, or national origin. Thus a boy who engages in such behavior *in an American context* is resisting the dominant or hegemonic form of masculinity.

Furthermore, scholars of Latin culture have noted that "withholding affection emotions" is also part of "traditional" Latino culture.[34] Thus, the pressures to be emotionally stoic may come not simply from the Anglo American power structure but also from Latino culture itself. Finally, the Puerto Rican boys in my studies became, like their non–Puerto Rican male peers, less resistant, less emotional, and more isolated as they became men. If the Puerto Rican boys were simply accommodating to their Latino culture when they openly expressed their emotions for their male friends, one would not expect a decline in this pattern as they grow older.

The Dominican American boys in my studies also challenge the belief that emotional expression is simply what "Latinos" do. While these boys also had emotionally intimate male friendships and thus resisted gender stereotypes, they did not reveal this pattern as commonly as their Puerto Rican peers. The fact that the Dominican Americans sounded different from the Puerto Ricans underscores that Spanish-speaking countries are not homogeneous, that the gender socialization of Latino children is not homogeneous, and that socialization processes do not happen in a vacuum. The social, economic, and political aspects of boys' lives influence each other and create pockets for possible resistance for some boys and challenges for others. While Dominican American students share with their Puerto Rican peers a Latino culture, they do not share a similar history in the United States (e.g., immigrant versus U.S. citizen), nor do they share similar racial histories; Dominicans have more African ancestry than Puerto Ricans. Dominicans also do not share the same economic and political conditions as their Puerto Rican peers. Dominicans in the United States are, on average, poorer and less politically established than Puerto Ricans.[35] Among the Latino population, they are also significantly fewer in number. Dominicans make up 2.6 percent (1,198,849) of the Latino population; Puerto Ricans make up 9.1 percent (4,114,701).[36] Given these demographics, it is not surprising that the Dominican American teens have less social clout than their Puerto Ricans in cities within the United States.

Furthermore, the Dominican American boys in my studies were often the target of direct verbal harassment by other boys, including the Puerto Rican boys. Bennie, a Dominican American student, says: "I mean my friends [who are Puerto Rican] will joke around with me and call me 'dumb in a can.' Why? 'cause it's like Domini-can . . . he's like 'DUM–I N–A–CAN.'" Edwin, also Dominican American, says: "Well, sometimes [the Puerto Ricans] joke around and call me 'Platano' [plantain]."[37] Such experiences of overt discrimination and teasing will likely make boys feel more vulnerable and thus less "masculine." As a consequence, they may be more inclined than their Puerto Rican peers to want to "prove" their masculinity by accommodating to gender stereotypes.

However, many Dominican American boys did have emotionally intimate friendships, especially during early and middle adolescence. These resistant patterns are likely due to many of the same factors that fostered resistance with the other boys (e.g., relationships with their mothers). The Dominican American boys simply had to face more challenges to their masculinity and thus appeared to have a harder time resisting such conventions over time, as was indicated by their lower levels of emotional expression when compared to their Puerto Rican peers.[38]

Like their Latino peers, the African American boys share a similar paradox of living with the stereotype of being "hyper" masculine yet being embedded in an ethnic and racial community where emotional expression is historically valued. African American boys and men share a history of "brotherhood," based on similar experiences of oppression, in which a core value is loyalty and connection to other Black males (e.g., the Million Man March).[39] Scholars have long argued that it is

European American culture that is dispassionate, aloof, stoic, and independent and not reflective of the traditional values of Black people of African descent, who are more passionate, emotional, and interdependent.[40] The "cool pose" of Black boys, in this view, signifies a distrust of White culture and not an inherent quality of Black culture.[41]

As with Latinos, the stereotype of "hyper" masculinity (and thus of heterosexuality) as well as the valuing of emotional expression and the connections among Black men may protect African American boys from being drawn too quickly into a form of masculinity that asks them to shut down their emotional lives. Evidence of this is found in the numerous examples of Black men in the media revealing a softer side when it comes to other Black men. In 2006, two Black rappers—Lil' Wayne and Baby—were photographed kissing each other on the lips, which created a media frenzy regarding the meaning of the photograph. A hip-hop website reports the following:

> What has set the email boxes abuzz is a photograph of Lil' Wayne and Baby planting a kiss smack dab on one another's lips. Immediately, the machismo-filled world of hardened rappers and wannabe rhymers explained away the image as something doctored or photoshopped, reasoning that manly heroes like Lil' Wayne and Baby would never attempt such a move. Yet recently, Baby finally addressed the firestorm of controversy in an interview and admitted that the photo only expressed the real father/son relationship that exists between Baby and Lil' Wayne. "Before I had a child, Wayne and all of them were my children, you heard me?" Baby said, using the same colloquialisms often spouted by other New Orleans native sons like Master P and Juvenile. "Wayne to me is my son—my first-born son—and that's what it do for me," Baby told Uptown Angela. "That's my life, that's my love and that's my thing. That's my lil' son. I love him to death."[42]

Framing his love for Lil' Wayne as a product of a father-son relationship rather than two men—only 13 years apart in age—

who have strong feelings of mutual love, Baby backs away from any homosexual insinuation. However, Baby, one of those "hardened rappers," is still able to describe Lil' Wayne, a peer and co-rapper, as "that's my love, that's my thing. . . . I love him to death" and is willing to kiss Lil' Wayne on the lips for the public to view. His heterosexuality/masculinity is not challenged. Like a football player who smacks another man on the butt after a good play, only a man who is perceived as the epitome of a man's man could get away with it.

Psychologists Howard Stevenson and Michael Cunningham are quick to point out, however, that while "hyper" or extreme masculinity may protect Black males from literally getting killed, it is only protective in a culture that requires boys to prove their manhood in the most destructive of ways.[43] In other words, "hyper" masculinity or the reliance on such stereotypes in public spaces may feel functional in the moment for young Black men, but it's not a long-term strategy for liberation. These stereotypes also insinuate that if a Black boy or man is not "hyper" masculine, he is not only not male (i.e., female), but also not Black (i.e., White).[44]

As with all of the boys in my studies, patterns of friendships and emotional expression and thus of resistance among Black boys are shaped by social class, geography, immigrant status, and of course, sexual orientation. While we did not have samples of middle class, rural, non-American, or gay youth with which to make comparisons, it is clear from an examination of the existing literature that friendships and emotional and social skills vary depending on the contexts and identities of the youth themselves. Middle and upper class Black boys living in the suburbs, for example, often feel like they have the most to prove in terms of their masculinity, given that they are not "protected" by the thug stereotype of their urban, low-income peers.[45] In addition, they must contend with the accusations by their peers of not being "Black enough," given their middle and upper class status. Thus, such boys may be less resistant to gender stereotypes than their working class Black and urban peers.

Sociologist Clyde Franklin finds in his research on Black men's friendships that working class men were significantly more likely to have emotionally intimate friendships (e.g., friendships in which men "shared everything together") than were middle class men. Franklin posits: "Because working class Black males experience greater isolation from mainstream society than upwardly mobile Black men, they may not internalize the same taboos against male same-sex friendships, which result in non-self-disclosure, competitiveness, and non-vulnerability."[46] Drawing attention to the power dynamics of friendships and masculinity, Franklin underscores the ways men who have more access to economic power may be less likely to risk that power by implicitly or explicitly challenging gender stereotypes than those who have less to lose but who are also confident in their own masculinities.

Gay Black boys, like gay Latino, White, and Asian American boys, will also face a different set of supports and challenges from their heterosexual male peers. For gay Black boys, accommodating to stereotypes of gayness, like being emotionally astute, may in fact be good for their health. However, gay boys are still boys who often attend homophobic schools, and the expectation to "man up" is likely as intense for them, if not more so, than for their heterosexual peers. In fact, because Blackness or being Latino is equated with masculinity and with explicitly not being gay, the pressure for Black and Latino gay boys to act not only like stereotypic men but like stereotypic *Black* or *Latino* men may be particularly strong. They may feel that they have much to prove in terms of their manhood *and* their race or ethnicity.

The supports for resistance to gender (and racial) stereotypes among Asian American boys in my studies come from a set of social, political, cultural, and economic factors that are both similar to and different from those in play for their Latino and Black peers. Chinese American boys, the dominant group of Asian Americans in my studies, share a Chinese culture with a long history of valuing friendships. Confucius, the most famous of Chinese philosophers, indicated that friendships are one of the five most important human relationships. In the first paragraph of his most famous text, he underscores the importance of friendships by placing it alongside the other fundamental pleasures of life: "To learn and to practice what is learned time and again is pleasure, is it not? To have friends come from afar is happiness, is it not?"[47] In addition, poets down through numerous Chinese dynasties have written about the importance of *intimate* friendships in particular. A poem written during the Tang dynasty by the most renowned Chinese poet, Li Bai, says:

> To Wang Lun—
> I am on board; I am about to sail;
> When there's stamping and singing on shore
> Peach blossom pool is a thousand feet deep,
> Yet not so deep, Wang Lun, as your love for me

Li Bai also wrote:

> To my friends—
> a. The most valuable thing in life is having a friend who knows
>   you; it is irrelevant to gold and money.
> b. The most valuable part of having someone who understands
>   you is about having someone who knows your heart.[48]

The core element of friendships in the Chinese Confucian tradition is having someone "know your heart." Even in modern China, this aspect of friendships is among the highest values. In a study I conducted along with psychologist Yueming Jia of 700 Chinese adolescents in China, 350 of whom were adolescent boys, we found that early adolescent boys, just like the boys in my studies in the United States, often have and want emotional, intimate male friendships—friendships in which their friends "know their heart."[49] A 13-year-old Chinese boy attending a middle school in Nanjing China says to his interviewer in our study: "If I don't have a friend, I would be crazy. The feeling would be depressing. No one would know what my heart wants to say, nobody would listen. Then I would be forced to become crazy." Another Chinese boy of the same age and attending the same school: "Our relationship is intensely close . . . that means that he tells me something inside his heart." When asked what he usually talks about with his best friend, he says: "Something that you don't want parents to know, some difficulties that you don't want to say [to others] . . . [I] am misunderstood at home sometimes or at school or when I am criticized by teachers. . . . He would comfort me and encourage me." These responses sound strikingly familiar and underscore the pervasiveness of the desire for and the existence of emotionally intimate friendships among boys and the extent to which boys, including Chinese American and Chinese boys, seek out such friendships. Like the norms surrounding Black "brotherhood," Chinese ideals of friendship may strengthen Chinese American boys' ability to speak in emotional terms about their own friendships.

Other "supports" for resistance—or factors that likely make it easier for youth to resist gender and racial stereotypes or both—among the Chinese American boys are embedded in a set of racial stereotypes similar to those of their Latino and Black peers. Images of kung fu fighting and martial arts are almost as pervasive in the media as the images of Latino gang members or Black "gangsta" rappers. This fighting image presents a masculine pose that likely serves as a cover for emotionally sensitive Chinese American boys in much the same way stereotypic images of Black or Latino gangsters serve as masculine fronts for Black and Latino young men. However, Asian American boys are also feminized in the media and in popular culture.[50] These feminine stereotypes place Asian American boys in a weaker position than their non-Asian peers. Thus they may be more likely to accommodate to gender stereotypes. My studies found, in fact, that while boys' desires for emotionally intimate male friendships were evident across racial and ethnic groups, such friendships were least likely to exist among the Asian American boys, particularly by late adolescence. The burden of having to defend their masculinity appears to pay a heavy cost.

As with their non–Asian American peers, patterns of resistance among the Asian American boys likely vary across numerous social demographic factors. Middle class, third generation and heterosexual Chinese American boys, for example, are less at risk for being feminized by their peers than poorer, more recent immigrant, or gay Chinese American boys. However, more recent immigrant Chinese American boys may be more connected to the Chinese tradition of valuing intimate friendships. Thus, such immigrants may be more likely to implicitly challenge American conventions of masculinity by having intimate male friendships than their middle class, second or third generation Chinese American peers. Again, boys' ability to stay connected to what they know about the world is deeply bound by their micro and macro contexts.

Finally, the supports for the European American or White boys in my studies that foster their friendships and their emotional acuity are also linked to these boys' cultural, political, and economic status. European American boys share a Western tradition in which friendships between boys and between men have a long history.[51] Philosophers and writers of fiction, such as Homer, Aristotle, Shakespeare, and Mark Twain, have long celebrated intimate male friendships. White, middle and upper class boys, furthermore, have social, economic, and political power that likely protects them from having to prove their manhood to the same extent as their less powerful, poor and working class peers. Being at the top of the power hierarchy—constructing the ideals of manhood because they are *the* man—allows for flexibility in their assertion of masculinity.[52] The phenomenon of "emo" teenagers—those who "emote" as part of their very essence and whose heavy eyeliner, body-hugging t-shirts and floppy hair dyed black makes them look "gay"—consists primarily of White heterosexual teens, many of whom are boys. Only the power that comes with being White, male, and heterosexual could allow for an entire subgroup whose schtick includes the expression of emotions and the wearing of eyeliner. Unlike Black superstars who are able to "get away" with kissing each other on the lips or express strong feelings of emotion, White boys in the "emo" peer group do not have to be wildly successful to get away with stereotypically feminine behavior.

Evidence of White males' privilege to bend or implicitly contest gender stereotypes is found in the growing number of books, television shows, and movies that have intimate male friendships as a central theme. In popular entertainments ranging from children's cartoons, including *SpongeBob Square Pants,* to the Harry Potter series, to the MTV series *Bromance* and movies such as *I Love You, Man*, or the television series *Men of a Certain Age*, intimate male friendships are promoted and celebrated. Yet these media products are often wolves in sheep's clothing. They promote male friendships but only for the purpose of "getting girls," "partying," or, in the case of Harry Potter, solving a mystery. In other words, the friendships are vehicles to achieve an end rather than an end in themselves. Few of these books, television shows, and movies reveal the intrinsic value of intimate friendships. Nonetheless, White boys, the audience for most of these media products, do get a consistent dose of the importance of male friendships.

Yet the "privilege" that White boys may have, particularly those in the middle and upper classes, to contest gender stereotypes is made more complicated by the conflation of "whiteness" with "gayness." The youth in my studies, both racial minority and majority, have repeatedly told us that White boys, particularly those who are emotionally sensitive, are assumed to be "gay."[53] Thus, the "protection" of social class and of race is counteracted by a racial and homophobic stereotype. In addition, the "privilege" of White middle and upper class boys can be a double-edged sword: both allowing them to break the rules and making that rule-breaking more consequential for them, since they are contesting the dominant power structure. This pattern is evident in the numerous examples of "hyper" masculinity in White middle class suburbs, including the raping of disabled girls and the shooting of school peers. Those who live in White suburban neighborhoods may feel extreme pressure to rigidly adhere to gender stereotypes *because* they are closer to the power structure, as Clyde Franklin noted about Black middle class men, than their less advantaged White peers, and thus have more to lose. The "protection" of being a part of the social elite may not, in the end, protect their social and emotional lives. In fact, their poor, working class, and urban White peers, who are often stereotyped as "hyper" masculine due to their social class and urban location and thus not gay, may be more likely to have intimate male friendships.

While I am not able to test these hypotheses regarding social class, sexual identity, and geographic location due to the social demographics of the boys in my studies, the evidence supporting these hypotheses can be found in other research.[54] Such findings draw attention to the ways social categories intersect in boys' lives. It is often, however, not the identities or social demographics themselves (e.g., being gay or straight) that intersect but the stereotypes of these social categories (e.g., being Black and "hyper" masculine) that come together to create opportunities for or constraints on intimate male friendships.

Underscoring the influence of the social context (including stereotypes) on friendships and boys' ability to resist gender stereotypes, I received a letter recently from an elderly British former teacher who wrote to me after reading a newspaper article describing the findings of my studies. He told me that the macho behavior we hear so much about is a product of American culture and its "excessive competition that excites more insecurity than boys naturally have." He claimed that in his years as a high school teacher in England, he rarely dealt with cases of bullying and never had anything like "jocks walking along the hallway shoving people into the lockers." Regardless of whether he is correct in his comparison between the United States and Britain, his letter draws attention to the ways the cultural context make a difference in boys' lives. Boys are able to resist gender stereotypes when they are embedded in contexts (e.g., supportive relationships at home) that support this resistance. When they adhere to gender stereotypes such as "shoving people into the lockers," they are also responding to a context that naturalizes such behavior for boys. Boys know that. Teachers know that. Parents know that. And yet social scientists and the media have a hard time seeing it.

SUMMARY

One of the primary supports for boys' abilities to have emotionally intimate male friendships and thus resist gender stereotypes is parents who offer a safe space for boys to talk freely about their thoughts and feelings. However, parents' willingness and abilities to offer such a space do not appear out of the blue. Parents are socialized into a culture in which mothers are considered the carriers of emotions and emotional talk and fathers are not. Thus, it is not surprising that we find that it is the mothers, rather than the fathers, who are offering the space for boys to stay connected to their thoughts and feelings about the world. The solution to the "boy crisis" should not be focused on absent fathers per se or on the "problem" of single mother households but on helping fathers remain emotionally connected to themselves and others so that they can stay with their families and provide better models of healthy relationships for their sons (and daughters). As Santos's middle school findings suggest, simply having fathers "supporting" their sons through engaging in various activities is not good enough if boys are to develop the emotional and social skills they need to thrive. Fathers must also help their sons maintain their empathic and emotionally astute ways of being in the world. As George has revealed, having both parents support his resistance to conventions of masculinity via encouraging his intimate male friendships makes it easier for him to have the relationships he wants and needs.

Another support for boys' intimate same-sex friendships (and thus their resistance to gender stereotypes) is found in the social power offered to those on the top of the social hierarchy in school. Schooling, it appears, is a more intimate affair than typically assumed affecting not only academic achievement but also the quality of friendships.[55] The social hierarchy creates possibilities of resistance for boys. The core factors that determine a boy's status in the social hierarchy, according to our observations of youth, are his social identities (e.g., race, sexuality, nationality). Students with social identities that are privileged (e.g., athlete, heterosexual) have more power and thus more freedom or flexibility in self-expression and behavior than others who have identities that are less favored by their peers (e.g., gay, immigrant).

Yet schools, like parents, are embedded in a larger macro context of patriarchal expectations, norms, and stereotypes that shape the dynamics both within and outside schools. Boys (and girls) are continually contending with stereotypes about gender, sexuality, race, nationality, social class, and immigrants, to name only a few, and these "ghosts in the house" profoundly influence the ways boys experience their relationships.[56] When particular stereotypes "favor" them (e.g., being "hyper" masculine and thus heterosexual), boys experience more freedom to resist other types of stereotypes (e.g., to be sensitive is to be gay). Boys, furthermore, are coping with multiple stereotypes and identities in and out of school settings. While one boy may be heterosexual and White, he may also be a recently arrived immigrant from a country that does not have English as its mother tongue and may have a very small physique. Thus the challenges to his masculinity may be just as difficult as if he were Chinese American and poor. And if that Chinese American boy is a third generation immigrant, is heterosexual, and has a large physique, he may actually find it easier to resist gender stereotypes by having emotionally intimate male friendships than his White immigrant peers. Stereotypes that boys confront in and out of school settings, in sum, may both protect boys *and* reinforce the very norms they know are not good for their health.

Among the questions that remain regarding the intimacy of boys' friendships, a core one is why we have had such difficulty seeing that boys speak in such emotionally articulate ways and have intimate male friendships that entail deep secrets and much vulnerability. Although boys are regularly contesting stereotypic representations in their close male friendships, and are being supported in their resistance in various ways, we often insist on only portraying the ways boys (and men) repeat stereotypes. We have trouble seeing the hand in front of our face when we are so focused on trying to see beneath the surface of our skin (i.e., our fascination with all things biological and brain focused). We focus on the thin culture and ignore the thick culture that shapes our desires and our interpretations of our skin and what lies beneath. We convince ourselves, in other words, that we can put culture aside when we speak about boys, friendships, human development, and human nature more generally. But as sociologists, historians, psychologists, philosophers, anthropologists and even neuroscientists have been arguing for decades, if not centuries, we are always already in culture and any understanding of human processes must acknowledge that thick culture fact.

CHAPTER 5

NICK AND GEORGE

One of the central lessons I learned from being a counselor with adolescents is that any theme that you hear across adolescents sounds different when you listen to an individual's life story. Intimate male friendships were common across the boys, particularly during early and middle adolescence. Yet there were subtleties to these patterns and ways they fit into the larger context of a life that get lost when one only focuses on the patterns. To reveal both the similarities and differences across boys, the friendship experiences of four boys are presented in this book. Nick and George are the focus of this chapter, and Fernando and Danny are the focus of Chapter 8. While all four boys reveal the pattern of having close friendships during early and middle adolescence and then becoming more wary of their peers and, for three of them, losing their close male friendships as they enter late adolescence, Nick and George suggest particularly strong patterns of emotional intimacy in their friendships, while Fernando and Danny suggest the opposite. Nick and George, however, reveal these patterns in distinct ways.

Both Nick and George have grandparents of Puerto Rican descent, were born and raised in New York City (as were their parents), and strongly identify as Americans. Their stories of friendships underscore the nuances in individual lives and the fact that being boys from New York, having similar ethnic backgrounds, and going to the same school does not produce the same story of friendships. While Nick openly talks about his love for his best friends and thus actively resists conventions of masculinity, George is more subtle and less emotional in his stories, but equally suggestive of resistance in his ability to understand the complexities of his friendships and in his desires for emotional intimacy with other boys. I selected these two boys as case studies because, while they share similarities that resonate with the larger sample of boys, they reveal the diverse ways boys experienced their friendships and challenged gender stereotypes.

NICK'S STORY

Freshman Year: Feeling His Way Through

Looking like a typical American teenager with his loose, low-riding, long shorts made for playing basketball and a New York Knicks white, blue and orange sleeveless jersey, Nick, at 14 years old, is the youngest of five children. He has a medium build, dark brown hair cut short and close to his head, and large brown eyes; he lives with an older brother, two older sisters, and his mother in an apartment building near the high school he attends. His father left the family soon after Nick was born and hasn't had contact with them since. Born and raised in New York City, Nick is an avid basketball player, often carries a basketball around in school, and wants to be a professional basketball player when he grows up. He proudly tells the interviewer in his freshman year: "No kids for my weight can do things that I can do. Like, I play more sports, they call me 'The Boss' down my block. We have a Boss down for each block, and I'm the Boss down for my block. I play handball, basketball, football. I play all sports." In his freshman year, Nick looks and acts like a stereotypic boy. But he does not speak like one.

Nick says that his relationship with his mother is close:

> I get a lot of attention from her. Like, just, I'm the baby. She always spends time with me, like, she'll take out all her time just to spend with me, like whatever I need, like, she'll, she'll be kinda a friend, if I really need her. Let's say, I just broke up with my girlfriend, and I really liked her, and I was with tears, she'll come and say, "It's okay, it's okay." Um, you know, I'll cry on her shoulder, and we'll stay, laying down in the bed, and, like, we'll stay, and we'll talk for a long time and finally we'll just fall asleep . . . and when I wake up I won't feel the same. I will feel better.

Nick's ability to be expressive with his mother is likely deeply affected by the fact that she has been diagnosed with ovarian cancer. He has been trying to spend more time with her lately, as he doesn't know how long she will be alive.

Nick describes himself as a "friendly" and "very funny person" who "loves to joke around with [his] friends." "If I meet a person, I'll try to give my best impression so that they can say hello the next time and not be, like, wave their hand [clears throat] or be shy. I'll try to give as good impression so I can make that person feel comfortable, like, whether it's a new student, or a new kid on the block." Nick is proud of his sociable nature and is clearly well liked by his peers. His entire social network consists of boys from the neighborhood whom he has known from a very early age and who mostly attend his school.

Nick's best friend, Noel, who is also Puerto Rican and whom he has known since he was three, lives below him in the same apartment building. His friendship with Noel, like many of his close friendships, is remarkable in its depth and intimacy. Even during the latter years of high school, when Nick is increasingly distrustful of other boys, he will continue to describe his love for Noel and the ways Noel has helped him through many difficult times.

When asked about his friendships at the beginning of his freshman year interview, Nick sounds like a gender stereotype:

> [With my friends] like, we talk about basketball and sports mostly, and girls, so there's never like any problem, between us, so, it's pretty good, our relationship. It's real good . . . You know, I don't have any problems with them, never have problems and if we do, you know, it's like, little things like little problems with the, problems, like we argue about sports, about sports players, how good they are. Little problems but not that bad.

Yet as Nick begins to lay out the details of his friendship, a different image emerges:

> [What I like about my friendships] is that like, if I'm in a fight, they'll jump in. If I'm having a problem, they'll be like, "What's wrong?," and then, "Would you wanna talk to me about the problem?" . . . When I was feeling down, when my mother went to the hospital . . . they saw it on my face and they was like, "Yo, what's going on, dude, what happened?" And I was like, "Nothing, my mom's in the hospital," and later, all my friends was coming up to me, asking me the same question, and they were like, "You wanna talk?"

Physical toughness frames a more vulnerable image and becomes the theme for his freshman year interview. Often embedded in a masculine language ("Yo, what's going on, dude?"), the language of sensitivity and explicit vulnerability ultimately comes through ("you wanna talk?").

When asked what he and his best friend do together, Nick says: "Everything. We hang out. We talk to each other about serious things, share some deep secrets." Responding to a question about what he *does* with his friend, Nick reveals implicitly how he *feels* about Noel.

The intimacy between Nick and Noel is also revealed in the blending of their families:

> Noel and I are close and everything, like I sleep over at his house, he sleeps at my house; I call his mom "Moms," he call my mom "Mom." We're serious, like his family is real close to me, like my second family, like as if they were my first. [His family] has a room to stay in 'cause I stay there any time I want. If I wanna talk, anybody's

open ears are there. If I wanna cry there, they'll show that they're there for me.

The families of the friends of the boys in my studies were often central to the boys' experience of friendships. Armondo says in his freshman year: "if you know [your friend's] parents, then you know how far the trust [with your friend] can be stretched." Eric says that the fact that he knows his friends' families so well and that his best friend's "little sister loves me" makes him feel closer to his best friend. In the context of a culture in which being close with another boy is ripe for misinterpretation, boys' close connection to their friends' families likely makes the intimacy with the friend more acceptable, as it involves loving family members rather than simply another boy.

When the interviewer asks Nick in his freshman year what has changed in his friendships with other boys since he was younger, he says:

> It changed a lot. Just like my other friends, changed a lot. When we were younger, it used to be, like, not so tight, not so tight as we are now. Not like, if something goes wrong, like one of us will shed a tear, the other one'll cry. When we were younger like, one of us, it was just like fun and games, but now we're serious, 'cause we're growing up and life got serious.

Even at the age of 14, Nick understands the importance of emotional expression in this newly discovered "serious life" and his "tighter" relationships.

When asked what he means by "serious," Nick says: "Like, at times, like, um, when it's time to get down, like, when one of us [Nick or Noel] is in trouble and the other one needs help, we both stick together and be there for each other." Repeating the intimate thread that runs throughout his discussions of friendships, Nick draws attention to the mutually supportive nature of his friendship with Noel. Yet when asked to provide an example of this "sticking together," Nick moves back into a masculine mode and resorts to the familiar terrain of physical toughness: "Let's see, if one person is in trouble with another guy, and he might get killed and everybody else could stick to each other so that that one person won't kill him, we'll get, we'll get help for that one person." Although he admits that this scenario has never happened to him, a scenario that sounds straight out of a Hollywood movie, he uses it to define "sticking together" to make, perhaps, his friendship with Noel appear more acceptable to a masculine norm.

The movement between speaking on more vulnerable terms and speaking in masculine clichés is constant in Nick's freshman year interview. Overtones of masculinity often followed on the heels of expressions of fragility as if out of fear that he was venturing into territory that will surely be misinterpreted. However, his sensitivity is always present: "a best friend is good so he'll stick with you, like the one I have, he'll stick with you through thick and thin, 'cause that's what he's doing to me now, and it seems like he's not gonna leave me."

Like so many of his peers, Nick feels threatened by the girl-friends of his closest friends and sees girls as an impediment to their intimacy:

> Like my best friend's girlfriends are like trying to take him away from me, 'cause they know I'm spending a lot of time with him, and he won't let that happen. Now he has a girlfriend and he's real serious with her, and no matter what, he'll always spend time with me. No matter what, I'm serious with my girlfriends or my family or he's serious with his girls or his family, we'll always spend time or make time to see each other, at least hanging out to say, "what's up?" or to talk on the phone at least.

Hinting at what will become a theme in the latter years of high school, Nick already seems worried that girls, especially those with whom the boys are "real serious," will steal his closest friends. He hopes Noel's loyalty will continue in future years.

Sophomore Year: With a Basketball in His Hand

When Nick is interviewed during his sophomore year, his interviewer already knows that his mother has died over the summer. She notes at the end of her interview with Nick:

> He definitely seems to be compensating for a lot of things by having fun and being silly and I've seen him in the hallways a lot and he does make a lot of jokes. I think that keeps him in bright spirits but when he does talk about his mom, it's like a cloud rolls over his face, it's really a great transformation. I mean he just becomes totally solemn when he talks about his mom. It's like a happy/sad feeling you get from him: happy because he has a really great memory of her and their relationship, and just sad because of what's happened. In addition, the whole time he had a basketball in his hand, and every time I've seen him he walks around school with this basketball in his hand.

Holding a basketball in his hands, Nick in his sophomore year interview talks about his sadness regarding the loss of his mother, his loss of his friendship with Noel (who continues to live below him in his apartment building), his emerging friendship with an older peer, and the fact that he no longer goes to church ("I don't have time"). His basketball seems to provide a literal and metaphoric safety net for his expressions of vulnerability, perhaps assuring him and the world that such expressions do not make him any less of a man. The basketball may also be a reminder of a constant—a thing that hasn't changed since last year—and thus may provide him with a sense of security.

Nick, who now lives with only his sisters and his stepfather, begins his sophomore year interview describing his friendship with a group of young men who are three to four years older than him. As in his earlier interview, he moves back and forth between a stereotypic masculine pose and a more resistant stance. When asked about how he and his friends are like "brothers," he says: "Like we give each other advice or they'll give advice like if I have problems with a girl, have fights, Latino fights." Coding the fights as explicitly "Latino" alludes to the ways that ethnicity and masculinity intersect with the "Latino" characterization emphasizing the macho quality of the fight.

Similar to his freshman year interview, Nick follows up this masculine posture with a description of how his friends have supported him since his mother died:

> My friends relate to most of the things I have to deal with. Like if they lost somebody in the family they love, they understand how it is to work that out . . . They understand what you want to do. Because it happened to me and it really hurts. [My friends say] "you just got to deal with it and I know it's hard, but if you loved her, she loved you, too." They'll be like, like sometimes they be telling me: "you got us now, we are like your brothers." And that really helps me.

Expressing the intimate details of his conversations with his friends, Nick reveals not only his own emotional depth but that of his friends (e.g., "if you loved her, she loved you, too"). Nick does not try to cover his hurt and insecurity (i.e., did my mother love me?), and they, in return, understand his emotional needs.

Nick says that the reason he likes his current set of close friends is that they love basketball and sports in general, but he adds: "[I trust my friends because] if I have a fight they are going to be there 100 percent." But as with all of his assertions of mainstream masculinity, open expressions of vulnerability quickly follow: "I trust my friends to respect my feelings . . . If I tell them something and tell them not to tell nobody they will keep my secrets, even to my other friends."

When asked about his best friend in his sophomore year, he says:

> Actually I have two best friends. One is Marcus, he's 18 and he goes to college and Noel, he's 15, *he wants to let me go.* [italics mine] So he's like really my best friend, but like he don't, he's not my friend, like he don't want to hang out no more because he's always with his girlfriend. So it's like he's still my best friend, he is still down to me, but like Marcus is the one I hang out with.

In a matter-of-fact tone of voice, Nick reveals his sadness over the loss of Noel due to a shift in Noel's priorities. His direct acknowledgment that Noel's desire has changed since last year puts Nick in an explicitly vulnerable position vis-à-vis his interviewer as well as toward Noel. He insists, however, that he is still "down" with Noel. Like the friend he wants Noel to be, Nicks maintains his loyality.

Nick does, however, have Marcus as a "best friend," as well as other boys with whom he spends time. "I trust them with mostly everything . . . I will give Marcus a hundred dollars and I will be like "hold that for me, next week, and I have it." Expressing a form of trust common between teenagers from poor and working class families,[1] Nick focuses on the material, and thus masculine, form of trust. Yet he is also willing to discuss the more emotional components:

> [For me to trust them, my friends] got to show me what they are about first. I have to know where they come from, how they really are. I want to know, you know, not just the basketball you, or just hanging out. You know like how you are when you go home, you know, how you act when you are at home.

In this sophisticated expression of his desire to *know* his friend, Nick once again reveals his astute emotional capacities.

Wondering aloud, his interviewer asks Nick: "How do you do it, just like what keeps you yourself?" Nick responds with clarity:

> Because I feel I have a lot of sorrow, you know like a lot of pain inside, since my mother's loss . . . you know, and like it hurts, so I don't want to walk around frowning and all sad and everything, all mad and taking it out, because I want to be happy, you know. I want to enjoy my life, you know, I don't want to walk around, you know, depressed, no, I'm not really depressed you know. I'm happy right now, because I have friends, I have a family still here, and I know that my mother is you know resting in peace. So right now I'm kinda

happy. So I'm not going to walk around crying and weeping and feeling sorry for myself. I'm going to go on living and doing what I got to do . . . Stay happy, and I'm not going to show the sad side.

Tracing the "I" statements in this passage (part of the analytic technique described in Chapter 2), we hear in this passage the tension for Nick between the real (i.e., his actual experiences of sadness and anger) and the "ideal" (i.e., that he shouldn't be sad or mad or depressed).

I feel
I have
I don't

I want
I want
I don't

I am not
I am
I have
I have
I know
I am kinda
I am not

I got to
I am not

While the loss of his mother affords him an expressive language, it also imposes an expectation of emotional stoicism. He both wants to be happy and feels "a lot of sorrow." He feels vulnerable but doesn't want to feel vulnerable. He knows that he is fortunate to have friends and family and also knows that he feels sad about losing his mother.

Nick is willing to continue to express directly feelings of vulnerability, however. When asked what happened to his friendship with Noel, he says:

> We just grew farther and farther apart instead of closer and closer, we were so close, best friends. It was so close, like real, real close. But like as soon as this girl came in, he just let me go and it really hurt. You know, it's like, you know, I understand you have a girl, you know, you have to spend time with your girl, you know, this time for me because, you know, I'm not saying you have to spend time with me. But, you know, as a best friend, you just can't, you know, you are just going to let me go like that. How you think I'm going to react? How am I going to feel?

Using, once again, the language of romantic love, Nick describes his feelings explicitly. His repeated use of "you know," furthermore, conveys a desire for confirmation that Noel's behavior was indeed unacceptable and that how he *feels* is important for Noel to consider.

In his sophomore year, Nick says that the best friend that he spends the most time with is Marcus:

> I mean, he's a best friend. . . . While Noel is pushing me away, Marcus is trying to, you know, he wants me to be his friend. Marcus needs a best friend. You know he's the type of person that I can get along with, you know, like he needs somebody just like me. You know he has problems at home, so he wants to share with somebody, somebody close that he could trust and will understand.

Basing his friendship on what Marcus needs and wants, Nick underscores his empathic capacity. Yet Marcus is not what Nick *needs and wants* as suggested in his discussions of Noel.

In the meantime, he is deeply responsive to Marcus's desires: "Yeah, he tells me everything that I want to know, when we talk. I mean I don't feel right, you know [his] mother's getting mad at home. I don't know what to do. . . . That's just how close we are. He tells me how he is feeling." His emphasis on his own and on

Marcus's feelings—his desire *to know* his friend's feelings—challenges, once again, the cultural construction of boys' friendships.

When asked about why Marcus is closer to him than his other friends, Nick says: "He understands me more. 'Cause he knows my problems, you know my mom passed away, he knows that I don't get that much love from my brother and sisters, so he's kind of being, you know helping me, be here for both of us, I mean." Even though Marcus is not Noel, Nick feels connected to Marcus and appreciates his warmth and understanding. At the end of the interview, Nick admits that he misses Noel and hopes that he will come back to him in the future.

Junior Year: Losing Friendships but Finding Noel

In his third year of high school, Nick continues to live with his sisters and stepfather, with whom he has had an extremely contentious relationship, especially since his mother died. Nick has a girlfriend this year with whom he hopes to eventually "settle down" and be a better father to his kids ("if I have kids") than his biological father was to him. Wearing his heart on his sleeve, Nick says he "wants to have a mother—I want to have a wife that—is like my mother was." His sadness over the loss of his mother remains palpable. Nick continues to be an avid basketball player and spends most of his free time playing basketball. He and his friends also spend much of the day "talking about sports, girls, and family issues." As in each of his interviews, he moves back and forth between masculine conventions and being more attuned to the nuances of the emotional world.

Nick's perceptions of his friendships in his junior year remain sensitive and astute:

> Best friends don't come and go. You know, best friends are for life. You know you're with—even though that best friend may be gone and goes and forgets about you and never comes back, you know? You are always gonna remember that friend because it's a best friend and you shared things that you wouldn't share with, like, a friend in school.

Speaking from what he knows, Nick reminds his interviewer that a physical loss does not mean a memory loss. He wants to believe that best friends remain best friends in feeling regardless of whether they are present or absent. Nick, however, is losing his friends this year and raises questions regarding the extent to which friends truly stay friends regardless of time spent together: "Well I feel like some of us have split apart 'cause of working or school, college. So I feel that my friends are not really there that much."

Following this discussion of loss, Nick justifies the loss in ways that remind us of the cultural context in which boys' friendships exist. Friendships become framed as immature and something that only a child needs:

> Friendships were actually more important when I was a kid because I—always needed friends. You can't really be in an environment by yourself, that's not really that good. So as a kid, I depended on having friends more when I was younger. [Now] we are just going to school, going to work, and we sort of separated.

Repeating the story we have heard so many times before—that growing up entails necessary loss—Nick tries to believe it. Yet in the midst of this discussion, he reveals the contradiction between what he should feel and how he actually feels:

> Like I really—really care, like my friends—you can't say to my friends that have gone, like you know, "come [back]." Um, I feel like, sort of sad that they are gone. But the friends that I have now, you know, we try to make the best of it. You know, like I said, friends do come and go but the friends that you have now, you try to make the best of it.

Nick tries hard to believe in the mainstream story of maturity but knows—like he knows about his feelings for his mother—that the story does allow him to feel how he really feels.

Despite losing some of his friends, however, Nick continues to have close relationships. With his closest friends he can "tell a secret or like about my family. Like my mother, like, I miss her and [they will say] 'I understand what you're feeling.' . . . They will just be there." He also continues to be deeply empathic:

> Like sometimes Noel will stay with his girl, and I'll have time for Marcus. Then everybody will say: "Oh, so Marcus is your best friend now," so like Noel will get jealous 'cause Marcus is your best friend. And then Marcus, will—and then I'll hang with José and the like—and then they're like: "Oh, so José is your best friend now." Like I try, you know, to spend time with them all.

Revealing not only Nick's sensitivity to his friends' feelings but his friends' sensitivity to Nick's behavior, this passage conveys the intensity of boys' friendships even as they enter late adolescence.

Nick and Noel are best friends again this year both physically and emotionally. According to Nick, Noel has promised never "to leave" him again and is making concerted efforts to spend more time with him than last year. Nick refers to Noel as "like a brother" because of "all the things we have been through and shared."

Nick says about Noel:

> I lost my mother, it was like him losing his. He was there at the funeral. He was there and he cried. And I told him, he hugged—I cried. He was really there for me. Even now, the conversation comes up and I come in tears, he'll say, "It's alright," and he'll give me a hug. He'll say, "I'll be there for you, you know, I've always been there for you,. 11 years." That's a long time. . . . You feel special. That person makes you feel special. And you try a lot to make that person feel special. To let that person know what—what he's been doing for you. . . . he knows that I'm his best friend. So he knows that I'll be there a lot for him. I spend time with him, you know. There's times that he'll need me or want to hang out, help, need my help for something, and I'll be there for him and I will say "Noel, you know, if you ever need anything, I'm here." Or, "If you need help with this, I'm here." I was there for him when he had a fight with his stepfather. He was like really emotional, you know. I say, you know, "I'm always gonna be there. If you need anything, I'm here, you know. If you want to come stay in my house." And he's done the same for me.

His repeated use of "you know's" in his response contains an implicit question for his interviewer. Does she know what he and

Noel know? As if to clarify to his interviewer, Nick adds: "A friendship means that the person makes you feel special and you make that person feel special. You give a little, get a little . . . Give love. You give a lot. You give yourself. Um, you give—you give time to that person . . . you are there for that person . . ." While his choice of the second person point of view may suggest a desire to distance himself from these feelings of mutual love, it also suggests that he wants to include his interviewer in the conversation. This is what "you" experience in a real friendship.

Senior Year: Protecting His Heart

In his senior year, Nick continues to live with his sisters and his step father, with whom he continues to argue about a range of topics including his curfews which he finds too strict. He is still with the same girlfriend from the previous year, but he spends little time talking about her in his interview. Most of his conversation is focused on his friendships, his desire to try to improve his poor school performance, his passion for basketball, and his arguments with his stepfather. He tells his interviewer that when he goes to college (he hopes to attend a local four-year college), he wants to play basketball and will try to make it on the college team until "hopefully" he makes it in a professional league. He also plans on majoring in music technology as he wants to work in a recording studio when he gets older if he does not make it in basketball. He continues to exude hope: "I'll be very successful in whatever I do, whether it's in music, whether it's in any sport—basketball, baseball, or football. I'm talented in most sports. I mean, whatever I do." His confidence remains, as does his close friendship with Noel.

Nick spends time with Noel regularly as well as two other friends, one of whom is Nick's cousin who was not mentioned in his previous interviews: "Noel has always been my best friend. It's like even though we went to different schools, we will always see each other either after school or on the weekends." He rarely sees the friends he mentioned in earlier interviews because they work "too much" and he finds them untrustworthy. Nick admits, as he has said for the past two years, that he used to not be as close to Noel because Noel spent too much time with his girl-friend and Nick spent too much time "on the courts." Now, however, they have found a good balance. They "work hard" to stay together and are each committed to "trying to do things to stay together . . . we don't want to grow further apart." He tries to take time off from school and basketball to see his friends and "getting to know them more to see what their person's about." Nick says that he trusts them with "anything . . . I trust them a lot. They won't hurt my feelings, and they will respect what I have to say if I told them something. I trust that they're gonna give me good advice, that they'll be there for me, that they'll always love me. I will love them too." Sounding like the Nick we have heard in earlier interviews, he suggests in his explicitly emotional language that he continues to be comfortable in his skin.

It is during this interview that Nick provides details about why he had a falling out with Noel during his sophomore year (before this interview, it had remained vague). Marcus had tried to "break up" Nick and Noel's friendship by spreading rumors that Nick had said negative things about Noel and his girlfriend. As a result, Nick dropped Marcus as a best friend following his sophomore year. However, Nick confessed that he did, in fact, feel frustrated with Noel's girlfriend at that time:

> I felt like she was taking him away from me. And it's like I would hang with her [and Noel], she would want to only hang out with him. So it's like, you know, we were pulling him by one arm and the other and he didn't want to split apart so basically what happened was, with the rumors that Marcus spread, Noel just moved more toward her way.

Sounding more like a love story involving three boys and a girl than a story of boys and competition, Nick frames the struggle for Noel's attention as one in which he and the girlfriend were pulling Noel in two different directions rather than as a product of Noel's girlfriend being unreasonable. Unlike many of his male peers, Nick's astute understanding of relationships remains intact even into his senior year.

Describing the difficulties he had with the loss of Noel, he says:

> That was hard when Noel left me in my sophomore year because my best friend's leaving me, you know. That's somebody that I love, you know. It was hard for me to hang out with Noel because he . . . Noel didn't want me around. And that really hurt, because your best friend, or somebody that you love, they don't want you around. You know. You feel hurt.

Wanting his interviewer to know what he *feels,* he repeatedly says "you know" as he describes what happened with Noel. Yet his love for Noel remains. His willingness to take Noel back was rare among the boys. Once betrayed by male friends, boys often left them permanently. The break was too much for them to bear.[2] Nick, however, pursues his close friendship with Noel despite the betrayal.

Yet Nick is not so forgiving with his peers more generally and admits to continuing to keep himself at a distance with them:

> [Because of what happened with Marcus and other things] I don't give—I don't give my heart out to too many people, you know, especially when it could get broken or hurt easily. I've been through too many times of that. So it's like I don't have any room—I have to recuperate from my heart broken. There's been death in my family, girlfriends, you know, guy friends. I don't have any more for my heart to get stepped on. So I've picked myself up for awhile. I'm walking. But you know, you never know when you fall down again. So I'm trying to just keep my eye out.

Following the "I voice" in this passage, we hear the tension between having and not having trust. He wants to trust but worries that if he does he will be hurt again.

I don't
I don't

I have
I don't have
I have
I don't have
I have

Tensions between wanting to trust and distrusting, wanting intimacy and fearing betrayal or loss were common among the boys
during late adolescence. Girlfriends, family members, *and* male
friends broke hearts and, in a few circumstances, passed away
and left them alone.

About his male friends in general (not Noel), Nick says:

> They are pretty cool. Just don't trust anybody, 'cause nearly
> everybody talks trash behind your back. . . . A lot of them are like
> dishonest in some ways. Like you can't trust them. I thought I could
> trust them before, but they're dishonest . . . I learned not to trust. . . .
> If I tell them like secrets, like if someone in my family was dying,
> that's none of your business. 'Cause if I tell them, I know they'd tell
> everybody and spread the word.

Nick wavers between sounding disconnected ("that's none of
your business") and talking about the process of disconnection.
Increasingly this year Nick tells stories of disconnection, distrust,
and losing faith in his male peers. But he remains remarkably
connected to the nuances of the emotional world. Describing a
time in which his friends didn't show up for a movie when they
were supposed to meet him, Nick explains how he felt:

> If you don't come [to where we are supposed to meet], I'm gonna get
> mad. I'm not gonna get mad 'cause you dissed me, I'm gonna get
> mad 'cause I missed you. But I'll probably show it to you like I'm
> gonna get mad 'cause you dissed me. But it's really, I'm gonna get
> mad 'cause I love you and I miss you. That's what it is.

Speaking directly about a culture that asks boys to pretend that they are mad when they are hurt—to "man up" rather than to express vulnerability—Nick reveals the central tension for boys especially during late adolescence.

Nick says that his friendships with other boys really started to decline during his sophomore year (after his falling out with Noel):

> I don't know. You could say that they grew but then they didn't grow. Meaning that it grew that like you know more people—we started hanging out together more, but then it didn't grow in the sense that when they started smoking and drinking as we got older, we grew further apart because . . . that's not what I'm about. . . . [I: How has it changed since middle school?] Just like I said, you know, it went downhill. It's like we was tight, you know, we were close. And then you know, like I said, it just grew further apart as we got older. . . . Some people, they got further apart. Some other people got closer. . . . For me, so while I got closer to some people in the group, I got further apart from some of the others. And now it's just like, I'm not close to anybody now.

Revealing the decline that is the theme for boys during late adolescence, Nick concludes he is no longer close to anybody.

Reflecting on the growing distance with his friends, Nick says:

> That's been like the biggest, like the biggest change. Like, I don't know. I can't explain it. . . . Yeah, we just go out, hang out, have fun. That's that. Now it's different, you know . . . things are always gonna change, you know. So we knew—we knew it was gonna come, but you know, it's like we could have prevented it, but we just let it happen. And I'm not saying I wanted it that way, the change. And I'm not saying that I didn't want it. But you know, things change. That's the way it has to be.

Acknowledging his own agency in the process of loss ("we could have prevented it") but choosing to "let it happen" anyway, Nick reveals the extent to which boys understand what is expected of them as they become men. And in line with this expectation, he is not willing to admit to his own desire ("I'm not saying that I wanted it that way . . . And I'm not saying that I didn't want it") because, he believes, it is inevitable.

At the end of his senior year interview, Nick says:

> Best friends will always be there for me. . . . It's like—it's deep . . . A best friend is someone you can talk to, share your inner thoughts with, and they could do the same as well. Someone, you know, to have a shoulder to cry on. Someone that you could be a shoulder to cry on for them, just share, share things and different experiences with each other and have fun basically. Just be like a family.

No longer looking for reassurance or connection with his interviewer with "you know's," he simply repeats his thoughts about friendships in the second person. Although the content is intimate, the monotone quality of his voice and his repetition of a cliché that he knows is not always true ("best friends will always be there for me") suggests a loss that he does not want to feel.

GEORGE'S STORY

Freshman Year: Easygoing and Empathic

George is a tall, 14-year-old young man, with light brown skin and wavy short black hair; he lives with his mother and father, both of whom were born in New York City, and a 20-year-old brother, who attends a community college in the city and lives at home in the same room as George. When he grows up, George would like to be an auto mechanic and he currently spends most of his free time after school working on cars with his father. George's mother works at two jobs: she is a nurse's aide at a local hospital and a volunteer at the church that the family attends. George and his mother have a very close relationship. He feels that they "understand" each other and his mother often tells him how much she loves him. George also feels very close to his father, who works as a manager for a grocery store in the neighborhood, and says that he spends a great deal of time with his father each weekend fixing his father's cars. Both of his parents encourage George to have friendships. George says that his father has always told him: "The more friends you have the more like . . . I mean you'll be happier more."

George describes himself: "I'm nice, I'm a good listener, I'm good in school, I'm smart, I'm kinda good in sports even though I don't like, like um sports like I only like soccer and football and like some volleyball." Although sports are mentioned, they do not form the core of his identity as it does for Nick. Fixing cars, however, does. He describes with great pride his father's cars, as well as the work they do together and the car shows they attend. George is proud of his gentle nature and says that he would never "make fun of anybody." He adds that he is also able to keep secrets and does not retaliate when others harass him. As an example, he describes a time when a boy from middle school picked on him and he chose not to respond: "My friends were like 'why don't you make fun of him back?' I was like 'because it's—that's not like how to solve a problem because it makes the other person get hurt and stuff like that.'"

George is explicit about the fact that he needs his friends and wants their support as well as their company. Rather than a particular friend, George has a circle of male and female friends in his freshman year that is more expansive than Nick's. At the beginning of his freshman year, George describes these friendships:

> We're close. Like we would speak out about our problems . . . Let's say like um, one kid was like, he was really messing around like, he was smoking one day and his mom caught him so he was like "What should I do? Like should I stop smoking?'" and I was like "yeah 'cause I mean it really messes you up."

Rather than focusing on the sports played, boys like George focus on the problems shared with their friends. When asked what he likes most about his friends, George says:

They know like when we're trying to get serious and when we're joking around. Like let's say you're angry and like one of your friends are like joking around and you don't really want to hear it. So like let's say, like in this situation where they know you're angry and then they're like "oh what's wrong" stuff like that. They won't like really joke around and stuff.

His vulnerability is especially remarkable given that it is in response to a question about what he likes most about his friendships. In the midst of much joking, mocking, and laughter, boys valued that their close friends knew how to "be serious" when necessary. Yet this skill is newly acquired and not something that was expected at an earlier age: "In the beginning, we just like joked around and had fun and that was about it, but like, later on, it just became closer like. I would say about in eighth and ninth grade, we became more serious."

As boys grow older, they become more skilled in understanding the needs of their friends. While this maturity in perspective taking has been noted,[3] the corresponding growth in the emotional intimacy in boys' friendship has not. Boys don't simply transition from having "chumships" with boys to "lust relationships" with girls,[4] they continue to have or at least want "chumships" throughout adolescence—friendships that entail serious talk and the sharing of secrets. George says: "I think friendships are real important because like you speak your mind. I mean if friendships weren't around like everybody would be like either angry or they would be like all, they would be all to themselves. They won't speak their minds." George knows, as do most of his male peers, that there are serious psychological consequences to not having a "chum."

George's mother shares his beliefs about the dire consequences of not having a friend with whom to talk:

Well she thinks it's really important because I mean, let's say, friends builds up self-esteem 'cause if you don't have a lot of friends I would think that you would have low self-esteem because you can't like

talk to anybody about your problems. You don't joke around . . .
Both of us think that way.

When describing the differences between girls and boys, George,
who has male and female friends, says initially that there is no difference between them. They are "pretty much the same. . . . I
mean I think with girls it's less, like they don't really talk about
like really serious problems." Among guys, however, he discusses
"family problems" and more personal concerns believing that
boys are more trustworthy than girls. George distinguishes, however, between types of boys. Some boys are "really a joke around
person and really silly, I wouldn't like say something personal to
them because I would know for a fact that they wouldn't keep it
to themselves" and the other type of boy is those with whom he
can share his secrets: "[These boys] are like really nice and they're
serious at times. They keep everything to themselves. I mean not
keep to themselves, but like they keep secrets to themselves."
Such careful distinctions between types of boys were often made
by boys, suggesting a sharp attunement to the relational world.

George describes his best friends, a group of four male friends
and one female friend (Samantha), as closer to him than any of
his other friends because "they know when like you're having
problems, like they can feel it out. It's like parents, like they always know like when you're trying to hide something. They always know when you're in trouble—stuff like that." George
trusts his friends with his personal issues, as he knows that they
"wouldn't tell everybody and everything like that." He admits,
however, to feeling closer to three of the boys within this group
of five because he has known these boys longer: "I mean you
know more about them and like what's wrong with them like
let's say they're angry, so you know, like when they're angry and
stuff like that." Being able to read each other's emotions is key
for George, as it is for Nick as well.

At the end of his interview, George says that the type of friend
he would like most in the world is one he could "trust and

they're trustworthy, you joke around, and you could stay to-gether for a long time." Mixing his accommodation to masculine conventions (e.g., "you joke around") with his more sensitive side, George describes his ideal and real friendships.

Sophomore Year: Struggling to Stay Close

In his sophomore year, George engages in the same routine he had as a freshman—doing his homework after school, working on cars with his father, eating dinner every night with both of his parents and, occasionally, his older brother. George continues to feel close with his mother, talking to her about girls and school, although they have been having more conflicts this year due to a curfew George thinks is too strict. George also continues to have a close relationship with his dad, referring to him as a "really close friend." At home, George struggles most with his older brother, but the source of conflict seems to be the stress his brother is causing his mother, which George says is "unfair" to his mother.

George describes himself this year in terms like those he used the previous year: "I'm understanding, I like to joke a lot. I'm a good listener. A good person really." His example of how he is "a good person" underscores his emotionally maturity:

> Well let—let's say you're talking to me trying to tell me something, I'd be [voice fades a lot] just like, "okay, yeah sure." And like, just like that, that word—saying "okay" a lot, is also like saying "I know," it cuts someone off makes them feel really stupid because, it makes them not want—it tells them like some idea of like, you don't really care. Like if you say, "Yeah, I know," it's just like "okay." So I usually don't say it as much.

George's deep sensitivity to the feelings of others is as obvious in his sophomore year as it was in his freshman year. When asked about things that bother him about his friends, he says:

> Sometimes like when you ask them what's wrong, like say they're down, they don't tell you what's wrong and like you, like you really

want to know to help them out but they're like nah. So it makes you feel like you're not as important as other friends as if they would tell some other people. . . . They probably think that I won't keep secrets but I do, so maybe they don't know that.

The emphasis for George, like Nick, is on *knowing* how others feel. His deep empathy is evident as is his comfort with expressing his emotional skills—skills that are underscored when he shifts from second person to first person in the last sentence of the above passage.

Drawing attention to his core values, George describes his friends this year in the same way as he describes himself: "kind, understanding, they joke around, they're good listeners." Mixing the stereotypically masculine ("they joke around") with the stereotypically feminine ("they're good listeners"), George reveals the borders that he and his male peers negotiate continually in their friendships. Yet in his sophomore year, as in his freshman year, he continues to wade deeply into stereotypically feminine territory defining trust with his friends as knowing that "I could tell them secrets. I can trust them. I know that they won't like tell lies. They won't make rumors about me. They won't—they'll keep my secrets and stuff. . . . They share their feelings and stuff."

George explains to his interviewer that he and his friends are more likely this year than in previous years to talk about family issues which he enjoys because "you get closer because you get to know more like what, like how they deal with problems in their family or girls, or like just in general really . . ." The emphasis for George, once again, is on *knowing* his friends. When asked why the content of their talk changed over the past year, George says: "I guess with family issues, it is because I guess my friends just have to let it out. I mean just like, sometimes it's just, they hold it in and they just have to try to find a way to let it out." Conveying a theme heard throughout my studies of boys, George understands the connection between sharing secrets and mental health.

This year, George claims to have two "really, really, really, really close" friends; one is Joaquin and the other is Samantha, the girl whom he has known all of his life and who was his best friend last year (the other boys he was close to previously are still close but are no longer "best friends"). Describing Joaquin, he says: "It's obviously pretty close since he's my best friend. Um, we talk about things, like if he's having any family problems or, um, like girlfriend-boyfriend problems, um, anything really." What he likes about Joaquin is that "he's like understanding, he keeps secrets to himself. He doesn't lie most of the time. Like if he needs to lie, it's usually something about, like joking around lying. Um, like he doesn't act stupid as in making rumors." The concern about betrayal and lying, which will start to consume George's later interviews, is suggested here but as a way to reveal why he can rely on Joaquin as a friend rather than why he distrusts him.

George has had Samantha as a close friend for over eight years. When asked to distinguish between Joaquin and Samantha, he says that with Samantha he wouldn't tell her about a new crush he has on a girl, or about the girl whom he is currently hoping will be his girlfriend, because she might tell her friends. However, he believes that he and Samantha have gotten closer recently because "it's me liking girls and she likes boys so it's just like since, let's say, I knew one of my friends and she liked him, so then I'd help her out, and it would just be likewise with her." The terms are similar across his closest friendships. He will tell them his secrets if he has confidence that they will not betray him and George believes, during his sophomore year, that he has friends who will not betray him.

Junior Year: Keeping the Faith

In his junior year, George and his mother continue to have a close relationship, but George expresses a lot of frustration with his mother's curfews and her "nagging" about schoolwork. He also remains close to his father and the two of them continue to work on cars during the weekends. This activity gives George much pleasure as his friends admire him for his mechanical ability and his father's "cool" cars. While he continues to want to be auto mechanic, he is no longer sure it will be a satisfying job and has thus chosen this year to become a tutor for young children with the hopes of finding his career path after high school. His self-description remains focused on relational qualities such as being a good listener and being straightforward with others, but incipient signs of the pressures of masculinity begin to appear. This year he says of himself: "I'm cool, I'm funny, I'm understanding." Rather than putting the relational qualities first, he puts them last and by his senior year, the relational qualities have disappeared entirely.

George begins his junior year interview by describing how his cousin follows him around in school which he finds annoying because, he explains, his cousin comes from a family that always tries to "cover the sun with their hands," which he explains means, "they always try to hide the obvious truth." In remarkably expressive language, George underscores his growing concern with betrayal and deceit—a concern that will be heard throughout his senior year interview.

As before, George's peer life consists of male and female friends, some of whom are best friends. This year, however, he divides up his male friends into those who "just want ass" and those to whom he can talk in a more serious manner about sensitive topics such as "feeling really stupid." "Serious things," he says, are only discussed with friends who *know* [his] feelings." As a way to underscore the importance for him of feeling known,[5] he provides an example of a girl on whom he has a crush who recently gave him a writing journal for his birthday. He reflects: "Everyone else would just give me like a hot wheels car or something and be like oh—that's like the outer shell. You gotta like know me inside before you do anything."

George thinks he has become more expressive as he has grown older. By way of example, he describes a time when a male friend stopped liking him: "He supposedly heard some like rumors about me and they were like totally retarded . . . he starts believing them and then he starts like not liking me. So I came up to him. I was like, 'what's up man?'" When asked why he confronted his friend, he explains:

> It's, it's stupid. So I mean, I was just like, "hey you know it's kind of dumb for like people to hate me, because I mean, there shouldn't be any reason to." So I just came up to him and I was like, "Hey, what's up?" And he was like, "Oh, I heard mad shit about you, blah, blah." I was like, "What did you hear?" I didn't say from who, because I mean, it doesn't matter. So he was like, "Blah, blah, that you were talking crap about my girlfriend's sweet 16." I was like, "Hey, I didn't even go, so I don't even know how it happened or how it went." So he was like "Oh, oh, oh, yeah that's right." So I mean now, it's just like getting back. We just talk about school and like stuff like that. We don't really get personal anymore.

George's story reveals boys' sensitivity to betrayal. Just like girls, boys have fights about and break up over "rumors." While they may attempt to repair the situation, the betrayal has permanent consequences ("we don't really get personal anymore").

While George's reflective nature is evident throughout this interview, it is most apparent when he describes his closest friends. Asked how he knows that he can trust his best friends, he says:

> I don't know. It's just like a feeling, where like you know he wouldn't like say something that would hurt you. Or like say something inappropriate when you're trying to be serious. . . . I guess you're just gonna have to like take the risk. And like, just like say something out of this world and see what he says. Now you know if he's gonna say something really ridiculous and you want something serious. It's obvious that, you know, he's not there yet, so.

Referring to the familiar trust test, George articulates the process of forming close friendships. His bottom line is that he wants to avoid being hurt and thus "tests" to see if a potential friend will hurt him. Although his use of the second person pronoun suggests a discomfort, perhaps, with his "feelings," his reliance on his feelings to assess the risks of a potential friend (i.e., "it's just like a feeling") draws attention to the extent to which George is grounded in his feelings.

Asked to describe the differences between his close and his best friends, George says:

> Maybe just like, the level of trust is even deeper when you can like say practically anything to your really best friends. And like your close friends, it's just like goes more in depth, like you can't say anything. . . . [With best friends], I could go like even deeper to like more problems with like personal, like, like family types of things. . . . With best friends I don't have to put this mask on and like say things that they want to hear. . . . It's not like this thing where like, oh yeah, I have to say what he likes, thinks, or likes.

Referring to the "mask of masculinity" that William Pollack describes in *Real Boys*,[6] George explicitly seeks and finds friends with whom he doesn't have to wear such masks. Only with best friends is George able to act like himself and freely express his "deeper" thoughts and feelings.

George believes that it is easier to find such trustworthy friends in high school than in junior high school:

> Because like now . . . you can have even closer relationships where you can talk about your parents. 'Cause you know, you either like them more or like you got more open or you can take more risks. I mean you just grow, you just grow out of that stage . . . 'cause like in the beginning, you know, you are really close like to your parents and you're really close to them because obviously they raised you. And then you start taking risks and talking to other people. So I mean, I guess by like this age or like high school, you start taking more risks and you realize it's not so bad.

Talking intimately and expressing oneself openly is perceived for George, as it is for so many boys in my studies, as a risk worth taking.

Yet, as George explains, having friendships entails many types of risks:

> Yeah, like people see me like [be close] with girls and they think, whoa that's kind of weird, and like some girl even came up to me, kind of got me like mad and she was like, 'Are you gay?' I was like, "No, what the hell, just because I'm close to girls and guys don't mean—doesn't mean nothing." But I mean, I didn't take it like at a personal level 'cause she didn't know me as much so I didn't really care.

George understands that he lives in an American culture in which friendships even with girls can be misinterpreted. And then, as if to acknowledge that his interviewer is also a part of this American culture, he clarifies his sexuality:

> I don't feel awkward against like gay people or anything. If that is how they want to be, that's how they want to be. It's not my problem. It's not like I have to like change that or it's not my goal to do that. I mean, what the hell, that's what they want to do. Go ahead. But I mean if you get me involved and like if you're trying to rap to me or something then that's kind of awkward. I need to like tell you like be like, "Whoa, I'm not like that." Or like if it's really serious, I'd just like walk away or something like that.

Like so many of the boys in my studies who walked the fine line between resisting and adhering to masculine conventions, George reveals in this clichéd response that it is hard to resist when directly questioned about being gay.

George, however, continues to resist gendered expectations when describing his friendships. He says he wants friends who are "really open with feelings" and appreciates Samantha's boyfriend, Jake, because he is "not like the guys, 'oh I gotta act tough and everything.' And just like, he's just like, says what he wants to say. He says what's on his mind and it's just like I don't know. It just like it emanates from him." Seeking authenticity in his friendships, George says:

We talk about like how he feels about things like family relationships and basic stuff like that, like how his family treats him, how he doesn't like his mother sometimes and stuff like that. Like you don't just come up to somebody like "damn my mom's acting like a bitch, blah, blah, and like we have so many problems with our family." You don't like go up to anyone and say that kind of stuff. . . . Jake is like really open, like the way he acts and everything. He's cool. And he expresses his feelings. Like I know what he thinks. It's not like I have to come out and say something. He'll be like, "Oh yeah, yeah, me too."

Rejecting the sharp division between feeling and thinking, George blends them together ("he expresses his feelings, like I know what he thinks"), acknowledging that one can be both "cool" and emotionally expressive.

George's description of his friendship with Joaquin is in stark contrast to the one with Jake. He describes Joaquin this year as constantly joking but also struggling with depression and not coming to school. George continues, however, to spend time with him because Joaquin can make him feel good whenever he feels down and Joaquin is trustworthy: "he wouldn't spread anything." George and Joaquin, however, rarely share secrets as they did in earlier years. When asked what he likes about Joaquin, George says:

Um, he's like really, he could joke around about anything. Or like take negative things and make something look really positive and like don't worry about it. Um, basically, I could trust him a lot . . . like he was saying like if you were to get drunk or something, I wouldn't take you to your house because I know your mom would be like really pissed off. You could sleep at my house for the day.

Describing a gender stereotypic friendship, George sounds like a different boy from the one we heard earlier. Yet he acknowledges that his friendship with Joaquin is "the obvious 'guy relationship,'" revealing an awareness of the limitations of the friendship.

At the end of his junior year interview, George says that he thinks that his friendships are very important:

> Yeah 'cause if you don't, I mean I don't really tell my mother
> everything. So I mean, if you just have your mother and your par-
> ents, then you're just gonna have all these ideas bottled up and
> you're just gonna go wacko because you can't express yourself even
> more. So I think, yeah, it's really important.

Sharing secrets and feelings is not perceived by boys to be something that simply fosters intimacy; it is also understood as essential for their mental health. George's mother concurs:

> [My mom thinks] you have to have friendships or else you'd be like
> wanting to commit suicide or something. 'Cause I mean, if you don't
> have anyone to talk to besides your parents, and if you don't like
> talking to your parent then you're just gonna keep all your feelings
> inside and you're just gonna feel like crap for like your whole life.
> She thinks they're like absolutely necessary.

Boys and their mothers, unlike the American culture in which
they are embedded, understand the essential nature of emotional expression and intimate friendships for psychological
well-being.

Senior Year: "Covering the Sun with Your Hand"

The tone of George's senior year interview is dramatically different from his previous interviews. While he presents himself as
someone who is doing "fine," it becomes apparent during his
three-hour interview that George is struggling this year. His relationship with his mother remains "close" but the conflicts have
increased dramatically because of his declining grades and the
fact that he continues to spend time with Joaquin who has now
dropped out of school. George's father, in addition, has had serious heart problems over the past year, and George worries about
him. Reflecting on his relationship with his dad, George says:

> Sometimes it is uncomfortable with my dad because like he knows
> me so much as to like—I can have like a certain expression on my
> face and he'd know how I, how I would be feeling. And sometimes

it's annoying 'cause you really don't want to tell him. So you be like, "No I'm fine. See?' And you just have to put on a smile.

His father insists on the type of honesty that was important to George in previous years. This year, however, George is frustrated with the implicit demand from his father for such honesty.

What George likes least about himself this year is that he is often pessimistic: "I sometimes just like don't like myself at all. Like it's just like, 'no' . . . I don't really think high of myself. I don't really think that low of myself. It's just like, you know, I'm just here. I mean I notice what I do. I notice like my qualities and everything. But I don't like take them for granted." Seeking a kind of neutrality, George struggles to describe himself. What he worries about most is the possibility of being a "zombie" like his 23-year-old brother who works at a fast food restaurant and still lives at home: "Like how am I gonna stop that? I can't." His fears seem to both impel him to move forward in his life.

George, for the first time in the four years of his interviews, tells his interviewer that he wants "to escape" with his friends which likely reflects the fact that his only close friendship this year is with Joaquin who has "escaped" school:

> Friends help you escape the real world . . . because it's like a vacation because like let's say you're at a job and it's just like really bitchy and stupid. I mean you have all that stress with you. But when you're with your friends, it's like it's a whole different atmosphere because you can loosen up and be yourself. And it's a lot less stressful because you don't have to worry about much 'cause like your friends are gonna be there and like not do stupid things. So you're just like at ease with yourself, at least for that moment, but that moment's like enough for you to go on.

Underscoring his discomfort with himself, George frames his friendships as a place to be at ease with himself. Yet his friends do not seem to provide the respite he seeks. George describes numerous conflicts with friends this year and of not telling any of his friends his more serious concerns because he doesn't want to "burden them."

> I felt like my friends didn't really need to know [about my dad's problems]. So it's no big deal. . . . I considered [telling them] but I mean I don't really 'cause it's like it's a bad, it brings like a whole bad atmosphere to things and it's just it's unnecessary. Like if you're feeling sad, why have others feel sad around you? It's not like it's gonna, you know help anything so . . . it's in the family so why not keep it in the family.

In stark contrast to his previous interviews, George sounds like a cliché of emotional restraint. His newly articulated desire "not to care"—a common desire for boys during late adolescence—becomes increasingly evident: "If I get the hint like my friend doesn't want me around or anything, it's no problem. I mean, do what you gotta do. I mean that's fine. I mean it would bother me a little like that—like, 'you don't like me now.' But I mean, what can I do about it?" If we trace his I statements in this passage, we hear him struggle to articulate his feelings.

I get
I mean
I mean
I mean
I mean
I do

His response suggests that the demands of maturity and manhood are hard on a growing boy. He wants to talk and does not want to talk about his hurt feelings. And then he says it explicitly:

> The big change is that next year is college and all that and you have to get ready and all this. And it's a big change because I mean you're going from being a teenager into being self-reliant and you have to just, like, be considered an adult. And it's like a whole load of responsibility. I mean it's like the security blanket's been taken away from you, so.

The "self-reliance" of manhood is frightening for George as he realizes that his "security blanket"—his family and his close friends—will be "taken away."

George skates on the surface in his friendships this year claiming that they are "all pretty cool" even though he isn't able to talk confidentially to any of his friends and he does not provide any examples of how these friendships are "cool." Describing a "close friend" whom he has never mentioned before in earlier interviews, George says:

> Victor was really an acquaintance. But now it's just like I can talk to him about anything 'cause I trust him. And I mean it's not like—he's a general friend because I don't hang out with him and like I don't see him as much. So that's really why, but he's cool. I mean I joke around with him and everything. I can be myself basically.

Although there is a possibility of intimacy ("I can talk to him about anything"), there is no evidence of intimacy ("he's a general friend because I don't hang out with him") in this friendship with Victor. He admits that he doesn't tell Victor his "most secret" secrets: "Like I can tell him secrets about—I can tell him like jokes—about people like I don't want the other person to hear or something—like that. I mean it's not all like trust as in I can tell him everything like what's happening with me personally. He doesn't know my family." Thus, while George is more inclusive this year of who is considered a close friend, naming numerous boys and girls from his school, each of these relationships seems remarkably superficial. He doesn't have any friendships this year with whom he shares his thoughts and feelings.

Most of his friends have "coupled" off, he says, and do not spend as much time with him as before. He too would like a girlfriend but the girl on whom he has a crush, the same girl he had a crush on in previous years, does not consistently reciprocate his affections. When asked how the "coupling" of his friends influences him, George starts to stutter and then starts to cough (the only time he coughs in the entire interview) saying: "I don't

know why my throat always acts up when I talk in these interviews." His physical reaction to the question answers the question. He seems troubled and unable to directly articulate what it
is that troubles him so deeply.

While George claims that Joaquin is his best friend this year,
he rarely sees him and does not share his most private thoughts
and feelings with him:

> My dad had a little problem with like his health and stuff. So I didn't
> really relay the message to Joaquin because I felt like he didn't really
> need to know. So it's no big deal . . . [I: Why didn't you tell him?] Um
> I don't know. Like it's not much of a big deal. Like my dad's still
> around and stuff so I mean, hey, you know? It's not like he's gonna
> die like tomorrow or anything. Geez. So I felt it wasn't. I mean not
> even Samantha knows. . . . But I guess I figured like I mean, hey
> what's the big deal? It's in the family. So why not leave it in the
> family?

Sounding like a stereotypic boy ("hey, what's the big deal?"),
George tries to convince his interviewer that he is being rational
in his decision not to share his deep secrets with Joaquin. His
repetition of the phrase "I mean" suggests, once again, a struggle to articulate what he means. He knows it was a "big deal"
when his father got sick, but he shrouds his response in a typical
"boy code" strategy of downplaying the seriousness of the problem to justify his silence.

George admits at the end of the interview that he does not
have a best friend and questions whether he has ever had one: "I
don't know . . . I guess I don't have a best friend, yeah, I'm not
sure . . . 'cause they are always just. They are not really best
friends. They are just like regular friends. I guess. . . . But I don't
know. I don't think I ever have had a best friend and if I did, like
they all like moved out or something like that." The reframing of
his history of friendships suggests not only a sharpening of his
conceptions of best friendship but also a sadness over the loss
of best friends ("if I did, like they all like moved out or some-

thing like that"). For George, both the past and the present seem bleak.

When asked directly what has changed in his friendships, he says:

> I don't know. I think that it did. Like some of them, like they obviously moved in different places as in like close friends and general friends. But I guess it's just like the years pass and like getting to know each other more often or seeing each other more often. And I mean you get used to that so I guess that's really why. You get to know the person more, so.

His lack of clarity suggests a disconnection. He stumbles searching for a way to express the changes without expressing what has most obviously changed.

Only at the end of his senior year interview does George speaks directly about the history of his friendships: "I think my friendships have gotten more important because like I used to rely on my parents a lot more from the ninth grade and back. And since like the tenth grade, I got to know more friends and I used to—now I hang out with them. *I—Well I did hang out with them, you know, more.* . . . If you don't have good friendships . . . you're not gonna get anywhere." George expresses both his deep understanding of why friendships are important and what happens when boys lose their close friendships.

SUMMARY

Both Nick and George describe having "deep depth" male friendships in which the sharing of thought and feelings form the foundation. They openly express themselves with and strongly value the emotional component of these friendships. They suggest, along with their male peers in my studies, what evolutionary anthropologists and primatologists have long claimed which is that part of what makes us human is our deeply empathic and intersubjective capacities.[7] Boys want intimate connections with their male peers that are based on *knowing* each other and sharing secrets and feelings and they believe that such relationships are necessary to prevent going, as George indicated, "wacko."

Yet there is variation between Nick and George in the factors that supported their abilities to have intimate same-sex friendships. The supports for Nick lay with his close relationship with his mother before she died and the fact that he was talented basketball player and very popular among his peers throughout adolescence. His athletic skills and popularity likely provided protection for him so that he could be expressive without being labeled as girlish or gay. The loss of his mother may have also provided him with a safe space to be vulnerable. The experience of trauma—especially the loss of a parent—may provide boys with a free pass from the "boy code." George, in contrast, was close with both of his parents and both parents encouraged him to have close friendships. Furthermore, George had a stereotypically masculine hobby (i.e., fixing cars) that also likely protected his masculine image. The simple fact, however, that he was asked if he was gay by a girl who thought it was odd that he was close friends with girls and boys may reveal that having such a hobby does not provide as much protection as being a talented basketball player.

Nick and George both, however, grew increasingly wary and distrustful of their peers by their junior and senior years. They began to lose their way and disconnect from their friends and from school suggesting that one may lead to the other. The boys' prediction that they would "go wacko" or "get depressed" if they didn't have intimate friendships seemed to become a reality at least for George. Yet like the themes of intimacy, these patterns of distrust and loss had variations across boys with Nick, for example, growing distrustful but maintaining his close friendship with Noel; while George grew both distrustful and lost the intimacy in his friendships. Exploring these patterns and their meaning provides the other essential piece to the map of boys' friendships during adolescence and is thus the focus of the remainder of the book.

FRIENDSHIPS DURING

LATE ADOLESCENCE

II

CHAPTER 6

"WHEN YOU GROW UP,

YOUR HEART DIES"

A simple question asked by an interviewer provokes a simple response that reveals everything about friendships among boys during late adolescence.[1] The question, asked of each boy in my research, is: "How have your friendships changed since you were a freshman in high school?" The responses of three boys in their senior years are:

I don't know, maybe, not a lot, but I guess that best friends become close friends. So that's basically the only thing that changed. It's like best friends become close friends, close friends become general friends and then general friends become acquaintances. So they just . . . If there's distance whether it's, I don't know, natural or whatever. You can say that but it just happens that way.

Like my friendship with my best friend is fading, but I'm saying it's still there but . . . So I mean, it's still there 'cause we still do stuff together, but only once in a while. It's sad 'cause he lives only one block away from me and I get to do stuff with him less than I get to do stuff with people who are way further so I'm like, yo. . . . It's like a DJ used his cross fader and started fading it slowly and slowly and now I'm like halfway through the cross fade.

We used to be like close, as far as always being around each other, now it's just like we're apart, like as far as—like if I need them, they'll still be there. If they need me, I'll be there but as far as like always being together, we're not as close as we were before.

Late adolescence for the boys in my studies is a time of disconnection and loneliness. Rather than being simply a period of "progress," as scholars of human development emphasize, adolescence for these boys is also a period of profound loss. At the age of 16 or 17, as their bodies are almost fully grown and their minds are increasingly attuned to cultural messages about manhood and maturity, boys began to distance themselves from the relationships they hold most dear—their closest male friendships. They became more distrustful and less willing to be close with their male peers and believe that such behavior, and even their emotional acuity, put them at risk of being labeled girly, immature, or gay. Thus, rather than focusing on who they are, they became obsessed with who they are not—they are not girls and not children, nor, in the case of heterosexual boys, are they gay. In response to a cultural context that links intimacy in male friendships and emotional sensitivity with a sex and a sexuality, the boys "matured" into men who are autonomous, emotionally stoic, and isolated. The ages of 16 to 19, however, are not only a period of disconnection for the boys in my studies, it is also the period in which the suicide rate for boys in the United States rises dramatically and becomes four times the rate for girls.[2] Just as the boys during early and middle adolescence predicted, not having friends to share their deepest secrets makes them go "wacko."

Yet boys continue to express their desires for intimate friendships. Danny says in his senior year:

> I guess, you know for me, in order for a friendship to work, you can't like just say "hi" and "how are you doing" and that's it. I mean sometimes you have to talk to people in order to find out how they are feeling so that they have somebody else to express themselves to and they don't have to feel alone and like they're the only person in the world that has this problem.

As Danny suggests, boys want to express themselves so that they don't feel alone and they seek the type of intimate friendships they had when they were younger. The transition to manhood for boys is a difficult one indeed.

The boys, particularly between the ages of 16–18, revealed themes of loss, distrust, and desire. They spoke of losing their closest male friendships and of feeling less trusting and more wary of their male peers in particular. Their fears of betrayal intensified as they grew older, and that meant, for many, that emotionally intimate male friendships were no longer possible. Yet boys also spoke of wanting such a relationship despite the fact that it was so difficult to find.

There were, however, variations in these themes. Some boys retained the emotional sensitivity that was so apparent in their freshman and sophomore year interviews when they spoke about their losses, fears of betrayal, and desires for intimate male friendships. They spoke openly of the hurt, sadness, and loneliness they experienced as a consequence of such losses. Others, however, spoke of the same themes of loss but used a language of toughness and stoicism. They spoke of "not caring" whether they had best friends, even though the edges of their stories often revealed another story entirely. In sharp contrast to their earlier interviews, the dominant emotion in the interviews of these boys was one of irritation and anger which was mostly directed at their peers but also, occasionally, at their interviewers.

However, both sets of boys—those who continued to be emotionally vulnerable in their language and those who did not—conveyed the same overarching themes. They used to have intimate male friendships in which trust formed the core and sharing secrets was the product of such trust, and now, during late adolescence, they no longer had such relationships and/or had the same levels of trust with their male peers as they did at an earlier age. Given the social and health research linking friendships and strong social support networks with positive mental, physical, and academic outcomes, these findings suggest that growing up may not be good for boys' health.

"My Man Is Gone, Damn, What I'm Gonna Do":
Expressing Loss in Vulnerable Terms

Addressing the question of what he likes about his best friendship with Mark during his freshman year interview, Carlos says: "Like we could express our feelings or whatever. And tell each other how we feel. Like if I feel bad one day, I tell them why." He uses language such as "we show each other love" to describe the bonds he feels with his close male friends. Asked how he knew he could trust his best friend, he says: "'cause I know the kid inside of him. 'cause I grew up with that kid, you understand? I know who he really is." By his sophomore year, however, something has shifted. When asked what he likes about Mark this year: "It's cool, man. We could do anything. We joke around whatever. 'Cause I don't want to have a serious friend. That's boring, yo. Like I want a friend that I could joke around with. If I mess up he won't, you know, just laugh or I don't know." Suggesting a "cool pose"[3] but then undercutting it with his more sensitive views ("If I mess up he won't, you know, just laugh"), Carlos reveals a central conflict for boys during late adolescence. They want to have an "understanding" friendship that does not entail hurt, but they also do not want to sound childish, girlish, or gay.

By his junior year, Carlos's fears are directly stated as he repeats "no homo" every time he says something intimate about his best friends. In response to a question about what he does with his close friends, Carlos tells the interviewer "that question sounded homo, that sounded homo." When the interviewer expresses confusion as to how her question sounded "homo," he nervously laughs and says that "we just do whatever, man, we like, we do whatever we can do. If we don't have money, we stay in his house, watch TV." No longer are Carlos and his friends "expressing feelings" as he indicated in his freshman year; they now do "whatever we can do." When asked about his "best friend" during his senior year interview, a friend whom he rarely sees but still considers a best friend: "The relationship, I mean it's a good relationship. It's um it's a tight bond whatever. Um,

I can trust him. I don't know how to explain it. Somebody you feel chemistry. No homo." His qualification of "no homo" on the heels of expressing closeness (in romantic terms) as well as his response of "it's a tight bond, whatever" suggests a discomfort with his feelings that was not evident in his earlier interviews.

Yet Carlos also adds that while he does not "hate" his best friend this year, he feels frustrated with him because he has chosen to spend so much time with his girlfriend. Just like Nick (see Chapter 5), Carlos resents his friend's choice—a choice that is perceived to be necessary in the pathway to manhood. When Mark, Carlos's former best friend, who also participated in my research, confirms that because of his girlfriend he does, in fact, spend less time with Carlos, Mark notes, "You gotta give up one if you are going to have the other." In his senior year, he says that he misses Carlos and hopes that he can continue to be close with him even if he does not see him that often. Even for Mark, who has chosen a girlfriend over his best friend, the desire to maintain intimacy with his best friend remains.

Dell had a best friend named D.J., whom he describes with great passion during his freshman and sophomore year interviews. By Dell's junior year, D.J. has moved to a different part of the city and changed schools; as a consequence, they rarely spend time together. When Dell is asked in his junior year what has changed since last year, he says:

> D: What's changed? Everything. The school sucks. The people suck. This neighborhood? Oh, that's always sucked. But, um, other than that, everything is just garbage. . . . All—Everybody's gone.
> I: Was there anyone in particular who left that—
> D: Yes, you know, D.J., my best friend from last year. He's gone. . . . D.J. was my right hand right there. He still is, really. But since he's gone, I ain't got no one else to turn to. He was the only person around. . . . Clarence and Jeffrey were kind of like D.J. and me. That was his right hand man right here and then like once Jeffrey

> left, you know, he felt the same way I feel now: "My man is gone, damn, what I'm gonna do?"

For Dell, the loss of his best friend means "everyone" is gone, underscoring the impact such losses have on teenage boys. Both his language and the emotional quality of his response draw attention to the ways boys expressed these losses in explicitly vulnerable terms.

When asked if he has a best friend this year, Guillermo, interviewed for the first time in his junior year, answers:

> Not really. I think myself. The friend I had, I lost it . . . That was the only person that I could trust and we talked about everything. When I was down, he used to help me feel better. The same I did to him. So I feel pretty lonely and sometimes depressed. Because I don't have no one to go out with, no one to speak on the phone, no one to tell my secrets, no one for me to solve my problems . . . I think that it will never be the same, you know. I think that when you have a real friend and you lost him, I don't think you find another one like him. That's the point of view that I have . . . I tried to look for a person, you know, but it's not that easy.

Guillermo's yearning is stark, as are his feelings of loss and inevitability. Like Dell, however, he retains his ability to express his feelings about the loss and about his desire for an intimate friendship even though he does not have one any longer.

Tyrone also speaks about the gradual loss of friendships and the corresponding sense of sadness. When asked whether he has a best friend in his sophomore year interview, he says:

> No, nah, it's like everybody I get close to, they either go away or, you know, so it's just like, nah, . . . and you know I have a friend that I chill with, you know, hang out with from time to time. But not one that I usually do everything with. You know, how like you just have that best friend and it's always like—say it's like you and him? Stuff like that. Nah. I did, I really did but you know . . . me and this other kid took up for each other, everything just came together, like, you know, it was

like it was made to be . . . If I had a problem I could always talk to him 'cause he knew mostly all my family. I knew mostly all his family and everything just worked . . . and they moved, and you know. Ever since then it's just like nobody . . . I don't want to get too close to somebody because I fear when I get close to people—the people I love have been taken away from me. And I just say, "Hey, I don't want to get too close to anybody 'cause I don't want to lose them."

Tyrone's response suggests a sensitivity to loss that is similar to his peers' responses to betrayal. Once a best friend is "lost" or commits a betrayal, the friendship is over and a replacement for that friend is difficult, if not impossible, to find. It appeared to be especially difficult during late adolescence. Thus boys, like Guillermo and Tyrone, give up in their search for a replacement.

While most boys experienced the loss of their best friends over time, other boys were able to maintain one or two of their closest friendships but grew increasingly distrustful, wary of, and angry toward their male peers more generally. Fitting with the masculine expectation that was articulated directly by Nick ("I'm not gonna get mad because you dissed me, I'm gonna get mad 'cause I missed you, but I'll probably show it to you like I'm gonna get mad because you dissed me"), anger and frustration were ways for boys to express their sadness. When we listened for emotional words in boys' interviews, words like "love" and "happy" were significantly more likely in boys' freshman and sophomore years than in their junior and senior year interviews. In their latter years of high school, there was a predominance of words such as "mad" and "hate" and "angry." The language of masculinity— where anger is the only emotion that is acceptable—was evident.

When Joseph, who had a best friend for ten years, is asked whether he has a best friend in his junior year, says: "No I don't trust nobody . . . Can't trust nobody these days." He says that the reason for this break in trust is that his former best friend got him in trouble for "breaking the elevator" in the school. Martin says in his senior year: "I don't trust nobody really. I trust only my brothers. Yeah, my family. I don't trust nobody because people are slick, once in a while, people are saying things I'm not expecting. I don't expect him to do something. So you don't have trust for nobody. I don't trust, I don't put, I don't put nothing past nothin' I don't." Mike, who said in his freshman and sophomore years that he can share "everything" with his best friends, says in his junior year:

> I can't trust nobody. Can't—that's what my mother always used to say. Can't trust nobody. I basically trust people who, like who's really tight or I've known really long . . . It's like, you always you always gotta watch out, you gonna trust somebody, you gotta really know him. You got to be really tight with him.

Although the degree of distrust varied, boys often feared, particularly by the time they were age 16 and older, "being dissed" by their male peers. "Being dissed" included having their friends spread confidential secrets, lie, steal their girlfriends, or talk about them behind their backs.

Milo, the boy who referred to the "circles of love" among him and his two best friends in his freshman year says by his third year of high school that he has been betrayed by them too many times to trust them any longer. Being teased by his "best friends" for his beliefs (e.g., he goes to church) and his friends not being "there" for him when he is having problems are the basis of why he feels angry and betrayed, although he does not provide the specifics in his interview. Instead of finding replacements for these friends, Milo says he no longer has any "real" best friends.

Similarly, when Mateo is asked during his junior year if he can trust his male friends, he says:

> I'm the type of person that I trust people too much 'cause over the years like in elementary school and stuff, I've always been backstabbed, I never had a real best friend . . . the people that I really thought were my best friends, they were talking behind my back or something. . . . Like a best friend to me would be some, a person

who has gone through, you know the worst, the good, the best and the worst with you. So then, like, a lot of years that you really know everything about that person. And like, you have, you know, a great feeling about that person and you know that that person would be there when you need them, 100 percent secure that that person is not gonna back-stab you.

Larry tells a similar story in his junior year:

> "Friend" is a word that people throw around. Friend is a word that shouldn't be used lightly, like the word "love" that's just another word that shouldn't be used very lightly 'cause they're strong words. You know I don't just meet somebody and call them my friend. The most they get out of me is an associate . . . A friend to me is a person that would be your friend no matter what, who will be there through thick and thin, you know someone to talk to about anything.

While the frustration and caution are evident in these boys' passages, so too are their desires. Mateo speaks about not having a best friend due to his fears of betrayal but also the "great feelings" that come with a loyal and trustworthy friendship. Using the stereotypically masculine language of "associates" but also the "feminine" language of marital vows ("through thick and thin"), Larry communicates both his distrust of his peers and his desire for an intimate friendship. And his desires are again evident by the end of the interview when he says that friends are important "because they could get you out so that you can take a breath from the world."

When Albert is asked in his senior year why he still does not have a best friend (he hasn't had a best friend since early adolescence), he says:

> You know, I can't trust—I don't trust 'em too much. I had a friend and he [tried to steal my tapes and my girlfriend] and you know I can't trust nobody else. [I have] a kind of friend, you know but to have another best friend, that would be pretty hard now, can't trust nobody else no more. . . . Can't trust people no more. Before you

could, but now, you know when you got a girl, and they think that
she's cute, they still might go try to rap to her and everything. You
can't trust 'em like before that they will be serious. Like that friend I
had in New York, my best friend [the friend he referred to in his
sophomore year], I could trust him with my girl, you know, and he
could trust me with his girl. People aren't like that anymore. Back
then you could trust.

Remembering a time in his past when he could trust his peers,
Albert describes what so many of his male peers remember as
well. When they were younger, their friendships were more intimate and trusting and now something has changed.

Malcolm also describes the change explicitly:

I might talk with people but it won't get real deep . . . there is nobody there to talk to . . . Right now, no [I don't have a best friend]. I
had a couple like once when I was real young, around ten, and then
when I [was a freshman]—and then me and this dude got real close,
we was cool. But right now, nobody really 'cause it seems that as I've
grown, you know, everybody just talk behind your back and stuff.
You know. So I just let it go because it seems like no people that can
hold—well not no people, but the people that I've been meeting can
hold up to their actions. Like you know . . . something might've happened like between me and a person where other people felt that we
couldn't even be friends no more. So they sit there and talk about me
to that person while I'm around or something. Then, then that person will just talk about me too, you know whatever, 'cause you
know all throughout my neighborhood, I always hear, "he talks
about you, he says this or he says that." . . . So I just don't really
bother with it, you know, trying to make best friends.

Resigning himself to the "reality" of his male peers, Malcolm
says that he is no longer interested in pursuing a best friend.

When asked in his junior year if he wants a best friend, Mateo says:

I really, it really doesn't matter to me no more. 'Cause when nowa-
days like you can't really have a best friend. It's like the person who
you think would never do something to you, out of nowhere some-

thing happens. And I don't . . . I ain't gonna be crying because something happens to me, or I feel like so badly through my inside and I
ain't tryin' to you know feel like that.

Like Mateo, boys often made the explicit connections between
being betrayed, hurting, and retreating from trying to find a new
best friend.

In his junior year, Phillip recalls a time in the recent past when
one of his close male friends offered to pay his way to the movies
because he didn't have enough money. Once they arrived at the
movie theater, the friend claimed not to have enough money to
cover Phillip and thus Phillip had to return home. He found out
later that the friend did, in fact, have money and treated his
friends to popcorn during the movie. Phillip says that this experience of betrayal hurt him "badly" and made him uninterested
in having male best friends because "you can't trust other boys."
When asked about the changes in his friendships, he says: "The
change is me decreasing my time with my friends. That's the
change . . . people have to be willing to be giving also. For me,
'cause I think I'm a very giving person. I give before anything so.
When you aren't giving. I can't trust you. I can't trust you."
Rather than understanding his betrayal as a matter of the friend's
loyalty—which would be consistent with a more masculine
take—Phillip makes it a matter of generosity and trust.

Shawn, at the age of 18, displays his heart on his sleeve. When
asked about friendships he says:

> I've got like a brick wall around me . . . gonna take a lot just to get
> inside me . . . 'cause I see many people out here, they be open [with
> each other] and many people could find a way to break them apart.
> But I don't want nobody knowing me and being able to break me
> apart and do anything they want with me.

He admits, however, that he is struggling to get rid of his "suit of
armor" so that he can have "real friendships." Shawn communicates both the fear of being *known* and the desire to be known,
connected, and vulnerable with another boy.

Looking directly at his interviewer, Jamal says in his junior year, "I don't label people as like my best friend, you know. I don't put, you know faith in people 'cause I don't wanna suffer." Similarly, Perry says that while he feels very close to his cousin, he is cautious with his peers. "I try not to be too attached to anybody when I first meet them. Let the relationship build on what we do and the way they conduct themselves. I try not to because if you start liking the person before you know who they are then maybe they could turn on you." Fernando, who has a girlfriend, says: "I feel a little more trust in girls than guys 'cause I find like guys a little snaky. I don't know. Like um, like they'll sit there and tell you lies and say it's true." Boys who have been portrayed in the scholarly literature as "object" or "activity" oriented spoke to us about "breaking apart," preventing boys from getting "inside," and being betrayed and suffering as a consequence.

"I DON'T CARE": EXPRESSING LOSS IN THE LANGUAGE OF MASCULINITY

After explaining the loss of his only best friend at age 15, Anthony is asked:

> *I:* Do you think friendships are important?
>
> *A:* Not really. People don't need friends. They don't. There's a lot of things people could do on their own.
>
> *I:* Do you think people need friends once in a while?
>
> *A:* Yeah, once in a while if something happens, you could talk about it.
>
> *I:* And do you think that friends are important to you?
>
> *A:* No, I really don't care. If something happens then it doesn't matter. I'll just be like, "Forget you."

Not wanting to care, Anthony claims not to care. Omar says in his junior year when asked how he feels about his friends this year: "*I don't feel anything,* [my friends] don't tell me anything, they don't put me down or nothing. Everything is cool." These boys may not want to care or feel, but they have isolated themselves precisely in response to caring about how their friends are treating them.

Mohammed sounds emotionally stoic and autonomous only during the last year of his interview. In his sophomore year, he said: "Trust means you can really, you know, keep things with him, you know what I'm saying? Like secrets, whatever. It's like a bank, you keep money and it's like safe. Like trust is that thing. You could put your words to somebody or he would really understand, you know, things." In response to why friends are important in the same sophomore year interview, he says:

> Yes, because, um, [pause] you don't want to be alone, you know . . . let's say you have a problem, and you can't face it yourself and at the same time you don't have anyone to ask for help to, and you don't want to get into problems like that and if you have a friend that can help you, they can help you. . . . Somebody who knows you well, who understands you. . . . Let's say you have serious problems, you know, you don't have anybody to talk about or that you're comfortable talking to other people about it as much as you are talking to your close friend.

Yet during his junior year (the last year he is interviewed), when asked if he can share his personal problems with his best friend, he says:

> I could tell him but you know I wouldn't feel that comfortable to tell him. [I: Why not?] Me, personally, first of all, I think like it's none of his business to get into it. You know, I don't see why I should tell him. You know? And I'm just not that comfortable. Actually with problems, if I had problems with my family or problems with anybody, I'm the kind of person that would keep it to myself.

Mohammed changes from a boy who values friendships because you "need someone to help you with your problems" into a boy who would rather "keep it" to himself. Boys grow older and become defensive ("I think like it's none of his business") and take the "manly" path of telling their secrets to no one. For Mohammed, the choice of telling no one is part of the natural process of maturity: "I have gotten more mature so I trust [my mother] with less things. I tell her less than I used to in junior high school because I feel like I could take care of it myself." Rather than resisting the push toward isolation that manhood insists on, boys like Mohammed simply become isolated.

During his junior year, Mohammed says he has no best friend this year, even though he had one previously: "Ramel [his former best friend] used to be my best friend but now that everything—I moved [to a different neighborhood although he remains in the same school], and I—something changed that I don't really quite see him that often. I think like I don't really have a best friend right now." As he struggles to articulate his thoughts, Mohammed knows that something has changed that is more than simply his residence. When asked about his desire to have a best friend, Mohammed says: "Yes, I wouldn't mind having a best friend but well, not really, but I wouldn't mind." Caught in the dilemma of manhood where having a best friend "sounds gay," Mohammed isn't willing to directly articulate his desire for such a friend by his junior year:

> I feel that, you know, . . . a best friend, you know is someone you could trust and someone you could, you know, tell all your personal things to that's a best friend, I think. But I don't think I have a need to tell somebody all my personal things or whatever it is. You know. I could keep it to myself.

Mohammed experiences a contrast between what he feels ("I feel . . . a best friend, you know, is someone you could trust. . . .") and what he should think ("but I don't think I have a need to tell somebody"). His repeated use of the phrase "you know" and his statements "I think" followed by "I don't think" suggest a struggle he can't acknowledge. In his junior year, however, Mohammed claims to have no "need" to tell his feelings to his friends and, also, has no friends. He admits to feeling "so depressed" and describes a physical fight with another boy at school, the first he has ever had, which gets him suspended for a few days from school. The following year, he tells me that he does not "have time" to do the final year interview.

When Yang is asked about his friendships in his freshman year, he uses words such as "safe" and "comfortable" to describe how he feels when he spends time with his friends. He says that he likes his best friend because he is "serious and honest" and does not "lie about personal things." Yang also indicates that his best friend is trustworthy and will "keep" his secrets. When asked about the fact that he speaks Chinese with his best friend, Yang notes that "friendship is not the way you speak. It's the way you feel for each other, the way you care about each other and all that stuff and not the way you talk, doesn't matter the way you talk." Friendships are important for Yang, "because you won't be that lonely, people care about you more and you really care about them." In his sophomore year, he says explicitly that what he likes about his best friend is that he "can really keep secrets." He spends a large portion of his interview this year describing what types of secrets each of his friends can keep and what types of secrets they are not good at keeping. He also discusses the process of "breaking up" and coming back together with his best friend and how the time apart allowed him to "release" his anger.

By his junior year, however, the content and tone of Yang's interview has shifted. His interview is consumed with stories of betrayals by his peers and there is a sharp increase this year in "I don't care" responses to questions from the interviewer. He has a close friend (whom he says is not a best friend), and when asked why he is only a close rather than a best friend, he says, "I don't know . . . I'm used to being alone." He has difficulty answering the questions about friendships and answers "I don't know, I don't care" to most of them. When the interviewer asks him why he is saying "I don't care" so much in answer to her questions, he says: "Probably I don't like my friends that much." Revealing an astute understanding of the emotional world, Yang links his anger at his friends with his desire not to care. The reason he doesn't like his friends this year: "It is probably the communication . . . 'cause this year we hardly have classes with each other and we hardly communicate with each other . . . I don't know." Yang knows precisely what he doesn't like about his best friend ("we don't communicate") but shrouds his response in "I don't knows," with the hope, perhaps, that by not knowing he will care less.

By his senior year, Yang seems entirely alone, and his ability to talk about his feelings is almost nonexistent. When asked by his interviewer if he has a close or best friend, he says: "I vote no one." He speaks of not being able to communicate with his friends anymore about the things that are important to him and says that the process of friendships during high school has been one of "more to less." When asked why he doesn't have a best friend, he says: "I don't know, and I DON'T CARE." Sounding like Pierre in Maurice Sendak's classic children's story about the boy who didn't care until a lion ate him up,[4] Yang doesn't want to care about the fact that he does not have a best friend and says, "I just want to be alone." And then in one of the few moments of vulnerability in the interview, he admits in a quiet tone of voice: "Sometimes, sometimes I don't want to be alone . . . probably [I would like to have a best friend] . . . I don't know, have that friend who you could talk to them and have them be there and I don't know." Yang has wrapped himself tightly in a stance of not caring and not knowing ("I don't know . . . I don't know") even though he *knows* he cares deeply. Yet when experiences of betrayal are mixed with the dictates of masculinity and maturity (i.e., emotional stoicism and autonomy), boys often end up alone.

Michael, who passionately discusses the intimacy, including the numerous arguments, he has with his best friend during his freshman and sophomore years, says in his senior year interview: "[long pause] Hmm, [we don't have disagreements about] nothing about nothing, really, we don't argue and so I can't say no, can't say that, so I don't know, not much, I don't feel anything." Sounding confused, Michael attempts to say that he doesn't have any arguments but then shifts into not knowing and then not feeling. He says that he and his best friend no longer share much personal information with each other because he does not trust him as much as he did before. When asked in his senior year why Hector is no longer his best friend, he says: "Well, he still is, but I would consider myself more [of a best friend] because I put me first now in a way, and then like friends, family, so I had to check for me first instead of Hector as like a best friend, because without me, I can't have any friends." Taking the culture of autonomy and isolation literally, he claims that *he* is his best friend and then adds: "If I wanted a best friend, I'd get a girlfriend, you know." Like many of the other boys, he sees his choices as limited. Michael "chooses" the route of isolation.

When Adrian is asked whether friendships are important in his freshman year, he says: "Yeah, you need people to talk to. You stay alone, you get lonely." In his sophomore year, he says: "If you didn't have any friends, you'd be lonely. You know? You don't have anyone else to talk to, or hang out with. You'd be lonely." Asked to define a best friend, he says: "A best friend? Somebody who's there for you. Somebody that'll listen to your problems and understand what you are talking about. That kind of friend." By his junior and senior year, however, his responses sound stoic. In his junior year, he says: "You need to have friends to have fun with, to talk to, to hang out with. If you don't have any, you'd be bored for the rest of your life." Adrian's willingness to express vulnerability has diminished, as being "bored" (versus being "lonely") is drained of any feelings. And by the fourth year, he simply says: "You know what I'm saying, if you don't have friends, you're gonna be bored for the rest of your life. You know? You need friends to hang out with." Asked why he doesn't have a best friend in his senior year: "I don't know, I really don't care if I have a best friend as long as I have friends." Like Yang, Adrian suggests that he cares by the intensity of his statements of not caring.

Omar, the same boy who says he "doesn't feel" with respect to his friendships spoke with great affection for his friends in his freshman and sophomore years and at one point proclaimed loudly to his interviewer that he loved his best friend and could tell him "everything." By his senior year, however, he sounds like a stereotype:

> *I:* What kind of things can't you tell your close friends?
>
> *O:* If I got sick and my girlfriend took care of me.
>
> *I:* Why can't you tell them that?
>
> *O:* Because they don't want to know about that, you know. . . . I don't wanna be too wussy. I don't want to get too sensitive around them . . . it's the way it developed, you know, like, I don't know, we're like real manly around each other.
>
> *I:* You are in what way?
>
> *O:* We talk about like sports, everybody spitting everywhere, people are drinking beer and smoking cigarettes, watching a basketball game, and talk about girls that we saw in the street, you know, stuff like that, so there's no room for like mushy talk.

Describing a scene that was almost entirely absent from boys' earlier interviews, Omar makes his desire for manliness explicit. When asked whether he will share anything intimate with his friends in his senior year, he says: "If it's real, real serious but like emotional type stuff, we usually leave that out. We give the more descriptive part to each other." He notes that with his best friend Jerome, he "basically just chills and talks, you know, we have like man to man conversations." Departing from his former effusive and open communication style, he says about his current girlfriend at the end of his senior year interview: "If she wanted like a sensitive man, she would have gone with a girl." And with this statement, as with Yang's similar statement, Omar makes explicit the cultural noose that tightens around boys' necks during late adolescence.

Asked how his friendships have changed since he was younger, Justin says in his freshman year: "I never really talked to people, I had a lot of guy friends when I was little but I was little I really didn't have nothing to say. . . . Since I'm older I feel that now that I have lots to say. I want, I have to tell it to some-body, I can't keep it inside." By his sophomore year, the cautious-ness creeps into his interview as he describes his ideal friend: "It would be close and everybody would be my friend but you can't always have everybody . . . you're always gotta decide, like they always got something up their sleeve." By his senior year, his de-cision to become emotionally stoic is openly pronounced:

> [My friend and I] we mostly joke around. It's not like really anything serious or whatever. Nothing like serious talking whatever 'cause I don't talk to nobody about serious stuff . . . I don't talk to nobody. I don't share my feelings really. Not that kind of a person or whatever. I don't even share with [my girlfriend] so I'm not really like open to that . . . Like I said I don't tell nobody my business so it's not a . . . like it's not a trust thing. It's just something that I don't do. So with money of course if [my friend] needs it, I give it to him, he'll give it back or whatever so it' s not really a big thing. So with feelings though I don't tell nobody. So it's not basically a trust thing, it's my personal reason not to tell nobody nothing.

Tracing the voice of the "I" in Justin's response, we hear him try to convince himself that he does not want to share his thoughts and feelings.

> I don't
> I don't
> I don't
> I don't
>
> I am not
> I don't
> I don't
> I give
> I don't.

The sheer repetition of "I don't," however, suggests that he has not successfully convinced himself of this new stance. Knowing that the admission of the link between trusting and sharing secrets would make him feel and appear more vulnerable, Justin denies such a link. He wants to be perceived as invulnerable. Yet this masculine "mask" is exposed as such when he says: "Don't want to tell nobody. My personal business is mine. So what goes on in my life I don't really wanna share 'cause if something hurts me, I don't wanna keep bringing it up so. I just try to forget about it." His confession that hurt is at the root of his "choice" not to share his feelings reveals just how much he cares and remembers.

Similarly, Max says in his sophomore year (the first year he is interviewed) that he tells his best friend "everything 'cause that's my best friend." When asked to define trust with this friend, he says: "You could tell him anything, you could give them anything, like you're giving yourself to him." Yet when asked in his junior year if he trusts his friends, he says: "No I don't trust anything. That's just the way I am. . . . I don't tell them niggas nothing. We just chill and that's it. We don't get into each other's personal lives. We just don't. I tell them to mind their own business. . . . It's nobody's business but my own." Max literally embodies the masculine convention with his statement that his distrust is simply "just the way I am." Even though he seems to know, given his earlier interviews, that he isn't who he says he is, he wants to project an image of manliness and thus claims that his personal life is "nobody's business but my own." By constructing a masculine identity, he provides a justification for his emotional stoicism and isolation.

Max's absorption of the "boy code" becomes more apparent when he tells a story about how a friend confided in him that his father was hurting him and he said to that friend, "I don't care, don't tell me. It's not my business." In his fourth year interview, Max says: "[I don't trust anybody] because, I don't know, that is the way I have always been." Revising the past to fit into his current masculine self, Max makes his lack of trust a "normal" part of his personality. Although he is able to admit, unlike Justin, that he doesn't trust others, Max repeats Justin's theme of not wanting to care. Boys were determined, by late adolescence, not to care. Like Justin, however, their masculine pose was usually shot through with vulnerability. When Max is asked about his close relationship with his cousin, he says:

> It's like no matter what, nothing will change between us, no matter what. Everything has happened that could have broken us apart, but it never has . . . If I have a problem with kids, [others] will run or if I'm feeling bad about a girl, he'll be there, no matter what. I will get kicked out of my house, he'll come no matter what.

In his repeated use of the phrase "no matter what," Max suggests a hope for a "forever" in his relationship with his cousin.

When asked why he doesn't have a best friend, 18-year-old Alejandro says:

> I'm really not that type of person like to let someone know everything I know about me. People always have the type of best friend that they always tell each other everything about each other and what happens in their life. I really don't think that should be happening. You should have something about you that should be kept with you, not tell to anybody just to make you feel better.

Again we hear the determination to present a masculine identity (i.e., "I'm really not that type of person"). Yet, as in the case of Justin, Alejandro's confession at the end of this passage ("not tell to anybody just to make you feel better") suggests that he understands that not talking to anyone is not good for him. These responses raise the question of whether the desire for autonomy is making boys lose connection with others or whether the loss of friendships makes them seek solace in the autonomy that manhood idealizes.

When Frank is asked, at age 16, about how his friendships have changed since he was younger, he says: "Well, when I was younger I had a lot of friends and most of them moved to other places . . . Everybody went their own way . . ." Asked whether he ever needs something from his friends: "Need? No, I never ask anybody, anybody." Frank's rephrasing from a question of

"need" to a question of "never asking" suggests that his autonomous stance is in response to a wariness of depending on
others rather than vice versa. Perry admits that he doesn't talk to
any of his friends because his friends "talk a lot. You tell him
stuff, he's gonna tell somebody. Yeah, and like some people,
that's why I don't tell a lot to anyone anymore." Perry makes it
explicit that betrayal, in fact, caused the desire for autonomy.
But it is also likely that the expectation for autonomy and stoicism causes acts of betrayal. Boys don't want to be perceived as
vulnerable during late adolescence, and the best way to cover is
to act as if they have no empathy or care, and thus betrayal en-
sues. Asked if friendships are important, Perry says, "I don't call
anybody 'friends,' like friends. I learned that when I was little. I
called somebody my friend and he did something. I don't call
anybody my friend any longer." In the midst of their seeming
lack of interest in close friendships, boys reveal a strong desire
for such friendships.

PATTERNS OF DESIRE

When asked in his junior year if he has a best friend, Victor says:

> I wouldn't say . . . I don't say I would 'cause I feel that a friend is go-
> ing to be there for you and they'll support you and stuff like that.
> Whether they're good and bad times, you can share with them, you
> could share your feelings with them, your true feelings. That's why I
> don't think I have any real close friends. I mean, things can travel
> around in a school and things would go around, and the story would
> change from person to person. Yeah. Basically, I hate it, I hate it,
> 'cause you know I wouldn't mind talking to somebody my age that I
> can relate to 'em on a different basis.

Like the route toward manhood, the expressed desire for intimate male friendships, heard so often in boys' junior and senior
year interviews, took different forms. For some such as Victor,
the desire was directly stated ("I hate it, I hate it") and for others, it was more reserved: "Yeah it wouldn't hurt to have one but

I just don't"; or, from another boy, "Well, no, I don't really wish I had a best friend, but if I had one, I wouldn't mind."

Francisco says in his fourth year interview that he would like a friend who is "sensitive like me . . . Like understanding like me . . . but um that's about it . . . Like I see movies, in the theater, I start to cry and stuff . . . No, none of my friends is like that." In their senior years, Keith said that what he would like to change most in his friendship with his "best friend" is to "spend more time" with him. Datong says: "I miss my best friend, just like hanging out together, we can't talk to each other much." When Alan is asked in his junior year if he wants a best friend, he responds:

> Yeah, always wanted a best friend . . . Kind of like in *Boy Meets World*, did you ever see that TV show? The [boys in the show] spend a lot of time with each other, they're pretty close to each other, they go to the same school, and they talk about everything with each other, and they trust each other. They get into arguments, but they always wind up being friends again and stuff like that.

Boys explicitly desired, even into late adolescence, "sensitive" boys with whom they could "talk about everything" and who were loyal and trusting. Lorenzo's wish is evident in his discussion of the importance of friendships: "Everybody needs somebody. Somebody, in other words, when you need a shoulder to cry on, inside, you need an arm to punch when you are mad and things like that." For Lorenzo, however, this type of friend in his junior year is an ideal rather than a reality.

The desire for a close male friendship was revealed in boys' responses to different types of questions but predominantly questions about what they liked, wanted, or thought was ideal or important in their friendships. After admitting that he doesn't have a best friend, Ryan, tells his interviewer in his third year of high school that he would indeed like a best friend "as long as like you know, I would, can talk to them about anything and you know if I tell them to keep a secret, they would keep it." When Tomas, at age 15 is asked what his ideal friendship would look like, he says: "Just a person that you could talk to." Asked to articulate why his friendships are so important, Jorge says in his junior year:

> 'Cause you always need somebody there for you. That's the way I see it. I always need somebody there. Someone that I could count on to talk to whenever I need anything. So I, I think they are really important, friendships. I don't, I mean if you're going to grow up being lonely like always, there's going to be something wrong. Either you're going to be mean to people, lonely, you're going to feel lonely all the time.

Boys during late adolescence were not interested in having friends to simply hang out and play video games with, they wanted friends they "could count on to talk to whenever [they] need[ed] anything." Similarly, Francisco says in his final year interview that friends are important because "there are sometimes you gonna have to just like tell people how you feel." Eddie says in his senior year about the importance of friendships: "Yes and no, both. I think no because sometimes friends do cause problems . . . then at the same time you need somebody to be there for you, and you need somebody to let your feeling out on, so it's both good and bad, positive and negative but in the end I think we benefit from friendships."

Strikingly, the expression of desire was heard both among boys who did not have intimate male friendships and from those who did. In his junior year interview, Fernando, who has a group of close male friends, when asked what he would like to change about his friendships, says: "[I wish for] nobody talking nothing bad about you behind your back and for all of us [his male friends] to be tight together. Like sometimes they turn their back on you, sometimes when problems get real real tough, they turn their backs on you and then you ain't got nobody else to go to." Fernando's desire for intimacy in his current friendship circle is evident, as is the desire not to be betrayed and isolated. In his junior year, Jorge, when asked what type of friendship he would like to have, responds:

J: The best of all? Well, I kind of have it now, but even better. But I would like it to get even tighter. I would like it—you know. I like . . . with the person, I can trust them with anything. But like— deeper, deeper than it is now would be cool.

I: Why is that important to you, to be even deeper?

J: It's not really important, it's just like—if you think about it, there's times that you want to be even tighter with a person, so that's what I am. There's times I would like to be tighter with [my friends].

Boys during late adolescence wanted "deeper" relationship with their friends than what they had, and boys, like Jorge, were will- ing to state it directly.

Occasionally, however, the desire for an intimate friendship is heard in more subtle ways, as when Malcolm says, in his junior year, that the difference between a hypothetical best friend and his current girlfriend is that "if you have a best friend, you know, you express yourself more, and you're like, you like, feel lost without them, so you know, with [my girlfriend] we have a close relation- ship where we express things but . . ." Similarly Glen, when asked in his junior year about his friends, says: "We have like lots of plans when we finish college or in college. We will get jobs, [and then] get a place like for guys only, like our cave where no one could bother us . . . a cave is where no one would bother us. That's what [my friend] said, then he started saying jokes about when you bring your girlfriend over we'll walk around the block and when it's our turn you go out and walk around the block." Moving from a more vulnerable place to a more macho one (a "boy cave" be- comes a "make-out" cave), Glen underscores the difficulties of ex- pressing desire for intimacy with boys during late adolescence.

After admitting that he and his friends occasionally cry, Glen says: "We're guys so we don't know emotional stuff like girls. It's like guys tend to . . . they don't show their emotional side, not all guys, I know my guys don't have an emotional part." Confirming the stereotype, which blatantly contradicts his own experiences, Glen faces a conflict. How does he have friendships in which strong emotions can be shared when such sharing is not what boys do? By his senior year, he has resolved the conflict by turning away from boys entirely: "Guys are so insensitive, females are better." His friendships are now exclusively with girls. The only problem with this strategy, Glen confides, is that some of his peers think he is gay. In a context where boys who don't have a masculine cover (e.g., sports) struggle, particularly during late adolescence, to win at the game of masculinity, Glen—who is not only sensitive and seeks intimate friendships but also is Chinese American—pays the price that most heterosexual boys fear.

SUMMARY

The story of development for the boys in my studies is a story of loss and disconnection from their peers. While some boys maintained their closest male friendships over time, all of the boys grew increasingly distrustful, wary of, and angry with their peers. As they grew older, they spoke increasingly of their fears of betrayal and their desires not to be hurt by their male (and female) peers. These patterns of loss are similar to the research findings on adult men from very different socioeconomic and racial backgrounds than the boys in my studies, suggesting that the patterns exist more broadly.[5] Adult men often note the losses that occurred during adolescence in their closest male friendships and their yearning to reestablish those connections. Informal interviews with dozens of middle class mothers of sons, as well as with my undergraduate students, also suggest that these patterns of loss and distrust during late adolescence and emerging adulthood are evident across social class, race, and ethnicity. Boys' desires for intimate male friendships are also evident in other research studies as well as in informal interviews. Boys during late adolescence and men seek the types of friendships they had with other boys during early and middle adolescence. The obvious question, in the thick of it, is why these patterns occur. Why do boys lose faith, trust, and sometimes even the friendship itself as they grow older? What makes their "heart die"?

CHAPTER 7

AS BOYS BECOME MEN

As boys grow up and become men who by definition are not supposed to have or reveal vulnerable emotions, they disconnect from their desires, their friendships, and ultimately from themselves. Some of the boys in my studies were able to directly express their sadness over the loss of trust and friendships; others were more firmly entrenched in dictates of manhood and simply said, "I don't care." The boys' desires, however, were almost always clear. They wanted the intimacy that they had when they were younger. They wanted to be able to share their thoughts and feelings with their friends so that they would not feel alone. They knew, just as they knew during early and middle adolescence, that being able to share their secrets and having intimate friendships was critical to their mental health. Yet they also knew that their desires for intimacy with other boys were risky and made them sound gay, girlish, and immature. So they "covered the sun with their hands" and claimed that their loss was inevitable or that they didn't care, didn't feel, or didn't need anybody.

Sociologist Victor Seidler writes about men's friendships: "We learn to do without friends . . . we learn not to acknowledge our need for friends and at some level to regard this need as a sign of weakness. Even if we would welcome friendship, we learn to live without it . . . most men do not let themselves think or feel about friendships."[1] Seidler's research, as well as others',[2] suggests that the loss that the boys in my studies experienced is not unique to them. The patterns detected in my studies represent the experience of many boys and men in different cultural contexts. They want the type of intimate friendships that they had when they were young, the ones in which they could talk until three in the morning about "everything." Health and social science research has consistently indicated that adults with strong social support networks, including friendships, are better off physically and mentally and are more successful in school and in work.[3] Thus, the loss of friendships is not a minor event. It has long-term consequences. Yet what are the reasons for this loss of friendships and trust as boys grow older?

Social scientists and policy analysts have long pointed out that while Americans are, indeed, "progressing," technologically and socially (e.g., Barack Obama's election), there is also a corresponding decrease in social connectedness and trust.[4] Scholars such as Robert Putnam in his best-selling book *Bowling Alone* describe the loss of social trust in communities across the United States. Sociologist Miller McPherson and his colleagues at the University of Arizona and Duke University found in a nationwide survey that from 1985 to 2004, Americans reported a marked decline in the number of people with whom they discussed meaningful matters.[5] Americans, according to their research, reported fewer close relationships with coworkers, extended family members, neighbors, *and* friends over a 20-year period. The percentage of people who depended completely on a spouse for important conversations, with no other person to turn to, almost doubled from 1985 to 2004, and the percentage of people saying they did not have *anyone* in whom they confided nearly tripled. Furthermore, the percentage of Americans who reported having four to five confidantes was cut in half between 1985 and 2004, falling to just 15 percent of the population. According to these scholars' research, almost half of all Americans now say that there is just one person, or no one at all, with whom they discuss important matters.

On the topic of trust more specifically, researchers have found that the extent to which Americans believe that others can be trusted has declined over the past four decades. In a study conducted in 1958, 58 percent of Americans indicated that "most people" can be trusted, while a series of follow-up studies conducted in the 1990s indicated that that number had dropped significantly to only 40 percent endorsing such a belief in 1998.[6] Similarly, Urie Bronfenbrenner and his colleagues report in their book *The State of Americans* that the percentage of high school seniors who say that "most people can be trusted" has declined significantly since 1981.[7] Others have reported similar findings.[8] As we enter, perhaps, our culture's "late adolescence" during the beginning of the twenty-first century, Americans appear to have grown increasingly disconnected and distrustful.

My studies of boys suggest that the ontogenetic pattern of the individual boy imitates the phylogenetic pattern of the larger culture. While boys clearly progress during adolescence in terms of their knowledge of the world (as do we as a technologically and scientifically advancing culture), they also experience a dramatic decline in the richness and quality of their social relations as they enter manhood. As a 17-year-old boy from a suburban school complained to his girlfriend, "I don't have any friends anymore. Where have they gone?"

The reasons for this loss and increase in distrust can be divided into thin and thick culture explanations. Thin culture explanations, as I explained in Chapter 1, repeat narratives that are familiar to many and only skim the surface. For example, the explanations the boys gave such as having no time for friendships or moving to a different residential location are "real" explanations, but they stay on the surface of the matter. They don't address why the boys are having such a hard time maintaining close friendships regardless of their lack of free time or number of transitions. Why do they betray each other? And why do they feel they have to make a choice between a girlfriend and a male friend when their nineteenth-century peers did not? Thick culture explanations, in contrast, address the subtle and not so subtle cultural forces that shape boys' abilities to have intimate male friendships. Thick culture explanations include Americans' emphasis on individualism, which produces a decreased sense of community, and gender stereotypes that link a fundamental human capacity (i.e., empathy and sensitivity) and need (i.e., close friendships) with a sex (female), a sexuality (gay), and an age (childhood).

In this chapter, I describe the explanations proffered by the boys—explanations that stay on the surface for the most part—and then, drawing from the scholarship across disciplines and from the boys' interviews, I propose thick culture explanations for why boys lose their closest friendships and grow increasingly distrustful of their peers. These thick culture explanations for boys' losses help us see the root of the problem and thus implicitly suggest strategies to help boys stay connected to what they want and need to thrive.

INTO THE THIN OF IT

When we asked boys directly why they were losing their male friendships, they often gave explanations that are widely shared by a culture obsessed with romantic relationships and autonomy. Their interpretations, however, only tell part of a larger story. Boys know a thicker truth and their continuing desire for intimacy in their friendships makes it clear that they know they are being asked to make a sacrifice they should not be forced to make as they enter manhood. During late adolescence, they "hide the sun with their hands" by restating thin culture interpretations rather than expressing what they know about their own needs and desires.

Boys, particularly those who are heterosexual, know by the ages of 16 or 17 years old that emotionally intimate male friendships are no longer possible in a homophobic context. They also know that their desire to challenge this context, if they revealed it, would put them at risk for ridicule. So they repeat well-worn stories about why friendships disappear. Girlfriends, work and school schedules, and changes in school and residence were risk-free reasons for the loss of friendships and trust. Thus, they invoked these excuses freely but not without expressing frustration, sadness, and anger at their losses and a persistent wish to regain what they had earlier in their development. They also, occasionally, expressed their frustration at not being able to express their emotions any longer, as when a boy in his junior year said that one of the nice things about being a girl might be that he would not have to be "emotionless."

When Eddie is asked about his male friendships in his senior year, he says:

> Sometimes [my friends] bother me too much about my girl. They get, I guess they get jealous that I'm with her more than I'm with them now. They say that I'm going to wind up leaving all of them. That I'm gonna get married you know and everything. They want me to stay around but I'm never around anymore. I say, it happens you know? It's nothing they can do about it.

Believing that he must make a choice, Eddie chooses his girlfriend. The loss and vulnerability that his friends feel is evident ("they say I'm going to wind up leaving all of them") but so is his own sense of loss as he repeatedly discusses his "difficult" situation with his friends. Though he was willing to share secrets with his friends in his freshman year, even telling his best friend about his parents' divorce, by his senior year he explains that he no longer shares confidences because he is male:

> Let's see, it's more of like a feminine and masculine thing. Like with [my best friend] it's like very masculine, like basketball and like rap stuff like that, you know, like things guys will usually do, as far as like sports and stuff like that. But with my girlfriend it's more like a loving, like comforting and stuff like that. It's more of an emotional relationship with a female. With my best friend, it's more of like a

masculine physical relationship, like let's box, or play basketball stuff like that.

Disconnecting from what he experienced just a few years earlier, he now fits the masculine standard. He is not, however, entirely happy with the changes: "Of course, you know, I miss hanging around with my friends but to get something, of course, you have to give up something. To have a relationship with my girlfriend, you have to give up like, not friendship, but I have to be apart a lot from my friends." The story is familiar. Heterosexual boys choose girls rather than having close male friends *and* a girlfriend. And what they will come to understand, as is evident in the health and social science research, is that by making such a choice, they give up something that is fundamental to their health and well-being.[9]

Boys also blamed girls directly for the loss of their male friendships. Fernando says in his senior year when asked how friendships have been different since the beginning of high school: "Like all my friends got girlfriends, so it's kinda hard [to maintain close friendships]. And sometimes the girlfriends don't get along with each other, so you kinda gotta separate, 'cause that's happened plenty of times." However, as Fernando explains, it's not just the girls who fight with each other:

> My girl and [my best friend's] girl got in an argument and [my best friend] was trying to act up, so I was kinda mad 'cause I was like, "How you gonna put your girl over me? No homo." But um, yeah sometimes I guess in instances [having a girlfriend] does change a relationship. Like I don't know. I look at it different now.

Fernando vacillates between saying what he knows ("'cause I was like 'how you gonna put your girl over me'") and repeating a macho mantra ("no homo") and then retreating into the "I don't know's" of late adolescence.[10] Fernando knows, however, that something is wrong.

In addition to girls, boys blamed school and work for the decline in intimacy in their friendships. Eduardo summarizes it well:

I: What has changed in your friendships over time?

E: Like, every year, like the number of friends I have like cuts down like I get less and less, I have less and less friends every year.

I: What do you think that's about?

E: I'm not sure, I guess it's because I don't associate with people any-more . . . Like I used to play basketball, be on baseball team, I used to be able to talk with everybody, have more friends than be-fore, but now I'm just, homework all week, and school, and work after school and on the weekends I relax and go out [with my cousins] so like the whole week is being used up timewise.

Like so many of the boys in my studies, Eduardo treats the loss of his friendships as natural. While school assignments and working are serious impediments to spending time with friends, Eduardo never examines why he only goes out with his cousins during the weekend when he used to go out with his friends from school and sports. Boys know, as do adults, that when they want to find time to spend with friends, they will find the time. Boys are not willing to find the time, however, when the costs of main-taining their close male friendships are so high.

Finally, boys claimed to lose close relationships when their friends moved away. While continual relocation is an American phenomenon, it is especially frequent among low-income groups[11] and thus may be particularly relevant for the poor and working class youth in my studies. It was clear from our inter-views that residential mobility was highly disruptive of close friendships. When Manny, a 16-year-old, is asked how his best friendships have changed over time, he says: "I never get to see [my former best friend] any more. Before, I used to live over there, that's it. I'm over here. I don't see him any more. We don't talk, we don't talk any more, I don't know. That's it. I don't see him anymore." Since he moved, Manny says he no longer has a best friend. Why he is unable to find a replacement in his new neighborhood is never addressed.

Residential mobility, however, is clearly not the only source of disruption. Boys who had not experienced such mobility spoke in similar ways as the boys who did. Changes of addresses, like having a job or a girlfriend, seemed to simply exacerbate an already existing problem of connection during late adolescence. Furthermore, the residential and school transitions that took place during *early and middle adolescence* did not prevent boys from having intimate friendships. The variation across boys' experiences of friendships mixed with the pervasive theme of loss and distrust by late adolescence suggests that these thin culture interpretations are not capturing the full story. Evidence of a "thicker" story is also suggested by the fact that boys rarely found a replacement for their former best friend, despite their continuing desire for "deep secret" friends.

INTO THE THICK OF IT

Exploring the ways social scientists explain the decline in social connectedness provides insight into the thick culture that infiltrates boys' experiences of friendships during late adolescence. Emile Durkheim, a sociologist of the late nineteenth and early twentieth centuries, described the process of increased alienation, or "anomie," as a result of a "mismatch" between the norms of a society and an individual's needs or circumstances. While the term "anomie" literally means "without law" and was used by Durkheim to describe the symptom of a lack of norms in society, he also used the term to describe the symptoms of an overly rigid society where rules are obsolete yet impermeable to change or adaptation. A society with too much rigidity and little individual discretion, he theorized, could produce a kind of anomie. A person commits suicide, he stated, when he or she is too rule governed and "when there is no free horizon of expectation."[12]

Durkheim's theory of "anomie" points to the possibility that our increased social disconnection, alienation, and loneliness are a product of an overly rigid society whose "norms," standards, and goals do not reflect people's desires, needs, or circumstances. Similarly, as boys are pushed to accept a construction of manhood and maturity that is a "mismatch" with what they want and need, they too experience anomie. And like the individuals Durkheim refers to in his sociological analysis of suicide, the boys in my studies experience depression and, perhaps, suicidal thoughts. They are yearning for a more flexible construction of manhood and of maturity that incorporates their desires for emotional intimacy with their male peers. Although constructions of masculinity may look as if they are changing, with more heterosexual boys and men wearing earrings and skinny jeans in 2011 than in 1989, they are changing mostly on the surface—in what people wear—and not necessarily in how we think and behave. Evidence of this pattern is found in the recent spate of suicides of boys who have been harassed by their peers for being emotionally effusive, liking to dance, different, and thus "gay."

Anthropologist Sarah B. Hrdy succinctly summarizes another view of why there has been such a marked decline in social connectedness during the twentieth century and early part of the twenty-first century: "The modern emphasis on individualism and personal independence along with consumption-oriented economies, compartmentalized living arrangements in high rise apartments or suburban homes, and neo-local residence patterns combine to undermine social connectedness."[13] This commonly held view is used to explain almost all social dysfunction in industrialized countries such as the United States.[14] In addition, the boys in my studies are shaped by an economy that makes it difficult for poor and working class families to remain in the same home for extended periods of time and that forces them, given their income status, to live in housing projects and high-rise apartments and to separate from loved ones in order to find work and a good education for their children.

Boys are also, of course, influenced by the "modern emphasis on individualism and personal independence." They repeatedly referred to the "need" for autonomy, although their desires were not necessarily consistent with these "needs." This combination of excessive individualism, hostile living spaces, and separated

families will inevitably produce boys (and girls) who are alienated from each other. Throw in homophobia, sexism, and a culture that equates intimate friendships and vulnerable emotions
with being girlish, gay, and childlike and you have the recipe for
boys' loss of friendships, their increased distrust, and their un-
willingness to share secrets with their friends even when they
know that such sharing will prevent them from going crazy.

Hrdy claims, however, that the trouble started earlier than
modern industrialization.[15] Using data from evolutionary anthropology, she argues that it is the patterns of the modern
family that have led to our social problems. Over thousands of
years, we have transformed from having communities in which
there are many "parents" or extended family members (i.e., allo-
parents) raising children to having just one or possibly two in the
nuclear family doing the task. Such families are isolated both
physically and emotionally from the others in their "tribe." This
movement away from communal parenting has resulted in children whose natural empathic abilities are increasingly limited.
Multiple caregivers, argues Hrdy, foster children's intersubjective and empathic abilities, as there are more people for children
to consider as they feel other people's feelings. Without such
communal care, children are less socially and emotionally skilled
than their ancestors who were raised in communal villages.
Hence, the decline in empathy and social connectedness during
the twentieth century and the early part of the twenty-first.

Epidemiologists Richard Wilkinson and Kate Pickett, in their
book *The Spirit Level* in which they analyzed over 30 industrialized countries, provide a more economic justification to the decline
in social connectedness and empathy. They conclude from their
analyses that the decline in social connectedness is linked to an increase in income inequality. In countries such as the United States,
where income inequality has gone up, social connectedness has
gone down. Furthermore, they reveal that this decline in social
connectedness is linked to a decline in the health and well-being of
people living in these countries: "For a species which thrives on

friendship and enjoys cooperation and trust . . . which is equipped with mirror neurons, allowing us to learn our way of life through a process of identification, it is clear that social structures which create relationships based on inequality, inferiority, and social exclusion must inflict a great deal of social pain."[16] This social pain, they argue, causes anxiety and stress which compromises the immune systems of both the rich and the poor. Thus the decline in social connectedness has long-term health consequences. The implications of their findings for boys, particularly for those who are from poor and working class families, are obvious.

Stephanie Coontz, an historian, provides a further possible explanation for the decline in social connectedness both in the society and among adolescent boys. She blames the decline of social connectedness on our twentieth-century notions of romantic love in marriage where a partner is expected to fulfill all one's emotional and social needs. In an article for the *New York Times*, she writes:

> It has only been in the last century that Americans have put all their emotional eggs in the basket of coupled love. But we have also neglected our other relationships, placing too many burdens on a fragile institution and making social life poorer in the process . . . [Men have] rediscover[ed] what earlier generations of men had taken for granted—that men need deep emotional connections with other men, not just their wives. Researchers soon found that men and women with confidants beyond the nuclear family were mentally and physically healthier than people who relied on just one other individual for emotional intimacy and support.[17]

Drawing from arguments used by the social historians who wrote about the prevalence of intimacy in men's friendships during the nineteenth century, Coontz argues that only in the twentieth century (and early twenty-first century), under the influence of Freudianism, have we found ourselves increasingly "suspicious" of same-sex relationships and focused exclusively on romantic partnerships. These patterns may indeed help to explain the patterns of loss in boys' friendships. As the expectation to enter into romantic relationships intensifies, boys make the sacrifice that an entire culture has made. Boys give up male friendships, focus on finding or having romantic partnerships, and "put all their emotional eggs in the basket of coupled love."

Sociologist Gregory Lehne blames the loss of social connectedness and friendships on homophobia and the cultural dictates of heterosexuality with its emphasis on competition and hierarchy. In a culture bent on proving its heterosexuality, according to Lehne, tolerance for those who engage in talk or behavior that is labeled gay or girlish will be minimal and thus male friendships and intimate social connections more broadly will not flourish. Lehne reveals the process:

> The pain that heterosexual males bear as a consequence of homosexuality is so chronic and pervasive that they probably do not notice that they are in pain or the possible source of their discomfort. Homophobia encourages men to compete. . . . Only certain types of relationships are possible between competitors. Love and close friendships are difficult to maintain in a competitive environment because to expose your weaknesses and admit your problems is to be less than a man.[18]

Homophobia, as the boys in my studies tell us directly, is clearly one of the primary factors explaining the loss of friendships. Homophobic statements (e.g., no homo) are scattered throughout the boys' interviews during late adolescence, whereas they are virtually absent in their first two years of interviews. Boys turned our questions about close male friendships by late adolescence into questions about their sexual orientation. "No homo" became a common phrase following statements of how they felt about their closest male friends. According to Urban Dictionary, "no homo" is a "slang phrase used after one inadvertently says something that sounds gay."[19] Boys came to believe that questions about close friendships "sound gay."

In his freshman year, Randy freely discusses the "feelings" he and his best friend express together. By his junior year, he says: "talking about feelings is like gay, so we don't talk about feelings." Discussing why he feels more comfortable talking to girls than to boys, Malcolm says: [With boys], it's just harder to like—'cause some of the things you may [want to do] make you seem as if you're gay or something. You know, it's more relaxing when you're with a girl." When asked about his close male friendships, Augustus tells his interviewer during the first two years of his interviews: "I can share my secrets with my best friend and he won't tell anyone." During his junior year interview, he discusses his best friend, but the tone is more distant and the feelings more cautious. Immediately following his description of closeness with his best friend, he adds the qualification "no homo." By his senior year, he says in response to whether he has a close friend that while he is tolerant of gay people, he himself is not gay. A question about friendship becomes a question about his sexuality.

Yet colleagues and friends have commonly noted that such homophobic fears, especially in a place like New York City, are not as pervasive as one might have heard decades before. My data suggest, however, that while the fears may be less intense, they are still quite strong. In fact, homophobic fears may be growing stronger as evidenced in the recent string of suicides that have taken place as a result of homophobic bullying in the schools. In her book *The Backlash against American Women,* Susan Faludi documents the ways people in positions of power have fought to push back the achievements feminists have made. This "backlash" blames girls and women for the troubles boys and men face in school and in the workplace,[20] and contributes to girls and women rejecting a feminist identity even though equal pay for equal work has yet to be achieved and we continue to see inadequate representation of women in positions of corporate, judicial, and governmental power. Similarly, in a context in which increasing numbers of gay and bisexual boys and men are coming out of the closet, where televisions shows have an increasing number of gay characters and where the lines between heterosexual and gay are blurred—even if only superficially—heterosexual boys may cling more tightly to their conventions of masculinity to prove their heterosexuality. Just as women's rights often provoke further oppression of women, gay liberation likely provokes heterosexual men to insist even more ferociously on their manliness in the most stereotypic of ways. Conventions of masculinity get reinforced with a new sense of vigor to distinguish those who are "in" from those who are "out." The consequence, of course, is not only emotional and social disconnection but an increase in acts of homophobia, as the very premise of manliness is based on such homophobic distinctions. Such a backlash may explain why it is so hard for boys to stay "sensitive" with their male friends during late adolescence and why it is even harder for young men to have intimate friendships now than it was in the nineteenth century.

This backlash is evident in the shooting sprees that boys and men have perpetrated over the past few decades, some of them aimed specifically at girls and women.[21] It is also evident in the increasing levels of homophobic and anti-girl bullying taking places in schools and neighborhoods across the country, some with deadly consequences. In one case, Mexican immigrant brothers in New York City who were walking home from work with their arms around each other were shot by men "because they were fags." The evidence of a backlash can also been seen in the case of the boyfriend killing the 17 month-old baby of his girlfriend because he acted "too much like a girl." He wanted to "toughen him up" by punching him and, instead, killed him.[22] These more extreme versions of boys and men asserting their heterosexual masculinity appear to be growing in prevalence even in the most liberal of cities and states. The less extreme version of boys trying to prove their manhood may lie precisely in the loss of boys' friendships and the social and emotional disconnection during late adolescence.

In addition to a backlash that appears to be sharpening the divisions between gay and straight (and man and woman), there appears to be another process at work that helps explain the loss of friendships during late adolescence. Embedded in the boys' interviews is a critique of our conceptions of maturity with its focus on autonomy, independence, and emotional stoicism (i.e., keeping one's problems to oneself). Such conceptions implicitly ask boys to make a choice between having a girlfriend or being alone (literally and/or psychologically). Boys know this is not good for their health. Yet they convince themselves that the trade-off—the loss of their closest male friends—is necessary to the process of growing up. In order to become a man, they must sacrifice the relationships that prevent them from becoming depressed and focus their attention on being autonomous, and independent.

Links between maturity and isolation were occasionally stated directly by the boys: "Now I'm a man, I need to take care of myself and not rely on others," or "I don't need to speak about my feelings anymore, I'm mature." Mohammed, who tells his best friend all his secrets during his freshman and sophomore years in high school, says in his junior year: "But I don't know. Recently . . . you know I kind of changed something. Not that much, but you know, I feel like there's no need to—I could keep [my feelings] to myself. You know, I'm mature enough." Interpreting a desire to share feelings as a sign of *immaturity*, Mohammed shuts down. In his junior year, he speaks of his increased sense of depression and isolation. Federico doesn't explicitly link the changes he has experienced in his friendships to maturity but suggests such a link. In his freshman year, he states that he tells all of his "deep secrets" to his best friend; by his senior year, however, he says: "I tell [my friends] secrets but not like deep secrets, um deep secrets 'cause you know you always have deep secrets that you keep to yourself." Making it seem inevitable ("you know you always"), Federico also suggests that there are costs to being "mature." Not wanting to sound gay or girly in concert with the goal of reaching maturity leads boys away from what they often seek—friendships in which they can share their true thoughts and feelings.

The boys' interviews as well as our observations of them over the past two decades has also suggested that stereotypes are fostering disconnection among boys and leading them away from their closest male friends. For Latino and Black teenagers, the same stereotype of "hyper" masculinity that may have "protected" their masculinity when they were younger may simply serve during late adolescence as a destructive force that encourages them to engage in "hyper" masculine behavior which disconnects them from their emotional and social needs. These young men carry the burden of having to resist gender, ethnic, and racial stereotypes (which are often embedded in social class stereotypes as well) in a culture where the very definition, according to the stereotype, of being Latino or Black *and* of being a man is macho. This is particularly the case for boys who are raised in low-income, urban contexts.[23]

In a study of boys attending an all-Black, all-male high school in Chicago, Onnie Rogers, a doctoral student in developmental psychology, found that boys are often confused about what is a "stereotype" and what is a "fact." In one of her interviews, she asks a ninth-grade boy:

I: Are there any stereotypes about African Americans?

P: Yes

I: Like what? What are some of the stereotypes?

P: Like one of the biggest ones is that they're in the lower class, which they are. Because I mean it's not a stereotype, it actually is, like not all of them but most of them, a majority of them are, and like uh they, African Americans, are thugs or whatever or gangsters and they get, and a stereotype or I don't even know if it's a stereotype or fact that African American and Latino boys drop out of high school and are more likely to drop out of high school and go to jail or whatever than other kids.

Although the last part of his response includes "facts," the most negative characterization—that African American men are in "thugs" and in gangs—is true for only a very small percentage of Black and Latino youth and is thus an unfounded negative stereotype. The confusion even for Black youth regarding what is a stereotype and what is a fact underscores the power of these stereotypes. The belief that Black and Latino males are gangsters and thugs will likely foster social and emotional disconnection in young men's search for admission into the world of Black and Latino manhood.[24]

For Asian American boys, the pressures to disconnect from their social and emotional needs during late adolescence also stems from racialized and sexualized stereotypes. On the one hand, Asian males are kung fu fighting titans; on the other, they are gay or feminized boys who will never "get the girl." In 2004, *Details* magazine published a picture of a young Asian man with the caption "Gay or Asian." Superimposed on the image were comparisons between Asian and gay stereotypes. Such stereotyping challenges Asian American boys' abilities to stay connected to what they want and need to thrive especially with respect to same-sex friendships. Even the stereotype of a kung fu fighter may not help in the face of accusations of being a girl or gay. The impact of these stereotypes of femininity on Asian American boys is suggested in the current fascination among Asian American boys with stereotypic "Black masculinity."[25] A new trend, noted by psychologist Jacqueline Nguyen, has Asian American boys calling themselves "pencils" to connote that they are "yellow" on the outside, white on the inside, and black at the core. Nguyen indicates that this trend grew out of the popularity of hip-hop music and styles and the desire to counter nerd stereotypes.[26] Yet the stereotypic Black masculinity that is admired by Asian American boys is often a "hyper" masculinity that entails disconnecting from their social, emotional, and academic needs and desires.

European American or White boys also face challenges related to stereotypes that make staying intimately connected to other boys difficult especially during late adolescence. A Latina in her sophomore year in one of my studies stated the stereotype directly: "being White is GAY."[27] Alluding to the fact that most of the gay public figures are White and that most gay characters on television and in the movies are White, teenagers in my studies and others have noted that while being Black is hypermasculine (i.e., heterosexual), being White is "gay." Thus White boys, like their Asian American counterparts, often seek the bold and heterosexual masculinity that is attributed to Black men.[28] Evidence of this desire to prove their heterosexuality can been seen in the long history of young White males emulating Black hip-hop style, as well as Black sports and music stars, in clothing, language, and attitude. From the White rappers of the early 1990s to the introduction of the term "wiggers" to the hoards of White boys who are trying to find and prove their "inner bro," White boys are "Black-identified" in the most stereotypic of ways.[29] Yet White boys don't actually want to be Black. They simply want to be perceived as cool and being cool is being manly (i.e., heterosexual) and thus Black. Yet the "brotherhood" seen among White boys is often a deeply distorted version of the Black model, based as it is more on a history of, say, "the time you puked at White Castle" than a history of shared oppression.[30] Thus what appears to be resistance to masculine conventions (e.g., "Bromance") is often the same old accommodation in which "boys" can act wild and "party." These boys are only skimming the surface of stereotypic "Black" masculinity and thus they miss out on what they could possibly learn from their Black "brothers" about intimacy and connectedness.

The evidence among White boys of the desire to be seen as manly and thus heterosexual can be found throughout the research on boys. Michael Kimmel's *Guyland,* for example, documents how White boys prove their heterosexuality in the most gender stereotypic ways.[31] In a qualitative study of White, middle class boys, psychologists Matthew Oransky and Jeanne Maracek find that the boys actively avoided any signs of emotional vulnerability and mocked such vulnerability in other boys. They also indicated that their peer groups "derided expressions of hurt and worry and of care and concern for others as "gay" or "girly"[32] and that the primary way that they connected with each other was by being "rowdy" and breaking things. Although this study, like most studies of White boys, does not examine boys' closest friendships in particular and makes the assumption that boys' behavior with their peers is the same as their behavior with their closest friends, the extent and ways that White boys set out to prove their heterosexuality with their peers is readily apparent.

SUMMARY

Integrating the scholarly literature with the boys' interviews reveals the thick culture that explains not only the loss of social connectedness but also the loss of friendships, the distrust, and the increased isolation that the boys in my studies felt as they reached late adolescence. Embedded in these theories across the social sciences and in my data is a critique of the constructs of masculinity (and its implicit homophobia, sexism, and racial stereotyping) and maturity. Both constructs idealize autonomy, separation, and emotional stoicism and lead boys (and girls) away from the social and emotional skills that are, according to many scholars, necessary to thrive.[33] Our constructs of manhood and maturity rest on an understanding of human nature, in other words, that is not natural. Identifying these distortions allows us to envision different goals for human development—goals that value friendships as much as romantic partners, relationships as much as autonomy, emotions as much as cognition, being a girl as much as being a boy, and being gay as much as being heterosexual. These goals would incorporate the knowledge acquired from the natural and social sciences and put that knowledge into practice.

Boys understand the sacrifice that they are asked to make as they mature and enter manhood. Larry says in his senior year: "How can anyone be happy without a friend or someone to talk to? That's impossible. I mean a person could have a girlfriend or a boyfriend, they're happy together. But . . . they're going to want that friend . . . It's healthy." The boys in my studies know what they want. The challenge is to help them have what they want and thus produce boys and men who stay connected to their friends and families and thus to themselves. We do not need to fix boys as much as we need to help boys remain confident in their knowledge of the social and emotional world.

CHAPTER 8

FERNANDO AND DANNY

As with closeness and intimacy, the themes of loss and distrust in boys' friendships varied across boys and within individual stories. The patterns presented in Chapter 6 only begin to reveal such nuances. Listening to Fernando and Danny, we begin to hear the more subtle variations that provide insight into the reasons for and the ways of experiencing such patterns in their friendships. Like Nick and George, Fernando and Danny have numerous similarities and differences, and it is precisely through this combination that we are able to see the form and content of the loss and distrust among teenage boys.

Both boys come from immigrant families; Fernando's parents came from the Dominican Republic to the United States before he was born, and Danny's parents came from China to the United States shortly after he was born. Both sets of parents work at blue collar jobs and provide stable homes for their teenage boys. Although both sets of parents are actively involved in their sons' lives, Fernando's parents are divorced and his father lives in another state; Danny's parents live at home together. Fernando, who speaks in affectionate and loving ways about his friends in his freshman year, becomes wary of intimacy over time with other boys, as we see in his repeated use of "no homo" in his latter year interviews. Danny shows only traces of affection for his friends in his early years of high school and then becomes more deeply immersed in a world of masculinity in which he struggles to speak honestly with his closest friends and feels alone. By their junior or senior years, both boys begin to show signs of depression as they increasingly disconnect from their friends and from themselves.

FERNANDO'S STORY

Freshman Year: Having Intimate Friendships

Fernando, a young-looking 14-year-old freshman with chubby cheeks, lively dark eyes, and short black hair that has been shaved on both sides of his head, lives with his mother, who is currently attending a local college with the goal of becoming a nurse, his 18-year-old sister, and his grandmother. His 22-year-old brother recently moved out of the home to find his own apartment. His father, who is a superintendent of an apartment building, lives in Los Angeles and calls Fernando every day to get an update on Fernando's life and to tell him how much he misses him. Fernando's parents, both of whom are from the Dominican Republic, immigrated to the United States before Fernando was born and separated when he was four years old.

During his freshman year, Fernando expresses feelings of closeness with both parents and says he wishes his father lived closer. He describes his mother as "funny" and a "good cook" and someone who can "keep a secret" and says he is able to express his feelings with her just as he can with his best friend, Juan. He describes his father as "cool" and someone who wants him to be "famous and have a good life." Fernando does not talk to him about things that are personal, although they will talk for hours about sports and television. Fernando says he wants to be a basketball player when he gets older, although his father wants him to be a doctor and his mother wants him to go into any medical profession. Fernando's parents, much like George's parents, strongly value friendships and advise him to have "lots of friends." He thinks that his mother may say this because she is compensating for her own lack of friends when she was little, while his father wants him to have friends because he has lots of friends himself.

Fernando describes himself as funny and smart and "able to keep a secret," reinforcing the fact that keeping secrets is not only valued but is a part of his identity. His "most important" values this year include education and friends: "Education's important 'cause I want to be somebody someday and having a lot of friends is important, that way I won't be by myself or you know, just lonely." His best friend, whom he has known since he was a little boy, currently lives in the same neighborhood and attends the same church as Fernando and his family.

Fernando spends a good deal of time during his freshman interview underscoring the importance of shared secrets with his friends. He defines "real secrets" as "something that happens at home," although among his "secrets" he also includes thoughts and feelings about girls, school, homework, and other people in general. Even in the parts of the interview that are not focused on friendships, Fernando discusses the importance of discretion: "Like you won't want to tell your family members 'cause it's probably about them or you don't want to tell them and you just tell your friend and they'll keep a secret." Fernando notes that in junior high school he was not able to trust his friends as much as he does now and appreciates the change: "I was lonely in junior high school . . . like by myself, independent," whereas now in high school it's "much better." Fernando understands implicitly the link between "independence" and "loneliness."

To his group of friends, he confides "a lot of secrets and they don't rat me out or spread out rumors." This trust contrasts to an earlier experience in junior high school when a close friend betrayed him: "I remember one friend—I told him a secret and the whole school ended up finding out. . . . Sometimes, I mean, I don't think everybody's the same though, but it made me a little bit harder." He, however, is not hardened yet.

Fernando's best friend, Juan, is also Dominican American and in the same grade, and Fernando has known him since he was four years old. Their activities include sleepovers, playing basketball, going to movies, and playing video games. When asked to describe the friendship, Fernando says: "It's private. I mean, yeah. I can't explain it. I don't know why . . . like he trusts me and I trust him." And then he says: "I mean it's fun. It's phat I guess . . . we just go to parties and have fun." Like his peers, Fernando embeds his more intimate statements in other statements ("it's phat I guess") that affirm his masculinity.

Responding to a question about what he likes about Juan, Fernando says: "We could talk to each other . . . because like, not every day I feel like I want to have fun. Like sometimes I would just be tired or just tired of school or—and we'll just talk. . . . If I feel bad, he'll just give me advice, talk to me, whatever." In addition to the talk, he and Juan know each other's families, and this, according to Fernando, draws them even closer.

Fernando claims that while he and Juan have few disagreements, they are likely to have more arguments in the future when they get older. When asked why, he draws on his older sister's experience: "Like she had a best friend ever since she was six and now [his sister is 19] they just started arguing for nothing, like for no reason." Like the other boys in my studies, Fernando sees the loss of trust and conflict as an inevitable part of growing up.

Sophomore Year: The Winds of Change

The biggest change for Fernando this year is his newfound romantic relationship. He began to date Lucy, who is Puerto Rican and also a sophomore, a few months before the second interview. He says, however, that he only sees his girlfriend "once in a blue moon" after school, because they would get "sick of each other" if they spent more time together. As with last year, Fernando feels close to his mother, sharing many of his thoughts and feelings with her about his siblings and friends. Although his mother knows about his girlfriend, he does not feel comfortable talking about this relationship with his mother since she would not approve of the sexual nature of it. His relationship with his father has grown more distant over the past year, and he admits: "I really don't trust him that much, I would not tell him like my deep secrets. I usually leave that to my best friends." He is frustrated that his father, who continues to call him on a daily basis, has not visited him for over three years.

One of the major shifts this year is that Fernando sounds increasingly like a male cliché: "I matured a lot [since last year]. More into girls, clothes. That's basically my environment and my world. Clothes, girls, and money." The most important things for him this year are "Sports . . . me being a guy, of course, I mean I love sports . . . girls . . . and money's important too because I mean I want to look hot . . . and I could buy my mom some diamond earrings or whatever." In stark contrast to the previous year in which education and friendships were most important, this year it is being a stereotypic guy, which he defines as "you think ahead, you think about your school, your future, what you like, like girls, and just sports and stuff. That's it." Fernando speaks in ways that are clearly coded for heterosexual manhood. Describing one of his friends, he says:

> Charlie is acting a little gay . . . he's like touching guys' butts and shit. I know he's joking around but. He says homo jokes . . . Well, me being a Christian, I should be homophobic, but I could live with it. . . . [If he were gay] I'd probably be his friend, like, "what's up?" But that's about it, 'cause I don't want him hitting on me or whatever.

Although he has shades of a more nuanced stance, the bottom line sounds like the "boy code."

Nonetheless, Fernando remains intimate with his close friends. The sharing of secrets, the selection of confidants, and the extent to which he is willing to share intimate information continues to be a theme. Although he trusts all his friends with

money (making the typical distinction between money and secrets), he only shares his "real secret secrets" and "deep secrets"
with his closest friends. He also continues to make sharp distinctions between types of friends based on the extent to which secrets can be shared.

For the first time, however, he admits to fighting with a friend.
By way of example, he says he had a brief fling with a girl in junior high school who eventually became his friend's girlfriend.
When his friend found out, he wouldn't talk to Fernando for
over a month. Fernando says he couldn't believe that this boy
would let a girl affect their relationship: "I mean we are close
friends and he's gonna let some girl get between us? . . . if it was
one of my closest friends, a girl wouldn't have broken us apart
that much. There is a little gap now 'cause now I know that he
could get jealous over anything." The anger at letting a girl inter-
vene in their friendships speaks to the bonds that Fernando has
with his friends and with his priorities in his sophomore year.

Boys often cited examples of other boys leaving them for girls
as a reason for difficulties in their friendships. Paul says in his
junior year when asked what he dislikes about his best friend: "If
he was hanging out with me for the whole day and a girl steps
up. He'll leave with her and leave me. That puts me down.
'Cause I was with him and he's gonna break out on me and
leave with a chick." Boys' sense of betrayal and hurt are readily
apparent.

Fernando names Juan and Jacob as his best friends this year
because he "was born with them" and because his mother is best
friends with Juan's and Jacob's mothers:

> Those are the first two people, I'll tell. . . . You can't be my best
> friend if I can't trust you. So trust is a big part of being best friends.
> Um, see I trust Juan with anything. Even if it's family issues—
> whatever. I'll tell him. And I'm pretty sure he'll feel the same way
> about me 'cause we've told each other secrets before.

Fernando's sense of trust and his willingness to share secrets are tightly woven together—those who are most trusted are those who are the recipients of his deepest secrets.

Yet even in the midst of this intimate talk, there is growing evidence of a hypermasculine narrative. Asked what he likes about Juan, he says: "Everything, the way that we just relate, no homo, just the way we talk to each other." The "no homo" qualifier, used rarely in his freshman interview, becomes a verbal tick during his sophomore year. Claiming that Juan "knows" when Fernando is afraid or angry even if Fernando doesn't say anything, Fernando adds: "he would know my facial expressions. He would just find out. I don't know how. He just finds out. That's how close the relationship is. No homo. We read each other's minds sometimes. Like I could actually tell what he's thinking at one moment . . . just by his facial expressions." Fernando expresses intimacy but then backs away to assert his heterosexuality.

Fernando continues this back and forth pattern throughout his interview:

> *F:* I think [Jacob and Juan] will be my best friends to the end. No homo. I know it sounds corny but it's the truth.
> *I:* It doesn't sound corny.
> *F:* Well it actually does "best friends 'til the end?"
> *I:* Well I feel that way about my friends.
> *F:* Well you're a girl.

Using code language (e.g., "corny") to refer to what he perceives as gay or girlish (as he makes explicit with his female interviewer), Fernando signals that he is aware of his masculine context but remains willing to use such language to describe his friendship. Asked to define a best friend, he says: "Someone I could trust, someone that, no homo, cares for me. Um that's it . . . Imagine a life with no friends. Pretty lonely. So you need friends." Saying "no homo," like being involved in sports, seemed to release boys from the threat of misinterpretation and allow the conversation of desire and intimacy to continue.

At the end of his sophomore year interview, however, Fernando succumbs to masculine "norms" and says about his best friends: "Well we mostly we talk about girls . . . 'cause we're both guys. We don't want to talk about feelings and stuff. It just sounds gay talking about feelings. So I—we just don't talk about it." Making the association explicit between "talking about feelings" and being gay, Fernando sinks deeper into gender stereotypes.

Junior Year: Equating Maturity with Manhood

Fernando begins his junior year interview by saying: "Well everything's changed . . . this year is pretty much more serious since it's the junior year," and then proceeds to discuss the jokes that he and his friends share and the ways he is messing up in school. When asked to describe how he has changed since last year, he says that while he used to do well in school he is currently "kind of backtracking" and being "lazy" this year. He also adds that he "used to be nice and calm" and now he is "joking loud." He describes in great detail his class clown antics and his growing apathy toward school. He admits that his mother still wants him to go to college, but he does not see this as his top priority anymore. Manhood has become confounded for him— as for so many teenage boys—with being "joking loud" and not taking his life, including school, too seriously.

In one of the few moments of vulnerability in his junior year interview, Fernando speaks about his growing distance from his father and how he wishes he saw his father more: "It's not really necessary now because I'm almost a young man, I can take care of myself"—suggesting, like so many of his peers, that manhood and maturity is equivalent to being independent and, ultimately, alone. His father continues to call almost every day, but he hasn't seen his father for almost four years, and when they speak on the phone, their conversations, he says, are brief. His relationship with his mother is described as "close," but, he says, "I'm not going to tell her some deep secrets of things that I've done wrong." Even his relationships with his parents have become more superficial.

Although Fernando continues to be involved with Lucy and some of the same friendships he had in previous years, the tension between his desire to be emotionally stoic and his craving for close relationships seems even stronger. When discussing his girlfriend, he says the relationship is "great," although he admits that he doesn't share with her what he does in the evenings, for fear she would be jealous and things would get "complicated." With his friends, he shares "everything," he says, but he isn't able to provide any examples of such intimacy and claims that the problems with his girlfriend are "none of their business": "I don't want to give them stuff about my girlfriend because that's too much information for them and they don't need to know that. But if I had problems like with another kid, then I would tell them and they would just come and have my back or stuff like that." While Fernando may want to share "everything" with his friends or have a romantic relationship that is "great," the truth appears to be that he can't and he doesn't. He has what most of the boys had by late adolescence—friendships that privilege humor over talking in which they skim the surface rather than maintaining the previous "deep depth" kind of relationship.

Fernando's growing lack of trust in his male friends also extends to girls:

> Ever since I'll say, about junior high, I trust this group of four girls with, like a couple of secrets, you know. And they just went off and told their other friends and sooner or later by the third day of the school week, the whole entire school knew that secret. And that's how I pretty much lost my trust in girls.

Often drawing a conclusion based on the behavior of a few, the boys did not take acts of betrayal lightly. Once boys felt betrayed, they often abandoned the friendship altogether. Boys wanted to avoid feelings of hurt and their strategy was one of survival rather than liberation.[1]

Fernando does, however, have best friends this year, including Juan and Lucy. Yet when describing these friends, his relationships sound as superficial as those with his parents: "Everything's fine. It's perfect. This is where it has to be. You know, we don't get into each others' deep, deep business." There is no indication of sharing secrets or feelings with anyone this year as he did in his freshman year. Describing his friendship with Juan, Fernando says:

> It's funny 'cause he is just like me in the same exact way. We joke around. We're mostly the jokers. We are like twins sometimes and that's what's funny about it. . . . Nothing I would trade in the world just to be with my best friend, Juan. . . . There's nothing I would really hide from Juan . . . if I have any family issues, he'll be like the first one I'll tell . . . trust me, we get real, real with each other. Trust me.

Although it sounds as if he has an intimate friendship with Juan as he had last year, when asked for specific examples, he is not able to provide any. Even his repetition of the phrase "trust me" and his stutter when he says the word "real" suggests that there may be reasons not to trust what he is saying. His seemingly surface relationship with Juan this year is confirmed when he says that his friendship with Juan, whom he has known since he was four, is now exactly the same as with his other friends. While he may want to have the intimacy he had earlier with Juan—an intimacy that did entail telling him "everything"—he no longer has such a friendship. At the end of the interview, Fernando makes his desires clear: "Yes of course friendships are important. One hundred percent because who besides your parents are you going to trust? And there's certain things you don't want to tell your family. So who else are you going to go to? So you need those people." Despite these needs, his entry into manhood has seemingly led him astray.

Senior Year: Being a Man

Describing himself this year as "tough to open up," Fernando, who is by now behind in his credits in high school which forces him to attend night school twice a week, rarely sees his best friend Juan, even though they continue to live close to each other. He spends most of the time with his girlfriend Lucy or by himself. He and Lucy seem to care about each other, but Fernando alludes to behaviors, as he did in the previous year, that he does not tell her about because he thinks it would "hurt her," even though he claims never to have cheated on her. As in the previous year, he sounds like a stereotype as he claims to think "mostly about girls, sports, and money." Following graduation, he hopes to attend college, but his larger ambition is to make a lot of money: "My first goal is to be rich."

His relationship with his mother continues to be "close" although he rarely talks to her about his personal life. As in previous years, his relationship with his father is a phone relationship, given that he hasn't seen his father for many years. In his senior year, he has not spoken to his father for almost three months: "He used to call every day but now since I don't make an effort to call him, like, he's trying to see how long it will take for me to call him. But I don't think I'll call him anytime soon." He admits to being angry with his father and says that since his dad has played such a small role in his life, he doesn't think much about their relationship. Unlike George's father, who modeled emotional intimacy for his son, Fernando appears to have no such model.

Repeating a theme for boys during late adolescence, Fernando says: "my friendships are not the same as it was. Before we used to do crazy stuff 'cause I guess we were younger. But now it's all about either making money or just trying to see what we're gonna do about our lives, think about our future, or whatever." Fernando no longer has the intimate friendships of his youth: "[my friendships] are just, no homo, it's great, it's cool. Um, we don't get along all the time. But even when we argue about stupid stuff, we get along." Insisting on neutrality, Fernando says that even when he is angry, he is not really angry. When asked what he would argue about with his friends, he says: "When guys argue, they usually argue about either sports or girls or who could get the most numbers in one day. Or something. It's stuff like that." Shifting the question away from himself, Fernando is stubborn by his senior year about toeing the mainstream line.

Even in his response about how he can trust his friends, his "cool pose" remains: "I could trust [my friends]with money, my girl, like if I was to be like yo, look after my girl for a week. I could trust them, everything. I could trust them, they won't steal nothing from my house." Although he continues to say "I could tell them everything" in reference to his close friends, he never follows up with examples of sharing particular types of information. Fernando is also back to saying "no homo" every time he describes any potentially intimate interaction: "Juan will be mad that I don't wanna go out [of the house], he wants to go out with me, no homo, we just start a little argument and then we'll cool down." Alluding to the existence of some remaining connection with Juan (who wants to "go out" with Fernando), he admits that they do in fact argue, but this admission is cloaked in the language of "no homo" that protects him from feelings of vulnerability.

Asked how his friendships have changed since the beginning of ninth grade, he says:

> It's different 'cause everybody's focusing on trying to get out of here. Everybody's going to college, different colleges. Um, everybody's older, you know. Everyone has left so the friendships in this school are gone, it's like everybody's hooked up too. Like all my friends got girlfriends, so it's kind of hard. And sometimes the girlfriends don't get along with each other, so you kinda gotta separate 'cause that's happened plenty of times.

Schooling and girls, the two most common explanations for the loss of friendships, are repeated by Fernando to explain his own losses. Although he is willing to hint at some vulnerability ("so it's kind of hard"), it is hidden in a more "normative" narrative.

In one of the rare moments of explicit vulnerability suggesting that there is another thicker story to tell, he expresses anger at boys who privilege their girlfriends over their guyfriends. Describing a conflict with a friend, Fernando says: "He was trying to act up so I was kind of mad 'cause I was like, 'How you gonna put your girl over me? No homo.'" Fernando, however, reverts to his old ways of exposing his desires and then quickly asserts his heterosexuality.

When describing his other friend, Santiago, he says: "he trusts me with a lot of things, a lot of secrets. So if he can open up to me, once again, I think I should probably do the same. But with my close friends, I don't know, they have like two sides to them sometimes. Like Marcelo, he acts real cool with you and then, I don't know, he's kinda sneaky. So I gotta keep my eye on him." Revealing the distrust that was so prevalent among the boys during late adolescence, Fernando indicates that he is no exception. His response also reveals that boys, even during late adolescence, continue to share and want to share secrets (e.g., "I think I should probably do the same"). The lack of intimacy in Fernando's friendships does not come from a lack of desire but a lack of trust that his secrets will be kept confidential.

These moments of vulnerability, however, are fleeting. Fernando's description of his friendship with Juan is: "[Our friendship is] perfect. Um, he makes me laugh, I make him laugh. We chill, we roll together, we got a lot of things in common. Like the love of music, um sports,—well he's not, he's getting into sports now. . . . it's mainly laughter . . . That's all it's about, it's mad humorous." Asked how he is similar to Juan, whom he rarely sees at this point, he says: "Friends, money, girls, uh sports, everything. Just I mean, I don't think there's that much things to talk about when it comes to guys, I mean it's pretty much the same thing. If it's not girls, if it's not money, if it's not sports, if it's not music. I don't know what it is." Fernando pursues main-stream masculinity, at this point, with a vengeance.

On the topic of ideal friendships, Fernando says at the end of his final interview in the study: "You gotta be funny, truthful, I just got to have fun with you, you know. I just don't want to get tired of you right away. 'Cause if I get tired of you, you are not really my friend. Um, you gotta, I guess just be there for me? I guess, I don't wanna sound too sissy-like." Boys want emotionally supportive relationships with other boys ("I guess just be there for me") but they veer away from finding what they want and need and instead focus on becoming a man. Fernando concludes his interview by saying: "I think I've matured in certain ways . . . I know how to be more of a man." Indeed.

DANNY'S STORY

Freshman Year: Speaking Freely

With pale skin and sharply defined cheekbones, wearing low-hanging jeans and a bright white t-shirt, Danny explains to his interviewer that he immigrated from China with his mother, father, and older brother when he was six years old. Presently he lives in the same neighborhood as his school. His mother works at a local factory and also manages apartment buildings in the neighborhood. His father works at a restaurant as a cook and immigrated to the United States a year earlier than Danny and his family so that he could find work and support them once they arrived.

Danny describes his relationship with his mother as "very close" and involving "a lot of talk about schoolwork" and how "it was back home in China." He does not have to "hide" things from his mother and says she will always make him feel better if he tells her about a problem. He describes his father as a "hard worker who provides for the family and he gives me money to buy things." He says that he and his dad are close, although he admits rarely seeing him since his dad works long hours starting in the early morning before Danny wakes up.[2] He wishes his dad didn't have to work so much and says that when they lived in China, his father was around the house more. Both of his parents value friendships and encourage Danny to have close friendships with other boys. Danny describes himself as a "friendly and patient person," particularly with his friends, and believes that friendships are among the three most important aspects of his life (next to family and school).

Danny claims that when he was a young boy, he was shy and didn't talk to any of his peers. During elementary school, after he immigrated to the United States, he became more talkative, and now: "I talk to everybody." Part of the reason for the change, he says, is his family's move into the same neighborhood as many of his friends, which has made spending time together much easier. When asked about his friends from school, he says he enjoys them because they "talk and laugh about things like computers, games, basketball, anything, like guy's stuff." Even in his freshman year, we begin to hear traces of gender stereotypes. But, like his peers, he remains willing to express a vulnerability that is inconsistent with such masculine poses:

> I think having friendships is good because it doesn't make you feel lonely. When you're by yourself, you feel lonely and you feel alone, as if nobody cares about you. . . . I like that my friends and I can always talk about things and everybody doesn't like say, you know, I'm better then you or you're better than me. When people say like I'm better than you, that means they think you're lower and you don't belong in the same group as them. It makes you feel down.

Even though he does "guy's stuff," Danny freely acknowledges the emotional benefits of friendships and the problems that occur when relationships turn competitive. He speaks openly about his friendships, relying on his feelings to gain additional clarity. Describing why he feels closer to certain boys over others, he says: "I know how they think and feel . . . I really don't know how the other guys feel." Friendships are only possible, according to Danny, when feelings are known.

Danny says that he likes that his friends are trustworthy and that they could "talk about things" and they won't share his secrets with others. Much of his freshman year interview focuses on explaining the nuances of trust and secret sharing—who can be trusted among his peers to keep his secrets. Danny is clearly embedded in an intricate web of relationships where the currency is how far "the trust can be stretched."[3] Trust, as Danny explains repeatedly, comes from knowing how someone is thinking and feeling, which then leads to feelings of care.

His best friend this year is Anthony, who is also Chinese, and whom he has known since he arrived in the United States. The most important component of this friendship is the trust they share: "I could trust him more with the important stuff than I trust the other friends. . . . having someone to trust, you don't have to worry about anything by yourself or care for yourself. There's like another person who cares about you too." His desire to be cared for is made explicit, as are the ways trust and care are intimately linked for him. Danny feels deeply cared for by Anthony and turns to him in times of distress as well when he simply wants to have fun.

At the end of his freshman year interview, Danny describes his ideal friendship: "It would be like I could trust him or he could trust me, and we could play together and he wouldn't get mad at everything. And then he could trust me when I get mad." Like the association between trust and care, trust and anger are linked for Danny, with trust providing the possibility for anger.

Asked why he thinks that friendships are important, Danny explains:

> 'Cause like it's like having a second, second voice from yourself. Friends, you can talk to them about a lot of things that you would normally talk about only to yourself. So having a friend is like um when you're in trouble you can talk to them about things. They could help you so you don't have to worry about yourself. . . . [Having a friend] means that I could have someone who's like always there, and always help. And then he doesn't tell people everything

about what we do and things. . . . It's like another way for you to think that you have somebody else to care for you.

Repeating the themes evident in his friendship with Anthony, Danny believes that friendships are intimate affairs—"second voices"—that allow him to feel less alone. He implicitly resists conventions of masculinity in his recognition of the social and emotional significance of having friends with whom he can talk. When the choice is isolation or friendships, friendships are chosen and—for most of the boys during early and adolescence—found.

Sophomore Year: Becoming Autonomous

In his sophomore year, Danny continues to describe his relationship with his mother as "very close," although he admits to sharing less with her now that he has grown older. Like Mohammed, Danny attributes this change to increased maturity: "Maybe like now that I'm older so I like to keep things to myself." Notably, growing up is not about expressing oneself more to peers than to parents but about becoming less expressive with anyone. His relationship with his dad continues to be "close" as well, but Danny rarely sees him and says he mostly talks to his dad about school and his grades. His father encourages his independence because "he likes for me to do things on my own and not rely on them every single time." Danny's parents, as parents of teenagers often do, push him to be more autonomous. Danny says he appreciates his father's push because "in the future, usually I'm going to rely on myself to get like good jobs." In contrast to his freshman year, when he describes himself as "friendly and patient," this year Danny says, "I would describe myself as a quiet kind of person."

In Danny's sophomore year, he still has a large group of friends with whom he plays basketball and handball. His close friends spend time together each week in school or, if they go to different high schools, on the phone or "chatting" online. While talking about his friends, Danny underscores the importance of emotional support: "'cause if nobody helps you out, the problem's going to get more serious. If somebody helps you and they could like help you out with the problem by telling you that you're not alone or something like that 'cause you don't want to feel alone when you're having a problem. That's why having friends to help you is better." Danny continues to make it clear that he does not want to be alone.

Danny makes sharp distinctions between close and best friends. With a best friend he could "get like close . . . and be more intimate" and "I would know him much better and be able to spend more time with him and know how he's like as a person." The key goal for Danny is to feel known and to know others deeply.[4] Yet it is unclear in his interview this year whether he has any close friends, as he sounds increasingly isolated from his peers. When asked to describe how his friendships have changed since he was younger, he says:

> I'm like more to myself now 'cause when you were little you just hang out with everybody like boys and girls, everybody. You're more open 'cause you don't have many problems . . . Like now you don't want people to know what's going on . . . like if you tell them what's going on in like, in school and maybe they'll like say something like "you're slow" or something like that. You may not feel as good anymore . . . and if you like fall back from the group [of friends] in school you will feel more lonely even though they're your friends.

Revising his earlier account of his friendships, he claims that it is only with growing up that he has become more cautious and distrustful. He recognizes the dilemma that boys often feel during late adolescence. If they do not say what they think and feel to their friends, they will feel even more alone, but if they do openly express themselves, they will be betrayed and not cared for any longer.[5]

In contrast to last year, Danny says that he keeps his most personal secrets to himself, including those about his family, "'cause it's a family relation and I wouldn't want anybody like saying that 'oh I should change my family' or something like that . . . 'cause I know my family is good." While his family secrets are off-limits to his friends, he shares his secrets about whom he likes or hates as he doesn't consider that type of information to have the same potential to hurt him as would a secret about the family.

Anthony remains his "best friend" this year and he sees him every day in and after school, playing basketball and "walking around." He likes that "we could openly express ourselves like I could tell him like, um, different things that I wouldn't tell other people." He describes Anthony as an "openly freely talkage person." Although Danny won't share his intimate secrets with other friends, he says he will do so with Anthony given the trust between the two of them. The reason for this trust is that they "know what each other's personality is like and how they might react to what the other would say." Again, knowing each other is a critical part of Danny's conceptions of trust.

Yet, as already alluded to in the early parts of his sophomore interview, things are not the same as they were the previous year. Danny confesses that he is beginning to doubt whether Anthony can truly be trusted with his secrets but doesn't provide specific details. Defining trust with him, Danny says: "It means that he would not go around and tell everybody what you have told him." The second person pronoun suggests a self-protective stance that is in response to a particular betrayal Anthony has committed. This is the last year Danny indicates that he has a best friend.

Junior Year: Becoming a "Closed Guy"

The most obvious change for Danny over the past year is in his self-description: "I'm kind of like a closed guy, I don't really like to express a lot of things." Shifting from his freshman year where secret sharing was a core part of his experience of friend-ships and being friendly and patient were core aspects of his identity, Danny has now retreated into being a silent boy who doesn't "express a lot of things." He continues, however, to feel "close" to his mother, although he expresses frustration that he often has to serve as a translator for his mother whose English is not good. His relationship with his father, he says, is "good":

> It's not totally closed in. I mean you can be open with him, and he could be open with you and I don't have to get like, having to pull back on some of the issues that are bothering me about somebody. It gives me the chance to tell him how I feel. I won't have to keep it inside. I mean, for some people it's hard because they don't have a real good relationship with their fathers. But I guess that's the thing I'm lucky for, 'cause I have that kind of relationship. I could tell him how I feel.

As in his freshman year, communicating *feelings* is central to his experience of closeness; yet it is now his father to whom he turns to express his feelings. The fact that his father fosters this dynamic speaks, most likely, to the roots of Danny's own emotional acuity.

Although Danny has some newfound friends this year, he does not feel close enough to share much of his life and says they mostly talk about what their plans are for the weekend, sports, and other things that, as Danny points out, do not entail confidences: "I won't tell anybody my secrets. . . . If I told them something that I know, secrets or something about how I feel about them, they may be shocked about it 'cause they all never heard me say these things before." His response underscores the extent to which he has become a "closed guy."

As in his previous interviews, Danny remains aware of the subtleties of his friendships and the importance of "talk" and trust to maintaining them. Asked what he doesn't like about his friendships, he says: "Not much, I mean we don't talk to each other a lot, so I don't really know the bad or good sides to them. . . . So there's not much, really I don't like about that." His response indicates that while his close friendships have disappeared, his emotional acuity has not.

In his junior year interview, Danny says that he doesn't have one best friend but that all of his 10 male friends are his "best friends." Boys often refer to everyone as their "best friends" when they feel that no one is their best friend. Having everyone be a best friend avoids having to admit to a lack of close friendships. The same pattern is true for Danny as he reveals that even Anthony won't be serious with him when he wants to be serious and doesn't seem reliable enough to entrust with his problems.

When asked whom he would pick as his closest friend among his 10 "best friends," he says in a firm way: "I'd pick me." When pushed to choose someone, he stubbornly says: "My shadow." And then he proceeds to explain: "I don't know. I mean, last year, I'd say Anthony was my best friend but things have changed now." Explaining the changes, he says:

> I'm the kind of person who doesn't really like to consider anybody a close friend or a best friend . . . I mean I guess it depends on different time periods. When I'm in school, I see them [the 10 friends he referred to earlier] all the time. But when I'm outside school, it's like a whole different world. I don't see them that much.

Repeating the masculine pose (i.e., "I'm the kind of person who doesn't really like to consider anybody a close friend"), Danny does not feel close to anyone. His explanation relies on the familiar story of emotional stoicism embedded in norms of masculinity and of maturity:

> Serious things are like you are having problems inside your family or with yourself, personal things. To me, I don't really like to express my personal feelings 'cause I'm your friend but I'm not your close friend. If you ask me for advice, I will give it to you. But in some cases, some topics may be like too serious so you want to keep it to yourself. I mean, you wanna kill yourself, I mean—If you say you wanna kill yourself to me, I would have to tell somebody but I mean that's a choice for you to tell me that you want do this or do that, it's your choice . . . I mean it's up to you to them whether they are gonna tell me.

Danny's struggles are suggested if we follow the "I voice" speaking in this passage.

I don't
I am
I am not

I will
I mean
I mean
I would
I mean
I mean

Struggling to articulate what he *is* and what he means, Danny sounds depressed and alone. He wants to tell others about his personal struggles ("I mean it's up to you, to them") yet fears they will betray him. He wants to be the type of "mature" person who doesn't express his personal feelings to others but knows that he should tell others what he is feeling, especially when it is something serious.

When asked why he chooses not to tell his personal concerns to his friends, he says: "I guess it's just what I have to deal with myself. I mean, everybody has to deal with their own personal situations. Life is complicated as I, as I see it 'cause if I don't deal with it myself and I rely on people my whole life, I won't be able to learn the lessons that I need for me to grow." Transforming isolation and disconnection into a "life lesson" and linking his retreat from others with maturity, Danny reflects his cultural context.

Danny's alienation is apparent as well in his discussion of his former best friend Anthony even though he begins his response by sounding positive:

[The friendship between me and Anthony] it's unconditional. I guess that means, for sure that we will be friends even if we don't see each other 'cause I've known him for such a long time and he's known me a long time. And we know how each other feels. And we don't have to tell each other every single day how we feel—how he feels. We know how each other feels already without telling each other. We don't have to worry about each other. I mean I don't have to worry about him when he has a problem. He knows he could come to me when he has a problem or something. And he knows I could go to him.

Although a "thin" read of this passage suggests closeness, there are signs of unrequited care as he struggles to connect to another boy (i.e., "how we feel—how he feels" and "he knows he *could* come to me . . . and he knows that I *could* go to him"). And then Danny tells a darker and seemingly more authentic story: "I don't trust Anthony because if I tell him how I really am and then he goes to other people and tells them that same thing that I told him . . ." He describes how Anthony told other students something (which he would not tell his interviewer) that Danny had told him in confidence and "then it all became one big mess." As a consequence, Danny became less trusting of Anthony and vowed never to fully trust another peer again. He adds: "Anthony is a jokester, he doesn't know when to become serious." Thus, he shares "nothing" with Anthony, even though he knows theoretically that he "could." Flipping between idealizing his friendship and expressing his lack of trust with Anthony, Danny reveals both his desire and his fears. He desires an "unconditional friend"—a friend who will "always be there" and will know his feelings without him having to express them. His experiences, however, have taught him that this type of friend is hard to find.

Danny admits, however, that talking about problems can be "helpful."

Talking is—it's a better way of expressing how you feel. I mean, having someone to talk to basically means you have someone that actually, like, wants to hear what you say and wants to know, like, how you're doing. So it gives you a sense that there's somebody out there who I can say is a close friend to me and they could listen to me when

I have a problem. And there, there's someone I could turn to when I have a problem or I'm someone they could turn to for someone who has a problem.

Rarely directly articulated, the desire for intimate friendships was often evident in the boys' descriptions of ideal friendships and explanations why, as in Danny's passage, trust is so important in a friendship.

After Danny says that he would not share anything "valuable" with his friends, the interviewer asks:

I: So what's something that's valuable that you wouldn't trust them with?

D: Valuable is in terms of my secrets, how I feel about each other people. Like, if I tell you how I feel about that person, they're not gonna go and tell that person. Basically secrets.

I: So you wouldn't trust your friends with secrets?

D: Not all.

I: Who would you trust with secrets out of all your friends?

D: I don't really know.

I: Have you ever trusted any of them with a secret?

D: No, because I don't have secrets.

I: So if you had one, whom would you tell?

D: None of them.

I: Why not?

D: I keep my secrets to myself.

I: Why?

D: Um, people say that you ha—if you have a friend, you could trust them with anything, and you could, like, tell people—tell them what—how things are. I mean—I don't believe that 'cause if it's your secret, you should keep it to yourself, 'cause why should you tell other people how you feel if it's personal to you?

Danny lays out explicitly boys' friendship trajectory during adolescence. In the beginning of the passage and of adolescence, the "value" and content of his secrets and his desire to have someone with whom to share his secrets is readily apparent. This vulnerability is then transformed in this passage, as well as in late adolescence, to a desire for autonomy ("you should keep it to yourself") but in Danny's case, as with most of his peers, this desire does not feel genuine.

Shifting from a need for friendship in his freshman year to a need for autonomy, Danny tries on the "mask" of masculinity:

> You know, friends could help you but you actually wanna do it— figure it out for yourselves before anybody could help you . . . It's just that you kind of feel in a sense that you're in a weaker state 'cause you can't figure out the problems yourself and the problems are happening to you because of that. And like none of the problems you have have ever happened to some people before and it's happening now and you don't know what to do about it.

While *wanting to want* autonomy given its association with maturity, Danny recognizes that the route to autonomy may not be the most effective strategy for helping him figure out his problems ("You know friends could help you but . . . you don't know what to do about it").

Yet he is working hard on dividing his thinking from his feeling as he tries to find a way out of his isolation:

I: Do you think that your friends know what you're really like?

D: They know the outside perimeters of my personal feelings, 'cause it's like—

I: Could you, like, clarify that?

D: My personal feelings are like how I feel about everyone. But I— But they only know what my personal ideas are of how I feel about someone.

I: You are gonna have to give me an example 'cause I just—I'm not getting it.

D: All right. My personal feelings about, like, some people in this school, like, all trying to be all gangsters and stuff, and I don't, I don't think that's the way they really are. That's my personal feelings. But

> my personal *idea* is that let them be what they wanna be, and I'll just leave my—I'll leave them alone and they'll leave me alone.

Splitting his ideas from his "personal feelings," Danny follows the conventions of masculinity according to which feelings are hidden ("I don't express what I'm really like to them") and "ideas," which are, in fact, false or inauthentic are shared. He hopes this strategy will protect him from the repercussions of honesty. Yet he knows that it will not because if he doesn't reveal his feelings, his friends will not *know* him, and thus he will not have "real" friendships. His dilemma is similar to the one Lyn Mikel Brown and Carol Gilligan describe for girls, namely, if he speaks what he feels, he will be abandoned, and if he does not speak, he will be alone.[6]

His wariness toward his peers becomes a growing wariness of the interviewer herself. After responding to numerous questions about his male friendships, Danny says in a loud and exasperated voice to his interviewer: "I do not like boys." Fearing that her persistent questions about friendships are framing him as "gay," he feels compelled to clarify the record. His irritation is heard again when asked about his ideal friendship:

> *D:* Ideal? The perfect friendship? The *Brady Bunch* style. I don't know I guess it's just everything goes well. You don't have any problems to worry about. Everyday you wake up and you walk to school. You meet the friends. And then you just have your perfect little day with the butterflies flying around outside, and that little music that you do. Stuff like that.
>
> *I:* Music? Butterflies? What is that?
>
> *D:* That's cartoon style. You said ideal.
>
> *I:* Well tell me real-life wise what a perfect friendship means to you?
>
> *D:* What I don't really believe in a real-life wise kind of perfect friendship. I don't believe there's anything as a perfect friendship for anyone. [If there were a perfect friendship] it would be having no problems whatsoever. You don't have any problems with that

person and you don't have any problems with yourself and that person doesn't have any problem with you.

Unlike most of his peers, Danny no longer has realistic ideals regarding friendships as he believes that such friendships would be impossible.

Yet he does retain his belief in the importance of friendships:

Well, of course, friendships are important. It gives you a sense of purpose in life. I mean it's part of, it's part of how you think in life. I mean, if I was—Let's say if I—everybody is gone in the entire world and I was the only one left that I would be happy 'cause I'll get anything I want without anybody to compete with me. However, like, even though I have all these special things, I'm not able to share it with somebody. I'm not able to share it with a family member or a friend. I'll be all alone. And that friend acts like a secondary family member to you 'cause you could turn to your friend for help and like problem-solving.

In his reveries about the possibilities of being the only one left "in the entire world," he recognizes that he would be alone and Danny does not want to be alone.

Senior Year: Being Alone

Now in his senior year, Danny is focused on getting ready to go to college and assume the responsibilities of manhood. He says he is still "close" to his mother, understands the way "she thinks and feels," and believes that she is sympathetic about "most things." He is less close to his father than in the previous year but still believes that his father is supportive and will encourage him to try new things and meet new people so that he has friends and new experiences. He reiterates that both of his parents want him to have friends and that they have friends themselves.

He begins his senior interview explaining the biggest change over the last year has been:

> The way I view myself has changed 'cause I mean I try to change in my own way too, like I am doing things differently, and like being more of my own character and not the character that like other people might try to be, somebody else they are not. Like I guess in truth, I was like trying to be somebody else I wasn't before. But right now, you discover new things like once you're like grown up, like once you get older, you discover new things and you don't have to be that type of person or have that type of style to fit in.

It is clear from listening to Danny over four years that this desire to be his own person—a more authentic self perhaps—grew out of his sense of alienation from his peers and, in addition, his disconnection from his peers stemmed from his desire for authenticity. The desire to be his "own character" rather than another's creation is firmly rooted in the process of identity development. Yet the missing part of the identity story—the search for who one is—is the way this process is deeply rooted in relationships and embedded in a set of masculine conventions where being "your own person" is valued over having quality relationships.

Danny continues to repeat the theme from his previous year's interview that he does not want to tell anyone his private thoughts and feelings:

> Maybe like your personal status, like what you're going through now, like if anybody's hurting you or stuff like that. I mean if it goes to a certain extent of course you would tell somebody but I mean if you think that you can fix it yourself like solve the problem on your own, you will. You might get advice, but I guess you wouldn't share it . . . it's just that, like I guess some people like to keep their own personal issues, like they like to solve it themselves before they kind of ask people for help and stuff. So I mean, sometimes you want to solve it like yourself and not have someone else.

Maturity, for Danny, is equated with silence. Alienation from one's peers is turned into a desire for autonomy that turns into silence that is implicitly justified for Danny in the name of manhood.

Danny does, however, have friends this year with whom he

plays basketball and "walks around" after school. He often goes to bed around two o'clock in the morning because he is online or on the phone chatting and sharing things—but nothing "really personal." Yet he continues to believe that "talking" to others is crucial: "You get a sense that you have somebody your own age to talk to about things, like that and I mean, you know, if you talk, if you think about it, you tell him and then he's not gonna maybe like, he probably won't laugh at you. But, I mean, he'll—you'll be able to talk to somebody about that." While his close relationships with his peers have, for the most part, disappeared, his sensitivity has not.

Danny claims that Anthony remains a friend but not a best friend. Asked to describe this friendship, he says: "It's like any friend, it's great, 'cause I mean, I've known him for that long. I know how he's like and I can like basically talk to him about almost anything that comes to mind. *I guess.*" His stoic cover (i.e., "it's great") is, however, exposed as false when he confesses to his interviewer that he never, in fact, talks seriously to Anthony because Anthony is never serious.

Asked what he dislikes about Anthony, he says:

D: I don't think that I don't have anything that I don't like. Like I don't really know. It depends on what kinds of dislikes that you are talking about, like what kind?

I: Umm, what do you mean?

D: 'cause I mean I don't know. I've known him for a long time, and like, if like, most of his dislikes I've gotten used to. I mean I don't really care.

I: Like what?

D: Like he's always making jokes and stuff like that . . . He's funny in a way and he's funny in a way that he goes like crazy sometimes and I can understand that, 'cause I've gotten used to that 'cause I know he that's type of character.

I: And is that something you didn't like about him at first, or—?

D: Not really.

I: No, so what is it that you dislike about your friendship with him? Even if it's something that you are used to already?

D: I really can't think of anything. Not really. It's just that we both annoy each other sometimes. But we always do it for fun. I mean, we all, we both know we got used to each other already so.

Danny's desire not to care stems from his desire not to be hurt. He knows by now that if he was not "used to" Anthony's insensitivity—his inability to be serious when Danny wants him to be serious—Danny would continue to feel hurt, so he gives up on trying to have a friendship with Anthony that entails being serious.

Asked what he is willing to share with Anthony, Danny says it is only the superficial facts of what he is doing that day or what "my family and I are gonna do like maybe next week or next month." He cannot tell him his "real secrets:"

> I don't know, I mean. Maybe it's not like a maybe. It's just that I know Anthony is gonna start messing around and be like, 'Oh' going up to [the girl I like] and be like, 'you know who likes you and stuff' . . . I mean I wouldn't say, I'd rather not tell him, I would just say, um. I would just let her find out first before I tell him.

Although Danny begins his response with claiming not to know, he quickly corrects himself and states bluntly that he *knows* that Anthony will betray him ("I don't know, I mean, maybe it's not like a maybe, it's just that I know"). His honesty and vulnerability is carried through the final parts of the interview when he confesses that Anthony does not know "many parts" of him and that he doesn't know Anthony either: "I don't know, maybe I don't know just how he feels inside. 'Cause he usually keeps his thoughts like most, I guess most important thoughts or what's he's thinking about like—what's going on for him. Maybe that's, maybe it's too personal to share, stuff like that." Trying to protect his friend, Danny struggles to understand why Anthony would keep his feelings to himself.

Asked to describe an ideal best friend at the end of his final year interview, Danny says:

> I guess we would just probably go to the same school, hang out every day, and talk to each other when you have problems, you discuss things. You keep in touch. That's all. I guess, for me, I mean keeping in touch is like an important thing for a friendship 'cause you gotta like talk to the person you are friends with and see what's going on so that they know that you care they know that um you're the type of person that wants to help you when you have a problem and wants to do something about it. I guess, you know for me, in order for a friendship to work, you can't like just say "hi" and "how are you doing" and that's it. I mean sometimes you have to talk to people in order to find out how they are feeling so that they have somebody else to express themselves to and they don't have to feel alone and like they're the only person in the world that has this problem.

Danny reveals how little has changed in his beliefs and desires over the four years of high school. What has changed, however, is his ability to find the friendships that he wants.

Summary

Both Fernando and Danny begin high school with an "open" and positive attitude about their friends and have intimate male friends with whom they share secrets and on whom they rely for guidance and emotional support. Gradually over the four years of high school, they become more distrustful of their peers, increasingly lonely and "independent," and less able to maintain close friendships. Both boys, however, continue to desire intimate friendships. They tell the story that so many of the boys told. While boys diverged in numerous ways, they typically followed a pattern that went from being openly emotional and vulnerable in their friendships during early and middle adolescence to being emotionally closed, distrustful, and seemingly alone by late adolescence.

The reasons for the emotional acuity of Fernando and Danny as well as their losses are suggested throughout their stories.

Their mothers provide early support for their capacity to be emotionally expressive and their ability to sustain intimate male friendships in early and middle adolescence. In addition, both sets of parents had friendships of their own and valued their children's friendships. Fernando and Danny both came from immigrant families (from the Dominican Republic and China) with "Old World" values that include being emotionally open and interdependent. Yet being immigrants may also have caused difficulties for the boys in their abilities to maintain their resistant stance by staying emotionally sensitive and having close male friendships. In a world where being foreign makes you less "cool" and thus less accepted by your American peers, Fernando and Danny may have felt more pressure to conform to the norms of emotional stoicism, independence, and physical toughness with their peers. When immigrant youth have to fight the negative stereotypes associated with being an immigrant (i.e., being dirty, not speaking English), they may well not want the added burden of being perceived as gay or girlish.

In addition, while the boys' fathers were present in their lives, they were not, as George's father was, men who consistently modeled intimate relationships for their sons (although Danny's father seemed to do that for a brief period). The lack of male role models—men with emotionally rich relationships with other men, with women, and with their children—will make it harder for boys to stay connected to their own emotional and relational worlds. Fernando and Danny suggest that it is not father absence per se that is the problem but a lack of men who are able to show them how to have emotionally intimate friendships. George had such models with his mother and father, and Nick had this model with his mother before she died, and thus they were able to stay emotionally connected during most of their adolescence.

Both Danny and Fernando also faced the challenges of being less socially accepted by their peers due to their ethnicity and, in Danny's case, his language. Both the Dominicans and the Chinese

American boys in the schools in which we collected data faced constant ethnic and racial discrimination from their peers.[7] In addition, the feminization of Asian boys, which Danny most likely experienced, may have also fed into his exasperated statement "I do not like boys." Those who are low on the peer totem pole will likely be the most defensive about their masculinity and thus also about their sexuality. For both of these boys, their gender and ethnicity (and most likely social class) as well as their experiences at home and school created their capacity for resistance to gender stereotypes during early and middle adolescence but also their gradual drift toward manly stereotypes by late adolescence.

Brown and Gilligan make the following assertion about girls who speak with clarity and honesty during late childhood, only to lose these honest voices by early adolescence:

> What choices do these girls have, growing up in this time and this place, this society and this culture: What relational paths are open to them, what can they feel and know and say and still be in connection with others, what are the economic and political as well as the psychological and educational realities of their situation?[8]

Boys are sounding like gender stereotypes and accommodating to conventions of masculinity as they reach late adolescence because they have few options given the American culture of "hyper" masculinity in which they live. In our assertions of "emotional illiteracy" and empathic deficiency, we blame the boys for their struggles rather than the social, political, and economic contexts in which they reside. The challenge for those interested in helping boys is to both reveal the thin culture that creates the problem in the first place—the naturalizing of behavior that is not only a product of culture but is bad for one's health—and use that knowledge, once acquired, to create social change, even if it means, as I will discuss in the final chapter, changing our definitions of manhood, maturity, and of human nature more generally.

CHAPTER 9

THE CRISIS
OF CONNECTION

Dana Edell, a researcher at New York University who was interested in exploring the memories of teenage girls and how these memories reflected their desires, conducted a research project that asked girls to recall the story line of the classic fairy tale turned Disney movie *The Little Mermaid*. Sharing a widely held belief that memories provide insight into the psyche or into our current feelings and expectations,[1] Dana interviewed dozens of girls throughout New York City. Most girls, she found, described the plot as a love story between a girl who is a mermaid and a boy who is human in which the girl sacrifices her voice so that she can become human and marry the boy. Some girls described the independent nature of the "mermaid," while others focused on her relationship with the prince or with her father. All, however, spoke of the love story.[2] On one occasion, Dana asked the same question to the 17-year-old boyfriend of one of the girls in her study who had come with her to be interviewed. Damian, a large-framed and athletic looking young man with his hair in cornrows, was busy checking his text messages but acknowledged that he had seen the movie with his little sister a few years before. He proceeded to give his synopsis of the plot: "It's about a girl and her fish friend, Flounder, and how they explored the deep seas together." While girls see a classic love story, Damian sees a love story of a different sort. Mirroring the boys in my studies, Damian reveals that friendships are very much on the minds of teenage boys.

The boys in my studies had and wanted male friendships to "explore the deep seas together," to share secrets, and to "be there" in times of need. They revealed a complex understanding of their social and emotional worlds that parallels the knowledge girls have during late childhood.[3] And, like girls, they were willing to express their feelings openly and freely. The gender divide—where girls don't think and boys don't feel—the virtual "DNA of the patriarchy"[4] does not capture how boys actually experience their worlds. Boys yearned for friendships without which they would "feel lost." They articulated the nuances of their relationships and described in great detail the love they had for their friends. They told us about "this thing that is deep, so deep, it's within you, you can't explain it. It's just a thing that you know that that person is that person . . . and that is all that should be important in our friendship . . . it just happens, it's human nature." Boys from diverse ethnic and racial communities described the critical role that other boys play in their lives. They spoke what they knew. And then they grew up.

Growing up for the boys in my studies, as well as for those in the best-selling boys' books such as *Real Boys*, means buying into a world where females have intimate friendships and males have buddies—a world where no one, particularly no boy, *wants* to be a girl and where emotions are separated from cognition and given gendered personalities. As boys become men, they join the generations of boys and men before them who "gave up relationships for the sake of relationships"[5] or, like Ariel, the mermaid in *The Little Mermaid,* sacrificed their voices for the sake of maintaining false relationships. In a culture where needing or wanting emotional support or intimacy is the antithesis of manliness,[6] boys during late adolescence suffer the deep alienation that comes with such an equation.

Books, magazines, and newspapers often announce with pseudoscientific certainty that women "tend to attach to other people more strongly [than men]."[7] Even articles that ask us to challenge our assumptions about boys include implicit and explicit arguments that boys should be allowed to express their inner cowboy and desire for competition, adventure, and individuation.[8] Girls and women are emotional and want relationships, and boys and men are not and do not. This division occurs in spite of the fact that we know from our nineteenth-century social historian colleagues that this divide is a relatively new phenomenon.[9] And that the taboo regarding, for example, holding hands or expressing emotions with anyone except a romantic partner or family member is found in certain cultures, such as the United States, and not in others. We know, from my studies and studies throughout the twentieth and into the twenty-first century, that boys during early and middle adolescence are openly expressing their need and desire for close relationships with their male peers.[10] We also know from neuroscientific research that emotions are an integral part of reasoning, decision-making, and rationality more broadly, and thus the separation of emotion from cognition is incoherent and misleading.[11] In addition, we know from neuroscientists like Lise Eliot that "girls are not naturally more empathic than boys; they're just allowed to express their feelings more" and that boys, as infants, are more emotional than girls.[12] The size of the gender gap, as she indicates, depends on the type of socialization the child received. And finally, we know from research in evolutionary anthropology and primatology that what has fostered our ontogeny and phylogeny is precisely our empathic, emotional, and intersubjective capacities.[13]

Nonetheless, we continue to reinforce the gender divide with its insistence that boys don't feel and have the same need or desire for emotionally intimate friendships or relationships as girls. Thus responses to the "boy crisis"[14] are focused on creating more "explosive" curricula in school[14] and having more male teachers who can teach boys how to act like "real" men rather than on helping boys have and maintain the emotional connections that they seek and that are so essential for their ability to thrive in and out of school. These responses reflect a thin understanding of the problem. The very social and emotional capacities, needs, and desires that are associated with being female and gay are not only the very same skills that are at the foundation of our survival as individuals and as a species;[15] they are also capacities, needs, and desires that boys themselves have and are explicit about if one is willing to listen. As Eliot indicates throughout her book *Pink Brain, Blue Brain,* we have greatly exaggerated the extent to which boys and girls differ biologically in core human capacities like empathy, intersubjectivity, and other forms of emotional and social intelligence.[16]

Yet we live on the surface or in the thin culture, not believing that the very skills, needs, and desires associated with being female and gay could be the key to our continued survival. Thus while we advance technologically and, in some respects, socially, we ignore the growing evidence of disconnection, isolation, and even a decline in our social and emotional skills.[17] Psychologist Sara Konrath and her colleagues conducted a meta-analysis in which they reviewed 72 studies focused on empathy among college students conducted between 1979 and 2009. The studies relied on standardized surveys to assess empathy and had participants respond to items such as "I sometimes try to understand my friends better by imagining how things look from their perspective" and "I often have tender, concerned feelings for people less fortunate than me." They concluded that feelings of empathy have declined sharply among college students since 1979, with the biggest drop happening after the year 2000.[18] Yet this finding did not make front-page news. A dramatic decline in empathy among young people is considered interesting for the media but not as newsworthy, for example, as natural disasters. However, these research findings, along with the growing list of books and articles that suggest similar declines in empathy as well as in trust, friendships, and community, do suggest a disaster especially given the known links between these social and emotional capacities and needs and physical and mental health, as well as success in school and at work, and even the length of one's life.[19]

Further evidence that we are in trouble can be found in a recent *New York Times* article titled: "A Best Friend? You Must be Kidding."[20] The journalist described how schools and camps are trying to discourage best friendships between children as they see them as potentially disruptive for other children and for teachers. The article explains that the "classic best-friend bond signals potential trouble for school officials intent on discouraging anything that hints of exclusivity, in part because of concerns about cliques and bullying." The director of counseling at a school in St. Louis is quoted as saying: "We try to talk to kids and work with them to get them to have big groups of friends and not be so possessive about friends." A camp director is quoted as saying "I don't think it's particularly healthy for a child to rely on one friend. If something goes awry, it can be devastating. It also limits a child's ability to explore other options in the world." These strategies ignore the decades of social science and health research that underscore the necessity of intimate friendships in children's and adult's lives. The problem of bullying and mean behavior does not stem from having best friendships but from feelings of isolation and loneliness. Children and adults need close friendships to foster their emotional and social capabilities. The way to protect our children from bullies, cliques, and other mean behavior is to help children form close relationships in which they learn the critical tools for success in adulthood.

While some scholars claim we are in the midst of a "boy crisis," we appear to, instead, to be in the midst of a human crisis—a "crisis of connection."[21] Relying on thin culture interpretations of boys' (or girls') academic and emotional woes such as father absence or a lack of male teachers leads us to put a band-aid on the wounds rather than address why boys and men are so injured. We know from our own instincts as well as from the scholarly literature that there are negative consequences to being emotionally shut down, having no one to turn to for emotional support, and being alone. The boys in my studies know this as well. And they express this knowledge by telling us that they will "go wacko," "use drugs," be "lonely," or even kill themselves if they are not able to express their feelings and share secrets with at least one friend. The significantly shorter life span of men compared to that of women and the spike in suicide rates of teenage boys right at the moment when the pressures to be manly—independent and stoic—intensify testify to the negative consequences of ignoring the importance of close friendships, trust, empathy, and emotionally supportive relationships more generally. Evidence is also seen in the poor school performance and low graduation rates of boys, particularly, as the research reveals, those boys who feel disconnected from or unsupported by their teachers, their peers, or both.[22]

While one could argue that the research linking close friendships, social support, and other forms of social and emotional intelligence to positive outcomes do not indicate causality, experimental studies suggest otherwise. The research that revealed the perceptual impact of having a close friend nearby when assessing the steepness of a hill suggests a causal connection.[23] These types of studies suggest that the extent to which we perceive a task or experience to be difficult or challenging will be significantly influenced by the extent to which we feel supported by others.

We know this fact from the research but we also know it from our own personal experiences. Being well supported, having others to turn to in times of distress, and having others to celebrate with makes us feel better about ourselves, our academic (or cognitive) potential, and our lives more generally. And being expressive, recognizing a need for close relationships, and being vulnerable enhances the possibility of developing such close relationships. Friendships as well as our emotional and social intelligence are central to our emotional, cognitive, and physical well-being. Yet we continue to ignore the evidence and blame female teachers, mothers, fathers, and the "feminized" school curriculum for boys' problems. We fail to see that they stem from our idealization of a stereotypic version of manhood that emphasizes independence and emotional stoicism and our devaluing of a stereotypic version of womanhood that emphasizes emotional and social skills.

Just as our masculine stereotypes rest on constructs of autonomy and stoicism, so does our definition of maturity—revealing, of course, the patriarchy at work, with manhood meaning the same thing as adulthood.[24] Responding to our emphasis on competitiveness and aggressiveness in our conceptions of human nature, primatologist Frans de Waal, who has provided extensive evidence on the empathic nature of primates, states that we need "a complete overhaul of assumptions about human nature."[25] Scholars of masculinity have argued for decades for a radical change in our conceptions of what it means to a man.[26] We also need, according to the teenage boys in my studies, an overhaul in our meaning of maturity. Rather than privileging the self-sufficient and autonomous elements, boys (and girls) suggest that we should emphasize the relational components of maturity—especially given our current crisis of connection. Evidence of maturity should, according to the boys who equate independence with loneliness, stem from being empathic and having caring and mutually supportive relationships with family members and peers. Being self-sufficient and independent are, of course, valuable parts of being mature, but we are hurting ourselves, as the boys suggest, when we focus almost exclusively on those elements of maturity. Rather than seeing the loss of connection to peers and family members as an inevitable and necessary part of development, we should see boys' and girls' social and emotional skills and their ability to have mutually supportive relationships as a significant part of the meaning of maturity itself.[27]

Yet the story of the decline in trust, friendships, and social connectedness as well as the damaging effects of gender (and racial) stereotypes on both males and females has already been told. Scholars of American culture, boys' development, masculinity, and race, as well those studying girls and women, have long noted these patterns.[28] The missing story seems to be that boys are having trusting and intimate male friendships and thus challenging gender stereotypes, especially during early and middle adolescence. They are already redefining the meaning of masculinity, maturity, and of being human. While there appear to be ethnic, racial, and, perhaps, social class and geographic (e.g., urban v. suburban v. rural) differences in the extent to which boys are resisting such stereotypes, many boys are, as a high school teacher said to me, "already doing it!" Boys do not need to be taught emotional and social skills. They already have these skills and are using them to navigate their relationships during adolescence.

The proof of boys regularly engaging in intimate male friendships and thus resisting gender stereotypes is found not only in the empirical research but also when one listens to boys who participate in school-based interventions. In the spring of 2010, I sat in on a peer counseling group in an all-boys independent school run by Michael Reichert, the school's consulting psychologist and director of the Center for the Study of Boys' and Girls' Lives, a research collaborative operated in partnership with the University of Pennsylvania. The group of 25 boys, juniors and seniors in high school, had met weekly for the past two years and now came together to say goodbye to the seniors who were graduating. The group included boys who had been referred, but most had simply volunteered to participate. Some of the boys were part of the sports program at the school, with one boy in the group being the "star" of the football team and a Division 1 college recruit. Yet all of the boys looked like stereotypic boys, with muscular bodies, wearing sweats and t-shirts with sports teams advertised on the front. I listened for an hour while each of the 10 graduating seniors in the group came to the front of the room and reported with tremendous affect, and occasionally with tears, how much the other boys in the group meant to them. They spoke with shaky voices and nervous laughter about how much they cared for and would miss seeing the other boys in the group. One boy said that when he went to his college fair, he asked about the "peer counseling" and they told him that it was an "over the phone" program. He laughed as he told the story and said: "that's not what we need." After listening to this group of manly-looking boys emote to one another for an hour, my question became how is it that we don't know this about boys? Where do our stereotypes about their emotional illiteracy or "object" orientation come from? Furthermore, how do we stem the loss of these life-sustaining skills as boys enter manhood?

A part of the answer is to begin by exposing the realities of boys' emotional and social worlds. For close to a decade, my students at New York University (students who range in age from 19 to 35) have been sending me YouTube clips, movie trailers, and accounts of conversations they have with their friends that provide evidence that boys and men are yearning for intimate male friendships. My students tell me that since they have become attuned to this particular desire, they see it "everywhere." Even the Harry Potter books and movies revolve around this theme. At the end of *The Order of the Phoenix,* the fifth volume in the Harry Potter series, Harry fends off death by Lord Voldemort by thinking about his close friendships and remembering that without love and friendships, he would not exist. Although such portrayals of friendships are often entrenched in gender stereotypes, the fact that there is so much attention to this topic in novels and in the media speaks to the widespread nature of the desire.

A 66-year-old father of one of my former students—who de-

scribes her father as "very traditional and emotionally closed"—
sees a draft of the first chapter of my book sitting on his daughter's desk and begins to read it. He tells her after completing it
that he couldn't put it down because it so accurately captured his
experience growing up. For the first time in their relationship, he
tells his daughter about his own losses of friendships and how he
longs for the intimate friendships of his adolescence. His daughter has never heard her dad speak in such emotional terms. She
is stunned. Since we began listening to boys over a decade ago, I
have also been surprised. Men of all ages approach me after
hearing my findings and tell me how deeply they identify with
the boys in my studies—boys whose demographic characteristics
they do not necessarily share except for the fact that they are
male and American. Sometimes these men tell me how they had
and lost their closest friendships, and sometimes they simply tell
me that they never had the kinds of friendships that they wanted.
They even tell me, at times, that they have not had the types of
relationships they want with either men or women because they
have felt such enormous pressure to be, as the boys put it in my
studies, "emotionless."

On a Wisconsin public radio show, I was asked to address the
issue of friendships and whether we, as children and as adults,
need such relationships. Listeners were asked to call in to ask me
questions. Two patterns emerged over the one-hour interview.
One was that few listeners had questions to ask. Most of them
simply wanted to testify that friendships were critical in their lives
or that they had lost their friendships early on and yearned to reconnect. The other was that the majority of callers were men.
One caller told a story about how he went to an event where he
was asked, along with a room full of husbands, how many considered their wives to be their best friends. The wives were asked,
in a separate room, how many considered their husbands to
be their best friends. According to the caller, 80 percent of the
men raised their hands whereas only 20 percent of the women

(according to his wife) raised their hands. He wanted to know why. After I explained to him what our gender stereotypes do to our relationships, I asked him how many men would have raised their hands had the men been asked how many *want* to have male best friends. He indicated that it likely would have been the majority of men and then paused, as if out of self-consciousness over revealing such a blatantly vulnerable belief. Manhood comes with serious costs and men know this. That is why they divulge their stories in low voices and pause as if they are trying to keep their secret contained. But, as the boys tell me, it is a secret that is no secret.

Boys' and men's desire for intimacy with other males, as well as the larger crisis of connection, does not suggest, however, that the solution is more male role models or male teachers. Men often reinforce the thin culture of manhood and maturity and encourage boys and other men to conform to gender stereotypes. Elementary and high school teachers have told me numerous stories of how boys suffer from the messages that their fathers, in particular, give them about being a man. Santos's finding that father support among middle school boys is linked to higher levels of accommodation to norms of masculinity (i.e., higher levels of emotional stoicism, physical toughness, and autonomy) points to the complex nature of father-son relationships.[29] Thus, the discussion of male role models or male teachers misses the point. Boys' suffering is a product not as much of having few men in their lives as it is of a culture that tells them to disconnect from others, including their families, in order to be men, to be mature, or "find themselves."[30] Boys don't need male role models who encourage stereotypic beliefs and behaviors. As with girls, they need people—men and women—who help them stay emotionally and socially connected to the world by being deeply connected to them.

Yet men are not the only ones who reinforce messages that are bad for boys' and girls' health. In Celine Kagan's high school class in New York City, a humanities class focused on themes of masculinity in literature, students produced short films, essays, and poems for their final projects. Ellie Schnayer, a senior in the class, wrote this poem about the conflict she feels with regard to wanting her boyfriend to "be a man," yet wanting him to be sensitive to her feelings:

Women want him, men want to be him.
Sometimes I wish you would just relax, and sit down and gaze at the world around you.
Sometimes I feel like you are trapped in a silicone bubble,
Only seeing what is fake.
What is pushed on you?
Your strength is admirable. But you don't interest me at all.
    You're a tool.
You remind me of the boys I met this summer.
You remind me of the boy who said goodbye.
Sensitive one minute, then destructive the next.
I like it when you smile and I love it when you cry with me.
But this is just too much.
You cry too much and you are a pussy.
You don't stand up for me.
You let me push you around.
I messed up and you told me it was okay.
But it wasn't.
Man-up already. I don't want to be dating a girl.
Be the stereotype.
Be my ideology, the buff guy, the gentleman, the tough guy, the provoker, the super-human, push the limits, the provider, the frat boy, the villain.
Each of these personas clash with the notion of homosexuality. But you're not gay, you're not a gentlemen either. I don't want to be dating a girl.
I like it when you smile and I love it when you cry with me.
But this is just too much.
I told you to man-up but you couldn't.

And then it changed.

You briefly became a man.

Dinners and hangouts. You toughened up. And I melted.

But you got too tough.

I flip-flop. Masculine traits you'd drop and pick up.

It was like you had to be everything at one point.

You are trapped in the silicone bubble now, with your alcoholic
    vomit and oil paint thinner.

I told you to man-up. And you did.

If only I hadn't.

If only I didn't make you feel bad for being sensitive.

If only I didn't take advantage of you, and if only I hadn't
    pushed you around.

Then I wouldn't remind myself of the boys from this summer.

Because I was like them, the way they acted, to you.

Controlling, dominant, bitchy.

And you were sensitive, sweet, and caring.

Stereotypes of the typical male infiltrated my ideal as to what
    you should have been. But weren't.

It should have been balanced. But you shouldn't have stopped
    being nice.

You stopped being NICE.

You'd hit the bottle till you puked and I'd smoke until my lungs
    shriveled.

You ruined it, dude, You changed, dude. Was it 'cause of me?

I like it when you smile and I love it when you cry with me.

But this is just too much.

My fault for pushing. My fault for the pressure. You snapped
    and I collapsed. You don't stand up for me. I messed up and
    you told me it was okay.

But it wasn't.

After Ellie reads the poem, the students are silent. Celine and I,
and most of the girls in the class, have tears in our eyes. The bell

rings and the students begin to gather around Ellie and tell her that her poem was "amazing." It *is* an "amazing" poem in its honesty and its window into the conflict that girls feel in a world in which they want a "sensitive" man but a "manly" one as well. It also repeats a thin culture story where girls are to blame for boys behavior. As her poem shows, however, boys and girls suffer in a culture where the *human* qualities of sensitivity, empathy, and emotions are given a sex and a sexuality. Hence the struggles for Ellie and her boyfriend emerge.

Evidence of girls reinforcing the conventions of masculinity is everywhere. The halls of any American high school are alive with stories of girls who want boys to be masculine in the most stereotypic and harmful of ways. On a MTV reality show that focuses on the privileged lives of New York City teenagers, one of the main characters, a 16-year-old boy, tells the audience that girls like it when boys are "assholes." A young boy in a boys' public charter school confides to a research interviewer that "girls are really messed up. . . . someone should create an all-girls school for them." When asked what he means, the boy says that many of the girls he knows want to be hit by their boyfriends because it underscores the boys' masculinity.[31] Girls openly defend Chris Brown, the pop star, who beat his pop star girlfriend Rihanna so badly that she had bruises all over her face. Girls laugh at a joke about date rape made by the host of the MTV video awards in 2009. These signs of serious trouble among girls are the product of living in a culture in which "being a girl," like being gay, is an insult (i.e., "don't be such a girl"). Ben, a 16-year-old boy in Celine Kagan's high school class, states it directly: "We are taught from an early age not to like females." The other boys *and* girls in the class agree. Girls, like boys, buy into a thin culture that implies that girls "deserve" to be hit or treated poorly by their boyfriends and that they should consider themselves lucky, in the first place, to have a boyfriend.[32] And as Ellie's poem shows us so eloquently, they also buy into the belief that being sensitive is gay

and being insensitive is manly. And when girls and women accommodate to such conventions of masculinity, it is even harder
for boys and men to resist.

The extent to which we turn a deaf ear to boys' emotional and
relational capacities raises the question of why we are so resistant
to noticing these patterns. In a world where thin interpretations
dominate, where we only believe what we see in front of us or
what lights up on the MRI scan, it is understandable that we
aren't able to see or recognize a more complex and psychological
story. As the field of psychology—whose name comes from the
Greek *psyche* which means the soul, spirit, breath, or life becomes
increasingly unpsychological and the field of sociology "dies"[33] and
is no longer able to tell interesting stories, it is not surprising that
we are blinded to what is in front of our faces. Lionel Trilling, the
renowned literary critic, noted, as previously indicated, that the
greatest "accomplishment" of our culture is that we have convinced ourselves that our thoughts and behavior can be neatly divided into that which is influenced by culture and that which is
not.[34] We are blinded to what boys are, in fact, doing and saying
because we do not believe that our beliefs about gender are a
product of culture. We make our stereotypes about boys and men
into what *is* naturally rather than what ought *not* to be culturally.

Legal scholar David Richards and psychologist Carol Gilligan claim that the opposite of patriarchy is democracy.[35] The
democracy they describe is not one that skates on the surface and
proclaims that all should have equal access to opportunities,
only to repeat the same old repressive and oppressive subjuga-
tions of the well-worn patriarchy. A "thick" democracy rejects
the hierarchical divisions of woman/man, subject/object, na-
ture/nurture, reason/emotion that perpetuate the patriarchy. In
other words, it is a democracy in which the divisions that do so
much harm to boys, girls, men, and women are no longer accepted or acceptable. The absurd is exposed as such. The opposite of patriarchy is not a fictional matriarchy where emotions
rule and thinking is passé. It is a thick democracy where think-

ing, feeling, learning, and having a range of different types of re-lationships are possible and encouraged for every "citizen." A "thick democracy" does not mean that we simply combine the stereotypical attributes of "male" and "female" or "black" and "white" but *reject*, on fundamental grounds, the idea that males and females, blacks and whites, poor and rich, straight and gay, do not share a need for intimate connections, the desire to learn, or the ability to speak about personal thoughts and feelings. In a "thick" democracy, we understand that these desires, needs, and abilities are precisely what make us human.

In her thick culture description of our evolutionary history, Sarah B. Hrdy claims:

> From a tender age and without special training, modern humans iden-tify with the plights of others and without being asked, volunteer to help and share, even with strangers. In these respects, our line of apes is a class by itself . . . This ability to identify with others and vicari-ously experience their suffering is not simply learned: it is part of us.[36]

Providing extensive anthropological evidence, Hrdy underscores the "ultra social" nature of human beings. She argues that "allo-parenting," or communal parenting where sisters, aunts, uncles, cousins, and other non-blood-related neighbors help raise chil-dren, is what, in large part, has enabled us as a species to main-tain our empathic skills over thousands of years. Other scholars have made similar arguments about the social and emotional na-ture of human beings. Using evidence from developmental psy-chology and primatology, they argue that rather than simply being selfish and aggressive, humans are also deeply caring about others, are empathic, and want to cooperate.[37]

In their book *Loneliness: Human Nature and the Need for So-cial Connection*, neuroscientists John T. Cacioppo and William Patrick write:

> As individuals, and as a society, we have everything to gain, and everything to lose, in how well or how poorly we manage our need

for human connection. With new patterns of immigration changing established cultures throughout the world, the importance of transcending tribalism to find common ground has never been greater. We need to remember not only the ways in which loneliness heightens our threat surveillance and impairs our cognitive abilities, but also the ways in which the warmth of genuine connection frees our minds to focus on whatever challenges lie before us. Both as individuals and as a society, feelings of social isolation deprive us of vast reservoirs of creativity and energy. Connection adds more water to the well that nourishes our human potential.[38]

Reading the growing body of scholarship on the social and emotional nature of humans, listening to boys and girls for close to two decades, and feeling the pulse of the culture at large, it has become obvious to me that boys and men as well as girls and women need and want emotionally rich relationships and that both sexes are struggling to find and maintain such relationships. Boys during early and middle adolescence, like girls during late childhood, know something about themselves that they lose touch with as they grow older.[39] They know what is needed to stay healthy, remain engaged in school, and succeed in their future adult lives. Yet they succumb to cultural pressures of manhood and maturity out of fear that if they don't, they will be victimized and isolated. The irony is, of course, that accommodating to such pressures is precisely what makes them feel ultimately so alone.

As theories of evolution have long taught us, we actively adapt to and respond to our environments. We can also change our environments. This dynamic process means that our beliefs and practices vary over time and across contexts. Recognizing such human variation allows us to "see" our cultural contexts. My father told me when I was a young professor studying "urban youth" that if I wanted to truly understand American youth, I should go live in China. Only by seeing another context—a context that was, at the time, dramatically different from my own—could I see what was distinctly my own. By paying attention to the cultural context of boys' and girls' development, as well as the fields of neuroscience, anthropology, developmental psychology, sociology, and primatology, the gender bifurcation of basic human capacities is exposed as a fiction, and the importance of intimate friendships and of close relationships more generally—beliefs shared by our cousins from earlier centuries and by many of our non-American cousins—is remembered.

Countries across the world are already attempting to address their own crises of connection by implementing nationwide changes. After three teenage victims of bullying committed suicide in 1983, Norway began a campaign to build children's social and emotional skills and thus decrease incidents of bullying. Professionals of all kinds were trained to identify and respond to acts of bullying, while students at all grade levels participated in weekly classroom discussions about conflicts and friendships. A quasi-experimental study was conducted on 2,500 children from 42 elementary and middle schools to determine the effects of this large-scale intervention. The results indicated that the rates of bullying dropped by half and stealing and cheating declined during the two-year period after the program began. Furthermore, significant improvements were detected in the social climate of the classroom, "as reflected in students' reports of increased satisfaction with school life and school work, improved order and discipline at school, and more positive social relationships."[40] Additional studies testing the effectiveness of large-scale bullying intervention programs have also been conducted in the 1990s in Norway and in the United States in the past ten years. The findings have been remarkably similar.[41] Fostering empathy and positive relationships makes a significant difference in children's social and academic lives, and will most assuredly help children maintain their closest friendships.

Psychologists Susan Engel and Marlene Sandstrom argue that the United States needs to revise what we understand as the function of our schools. In order to more adequately address the pervasive problem of bullying in schools as well as cyberbullying, schools need to "teach students kindness, along with algebra and history."[42] According to the boys in my studies, we do indeed need to make our schools more active in the building of social and emotional skills. Yet we do not need to "teach students" such skills—as they already have them—but to foster their development.

In sum, what would it mean for us to let "boys be boys" by nurturing their natural emotional and social capacities? Social science and health research has already given us the answer. If we were to value a full range of relationships—a biodiversity of sorts—where cognition and emotion were understood to be deeply integrated, as neuroscientists have proven,[43] and where being emotionally literate and invested in relationships were not a "girl thing," "a childish thing," or a "gay thing" but an inherent and fundamental part of being human; if we could enter into the thick of it rather than staying on the surface, these changes would lead to better psychological and physical health, less bullying, higher rates of graduation, more school engagement, better marriages, better friendships, increased satisfaction at work, longer lives, and a healthier society more generally.[44] Francisco, one of the boys in my studies, already knows this. When he describes his ideal friendship, he says: "Sensitive like me." When the interviewer asks him to explain, he says: "Um, understanding like me . . . see, you don't know that though. I know that." Believing that his male interviewer does not know what he knows, Francisco states directly what he wants and needs. In Shakespeare's tragedy King Lear, Edgar says at the end of the play: "Speak what we feel, not what we ought to say" (act 5, scene 3). The boys in my studies know this as well. They know that they risk going "wacko" if they don't have someone with whom to share their deepest secrets. Like girls at the edge of adolescence, boys know what they need. It is time to expose their "secret" and respond to their plea.

Boys Don't Cry

A mother left her child on the doorstep of school's first day.
His weeping was more bitter because he was alone
for eternity, that time that never moves for one so small
trapped in a classroom. Boys don't cry! He was soon himself
    again,
or so it seemed but he had changed. Children always do.
One poet says they are like eggs stewing in their lives,
and we have no control over what the cooking will do.
Some get harder and harder. That's the way life works,
he says, especially for boys, young men to be precise.
In the afternoon, his mother came back and he was quiet, no
    tears.
That happens when we turn on the heat that first day of school,
when we distinguish boy tears from girl tears, and tell them
boys have to tough it out. Ah, the lessons we teachers teach
when we disperse the salts of human kindness according to
    gender.

    Joseph T. Cox[45]
    Headmaster, Haverford School for Boys

NOTES

1. THE HIDDEN LANDSCAPE OF BOYS' FRIENDSHIPS

1. All of the names of the boys used throughout the book are pseudonyms.

2. John P. Hill and Mary Ellen Lynch, "The Intensification of Gender-related Role Expectations during Early Adolescence," in *Girls at Puberty: Biological and Psychosocial Perspectives,* ed. Jeanne Brooks-Gunn and Anne C. Petersen (New York: Academic Press, 1983).

3. Frederick Bonser, "Chums: A Study in Youthful Friendships," *Pedagogical Seminary* 9 (1902): 221–236.

4. William M. Bukowski, "Friendship and the Worlds of Childhood," *The Role of Friendship in Psychological Adjustment: New Directions for Child and Adolescent Development* 91 (2001): 93–105.

5. Steve Biddulph, *Raising Boys* (Calif.: Celestial Arts, 2008), 40.

6. Mathew Oransky and Jeanna Marecek, "'I'm Not Going to Be a Girl': Masculinity and Emotions in Boys' Friendships and Peer Groups," *Journal of Adolescent Research* 24 (2009): 218–241.

7. Kenneth H. Rubin, *The Friendship Factor: Helping Our Children Navigate Their Social Worlds—and Why It Matters for their Success and Happiness* (New York: Viking, 2002).

8. Ibid.

9. William Pollack, *Real Boys: Rescuing Our Sons from the Myths of Boyhood* (New York: Holt, 1998).

10. Michael Kimmel, *Guyland: The Perilous World Where Boys Become Men* (New York: HarperCollins, 2008), 55.

11. Ibid., 53.

12. Stephen Frosh, Ann Phoenix, and Rob Pattman, *Young Masculinities: Understanding Boys in Contemporary Society* (Basingstoke, England: Palgrave, 2002).

13. Dan Kindlon and Michael Thompson, *Raising Cain: Protecting the Emotional Life of Boys* (New York: Ballantine Books, 2000), 197.

14. William Julius Wilson, *The Truly Disadvantaged: The Inner City, the Underclass, and Public Policy* (Chicago: University of Chicago Press, 1987).

15. Howard C. Stevenson, "Boys in Men's Clothing: Racial Socialization and Neighborhood Safety as Buffers to Hypervulnerability in African American Males," *Adolescent Boys: Exploring Diverse Cultures of Boyhood,* ed. Niobe Way and Judy Y. Chu (New York: New York University Press, 2004), 59–77.

16. David L. Eng, *Racial Castration: Managing Masculinity in Asian America* (Durham, N.C.: Duke University Press, 2001).

17. See "Gay or Asian," *Details,* April 2004, 52; Joy Lei, "(Un)Necessary Toughness? Those 'Loud Black Girls' and Those 'Quiet Asian Boys,'" *Anthropology & Education Quarterly* 34 (2003): 158–181; Stacey Lee, "Learning about Race, Learning about 'America': Hmong American High School Students," in *Beyond Silenced Voices: Class, Race, and Gender in United States Schools,* ed. Lois Weis and Michelle Fine (Albany: State University of New York, 2005).

18. Ibid.

19. Stephanie Coontz, "How to Stay Married," *The Times of London,* November 30, 2006.

20. Peter M. Nardi, "Sex, Friendship, and Gender Roles among Gay Men," in *Men's Friendships,* ed. Peter M. Nardi (Newbury Park, Calif.: Sage, 1992), 173–185.

21. Ibid.

22. Walter L. Williams, "The Relationship between Male-Male Friendship and Male-Female Marriage: American Indian and Asian Comparisons," in Nardi, *Men's Friendships,* 191.

23. Ibid.

24. Niobe Way and L. Chen, "Close and General Friendship Quality among African American, Latino, and Asian American Adolescents from Low-income Families," *Journal of Adolescent Research* 15(2000): 274–301; Niobe Way and K. Pahl, "Individual and Contextual Predictors of Perceived Friendship Quality among Ethnic Minority, Low-income Adolescents," *Journal of Research on Adolescence* 11 (2001): 325–349; Niobe Way and M. Robinson, "A Longitudinal Study of the Effects of Family, Friends, and School Experiences on the Psychological

Adjustment of Ethnic Minority, Low-SES Adolescents," *Journal of Adolescent Research* 18 (2003): 324–346; Niobe Way, and M. Greene, "Changes in Perceived Friendship Quality during Adolescence: The Patterns and Contextual Predictors," *Journal of Research on Adolescence* 16 (2006): 293–320; L. Mikel Brown, N. Way, and J. Duff, "The Others in My I: Adolescent Girls' Friendships and Peer Relations," in *Beyond Appearances: A New Look at Adolescent Girls,* ed. N. Johnson, M. Roberts, and J. Worell (Washington, D.C.: American Psychological Association Press, 1999); Niobe Way, B. Becker, and M. Greene, "Friendships among African American, Latino, and Chinese American Adolescents in an Urban Context," in *Child Psychology: A Handbook of Contemporary Issues* 2nd ed. C. Tamis-Lemonda and L. Balter (New York: Psychology Press, 2006).

25. Harry Stack Sullivan, *The Interpersonal Theory of Psychiatry* (New York: Norton, 1953); William Bukowski, Andrew Newcomb and Willard Hartup, eds., *The Company They Keep: Friendships in Childhood and Adolescence* (Cambridge Studies in Social and Emotional Development), (Cambridge: Cambridge University Press, 1998); Michael Thompson, Catherine O'Neill-Grace, and Lawrence Cohen, *Best Friends, Worst Enemies: Understanding the Social Lives of Children* (New York: Ballantine Books, 2002); Carlos Santos, Niobe Way, and Diane Hughes, "Linking Masculinity and Education among Middle School Students," paper presented at the Society of Research on Child Development, 2011.

26. Cynthia A. Erdley, Douglas W. Nangle, Julie E. Newman and Erika M. Carpenter, "Children's Friendship Experiences and Psychological Adjustment," *The Role of Friendship in Psychological Adjustment: New Directions for Child and Adolescent Development* 91 (2001): 5–24.

27. Ibid.

28. Ibid.

29. Yueming Jia, Niobe Way, Guangming Ling, Hirokazu Yoshikawa, Xinyin Chen, Diane Hughes, Xiaoyan Ke, and Zuhong Lu, "The Influence of Student Perceptions of School Climate on Socio-Emotional and Academic Adjustment: A Comparison of Chinese and U.S. Adolescents," *Child Development* 80 (2009): 1540–1530.

30. See Santos et al., "Linking Masculinity and Education among Middle School Students." See also Maria Hernandez, Diane Hughes, Niobe Way, and Rebecca McGill, "Relationships in school as a predictor of academic engagement." Paper in progress.

31. Simone Schnall, Kent D. Harber, Jeanine K. Stefanucci, and Dennis R. Proffitt, "Social Support and the Perception of Geographi-

cal Slant," *Journal of Experimental Social Psychology* 44 (2008): 1246–1255.

32. Rebecca G. Adams and Graham Allan, *Placing Friendship in Context* (Cambridge: Cambridge University Press, 1998).

33. Kristina Orth-Gomér, Annika Rosengren and Lars Wilhelmsen, "Lack of Social Support and Incidence of Coronary Heart Disease in Middle-Aged Swedish Men," *Psychosomatic Medicine* 55 (1993): 37–43.

34. Richard Wilkinson and Kate Pickett, *The Spirit Level: Why Greater Equality Makes Societies Stronger* (London: Bloomsbury Press, 2009).

35. Ibid., 198.

36. Eric Klinenberg, *Heatwave: A Social Autopsy of Disaster in Chicago* (Chicago: University of Chicago Press, 2003).

37. Tara Parker-Pope, "Well, What Are Friends For? A Longer Life," *New York Times*, 20 April 2009.

38. Jean Anyon, "Intersections of Gender and Class: Accommodation and Resistance by Working-Class and Affluent Females to Contradictory Sex-Role Ideologies," in *Gender, Class, and Education*, ed. Stephen Walker and Len Barton (London: Taylor and Francis, 1983).

39. Niobe Way, *Everyday Courage: The Lives of Stories of Urban Adolescents* (New York: New York University Press, 1998).

40. Peg Tyre, *The Trouble with Boys: A Surprising Report Card on Our Sons, Their Problems at School, and What Parents and Educations Must Do* (New York: Crown, 2008).

41. Patricia Cohen, "In Midlife, Boomers are Happy—and Suicidal," *New York Times*, 11 June 2010.

42. See Frans de Waal, *The Age of Empathy: Nature's Lessons for a Kinder Society* (New York: Three Rivers Press, 2010). See also Jeremy Rifkin, *The Empathic Civilization: The Race to Global Consciousness in a World in Crisis* (Tarcher Penguin: New York, NY).

43. G. Stanley Hall, "The Moral and Religious Training of Children and Adolescents," *The Pedagogical Seminary* 5 (1891): 206. Italics mine.

44. Sullivan, *Interpersonal Theory of Psychiatry*, 245.

45. See Judy Y. Chu, "A Relational Perspective on Adolescent Boys' Identity Development." In *Adolescent Boys: Exploring Diverse Cultures of Boyhood*, ed. Niobe Way and Judy Y. Chu (New York: New York University Press, 2004), 78–106. See also Nigel Edley and Margaret Wetherell, "Jockeying for Position: The Construction of Masculine Identities," *Discourse and Society* 8 (1997): 203–217; Brendan

Gough, "'Biting Your Tongue': Negotiating Masculinities in Contemporary Britain," *Journal of Gender Studies* 1 (2001): 165–185; Ann Phoenix, Stephen Frosh, and Rob Pattman, "Producing Contradictory Masculine Subject Positions: Narratives of Threat, Homophobia, and Bullying in 11–14 Year Old Boys," *Journal of Social Issues* 59 (2003): 179–195; Michael Reichert and Sharon Ravich, "Defying Normative Male Identities: The Transgressive Possibilities of Jewish Boyhood," *Youth and Society* 20 (2009):1–26.

46. Frosh et al., *Young Masculinities*.

47. William S. Pollack and Todd Shuster, *Real Boys' Voices* (New York: Random House, 2000), 268.

48. Ibid., 269.

49. Malina Saval, *The Secret Lives of Boys: Inside the Raw Emotional World of Real Teens* (New York: Basic Books, 2009), 144.

50. Thompson et al., *Best Friends, Worst Enemies*.

51. Ibid., 72.

52. See Judy Y. Chu, "Adolescent Boys' Friendships and Peer Group Culture," *New Directions for Child and Adolescent Development* 107 (2005): 7–22. P. M. Camarena, P. A. Sarigiani, and A. C. Petersen, "Gender-Specific Pathways to Intimacy in Early Adolescence," *Journal of Youth and Adolescence* 19 (1990): 19–32; Beverley Fehr, *Friendship Processes* (Thousand Oaks, Calif.: Sage, 1996); Beverley Fehr, "Intimacy Expectations in Same-Sex Friendships: A Prototype Interaction Pattern Model," *Journal of Personality and Social Psychology* 86 (2004): 265–284; L. R. McNelles and J. A. Connolly, "Intimacy between Adolescent Friends: Age and Gender Differences in Intimate Affect and Intimate Behaviors," *Journal of Research on Adolescence* 9 (1999): 143–159; R. Sharabany, R. Gershoni, and J. E. Hoffman, "Girlfriend, Boyfriend: Age and Sex Differences in Intimate Friendships," *Developmental Psychology* 17 (1981): 800–808.

53. Kimberley Radmacher and Margarita Azmitia, "Are There Gendered Pathways to Intimacy in Early Adolescents' and Emerging Adults' Friendships?" *Journal of Adolescent Research* 21 (2006): 415–448.

54. Lyn Mikel Brown and Carol Gilligan, *Meeting at the Crossroads: Women's Psychology and Girls' Development* (Cambridge, Mass: Harvard University Press, 1992).

55. Carol Gilligan, *The Birth of Pleasure: A New Map of Love* (New York: Vintage, 2003).

56. Thompson et al., *Best Friends, Worst Enemies*, 56.

57. Ibid., 56.

58. Stuart Miller, *Men and Friendship* (Boston: Houghton Mifflin, 1983).

59. Ibid., xiii.

60. Daniel J. Levinson, *The Seasons of a Man's Life* (New York: Alfred Knopf, 1978).

61. Amanda E. Guyer, Erin B. McClure, Nina D. Shiffrin, Daniel S. Pine, and Eric E. Nelson, "Probing the Neural Correlates of Anticipated Peer Evaluation in Adolescence," *Child Development* 80 (2009): 1000–1115.

62. Ibid., 1013.

63. See Lise Eliot, *Pink Brain, Blue Brain: How Small Differences Grow into Troublesome Gaps—and What We Can Do about It* (New York: Mariner Books, 2010).

64. Clifford Geertz, *The Interpretation of Cultures* (New York: Basic Books, 1977).

65. Ibid.

66. Robert Putnam, *Bowling Alone: The Collapse and Revival of American Community* (New York: Simon & Schuster, 2001).

67. Michelle Porshe, Stephanie Ross, and Catherine Snow, "From Preschool to Middle School: The Role of Masculinity in Low-income Urban Adolescent Boys' Literacy Skills and Academic Achievement," *Adolescent Boys: Exploring Diverse Cultures of Boyhood*, ed. Niobe Way and Judy Chu (New York: New York University Press, 2004)

68. Putnam, *Bowling Alone*.

69. Judith Rich Harris, *The Nurture Assumption: Why Children Turn Out the Way They Do* (New York: Touchstone, 1998); Coontz, "Intimacy Unstuck."

70. Harris, *Nurture Assumption*, 357–358.

71. Miller McPherson, Lynn Smith-Lovin, and Mathew E. Brashears, "Social Isolation in America: Changes in Core Discussion Networks over Two Decades," *American Sociological Review* 71 (2006): 358.

72. Ibid.

73. Eliot, *Pink Brain, Blue Brain*.

74. Ibid., 262.

75. Frans de Waal, *The Age of Empathy*.

76. This quote is taken from a mixed method study of middle school students conducted at the Center for Research on Culture, Education, and Development that is funded by the National Science Foundation. The principal investigators of the CRCDE are Catherine Tamis-LeMonda, Niobe Way, Diane Hughes, and Hiro Yoshikawa.

77. Miller, *Men and Friendship*, 2.

78. Coontz, "Intimacy Unstuck."

79. Karen V. Hansen, "Rejection, Vulnerability and Men's Friendships," in Nardi, ed., *Men's Friendships,* 43.

80. Hansen, "Rejection, Vulnerability, and Men's friendships."

81. E. A. Rotundo, "Romantic Friendships: Male Intimacy and Middle Class Youth in the North United States 1800–1900," *Journal of Social History* 23 (1989): 1–25.

82. Hansen, "Rejection, Vulnerability and Men's Friendships," 45.

83. Williams, "The Relationship between Male-Male," 197.

84. Stevenson, "Boys in Men's Clothing."

85. Joseph H. Pleck, Freya L. Sonenstein, and Leighton C. Ku, "Masculinity Ideology: Its Impact on Adolescent Males' Heterosexual Relationship," *Journal of Social Issues* 49 (1993): 11–29; Carlos Santos, Niobe Way, Courtney Adams, and Emily Smith, "Longitudinal Patterns in Middle School Boys' Depression and Adherence to Norms of Masculinity in Friendships," paper presented at the annual meeting of the American Psychological Association, Toronto, August 15, 2009.

86. Oransky and Marecek, "I'm Not Going to Be a Girl"; Wayne Martino, "Policing Masculinities: Investigating the Role of Homophobia and Heteronormativity in the Lives of Adolescent School Boys," *Journal of Men's Studies* 8 (2007): 213–236; C. J. Pascoe, *Dude, You Are a Fag: Masculinity and Sexuality in High School* (Berkeley: University of California Press, 2007).

87. Hrdy, *Mothers and Others*; Eliot, *Pink Brain, Blue Brain*; de Waal, *The Age of Empathy*; Tomasello, *Why We Cooperate.*

88. Hrdy, *Mothers and Others*; Eliot, *Pink Brain, Blue Brain.*

89. U.S. Census 2008.

90. Pollack, *Real Boys*; Saval, *Secret Lives of Boys*; Thompson et al., *Best Friends, Worst Enemies.*

91. See Edward O'Brien, Courtney Hsing and Sara Konrath, "Changes in Dispositional Empathy over Time in American College Students," paper presented at the annual meeting of the Association for Psychological Science Boston, 2010; Putnam, *Bowling Alone.*

92. Putnam, *Bowling Alone.*

93. See Hrdy, *Mothers and Others*; Eliot, *Pink Brain, Blue Brain*; De Waal, *The Age of Empathy*; Tomasello, *Why We Cooperate.*

94. See Brown and Gilligan, *Meeting at the Crossroads*; Pedro Noguera, *The Trouble with Black Boys: And Other Reflections on Race, Equity, and the Future of Public Education* (San Francisco: Jossey-Bass, 2008); Theresa Perry, "Up from the Parched Earth: Toward a Theory of African American Achievement," in *Young, Gifted, and*

Black: Promoting High Achievement among African-American Students, ed. Theresa Perry, Claude Steele, and Asa Hilliard (Boston: Beacon Press, 2003), 1–87; Michelle Fine, "Sexuality, Schooling and Adolescent Females: The Missing Discourse of Desire," *Harvard Educational Review* 58 (1988): 29–53; Bell Hooks, *Black Looks: Race and Representation* (Boston: South End Press, 1992); Anyon, "Intersections of Gender and Class.

2. INVESTIGATING BOYS, FRIENDSHIPS, AND HUMAN NATURE

1. Harry Stack Sullivan, *The Interpersonal Theory of Psychiatry,* (New York: Norton, 1953), 245.

2. See Niobe Way, *Everyday Courage: The Lives and Stories of Urban Adolescents,* (New York: NYU Press, 1998).

3. Reed Larson, Bradford B. Brown, and Jeylan Mortimer, ed., *Adolescents Preparation for the Future: Perils and Promise: A Report on the Study Group of Adolescence in the twenty-first Century* (Ann Arbor: Society for Research on Adolescence, 2002), 55.

4. See Way, *Everyday Courage.*

5. Orlando Patterson, "The Last Sociologist," *New York Times,* May 19, 2002.

6. The analogy of the kitchen stove is drawn from the work of Adrian Staub at the University of Massachusetts, Amherst.

7. Urie Bronfenbrenner, "Toward an Experimental Ecology of Human Development," *American Psychologist* 32 (1977): 513–531.

8. For further discussion of the ways stereotypes shape identities and relationships see: Cynthia Garcia Coll, G. Lamberty, and B. Wasik, "An Integrative Model for the Study of Developmental Competencies in Minority Children," *Child Development* 67 (1996): 1891–1914; M. B. Spencer, D. Dupree, and T. Hartmann, "A Phenomenological Variant of Ecological Systems Theory (PVEST): A Self-Organization Perspective in Context," *Development and Psychopathology* 9 (1997): 817–833; Joy Lei, "(Un)Necessary Toughness? Those 'Loud Black Girls' and Those 'Quiet Asian Boys,'" *Anthropology & Education Quarterly* 34 (2003): 158–181.

9. Jean Anyon, "Intersections of Gender and Class: Accommodation and Resistance by Working-Class and Affluent Females to Contradictory Sex-Role Ideologies," in *Gender, Class and Education,* ed. Stephen Walker and Len Barton (London: Taylor and Francis, 1983); L. Brown and Carol Gilligan, "Listening for Voice in Narratives of Relationship," in *New Directions in Child Development: Narrative and Storytelling: Implications for Understanding Moral Development,* ed. M. Tappan

and M. Packer 54 (1991): 43–62; Janie V. Ward, "Raising Resisters: The Role of Truth Telling in the Psychological Development of African American Girls," in *Urban Girls: Resisting Stereotypes, Creating Identities*, ed. Bonnie J. Ross Leadbeater and Niobe Way (New York: New York University Press, 1996); Carol Gilligan, *The Birth of Pleasure: A New Map of Love* (New York: Vintage, 2003).

10. Antonia Damasio, *Descartes' Error: Emotion, Reason, and the Human Brain* (New York: Harper Perennial, 1995); Sarah B. Hrdy, *Mothers and Others: Maternal Instincts and How They Shape the Human Species* (Cambridge, Mass.: Harvard University Press; Lise Eliot, *Pink Brain, Blue Brain: How Small Differences Grow into Troublesome Gaps—and What We can Do about It* (New York: Mariner Books, 2010); Frans de Waal, *The Age of Empathy: Nature's lessons for a Kinder Society* (New York: Three Rivers Press, 2010); Michael Tomasello, *Why we cooperate* (Cambridge: MIT Press, 2009).

11. For an exception, see Xinyin Chen, Doran French, and Barry Schneider, *Peer Relationships in Cultural Context, Cambridge Studies in Social and Emotional Development* (Cambridge: Cambridge University Press, 2006).

12. Peg Tyre, *The Trouble with Boys: A Surprising Report Card on Our Sons, Their Problems at School and What Parents and Educators Must Do* (New York: Crown, 2008); Leonard Sax, *Boys Adrift: The Five Factors Driving the Growing Epidemic of Unmotivated Boys and Underachieving Young Men* (New York: Basic Books, 2007).

13. Of the students who score a perfect math SAT approximately 70 percent are boys. See Richard Whitmore. *Why boys fail.* (Amacom, 2010). See also Nicholas Kristof, "The Boys Have Fallen Behind," *New York Times,* 28 March 2010: WK12.

14. Tyre, *The Trouble with Boys;* Sax, *Boys Adrift.*

15. Ibid.

16. Pedro Noguera, *The Trouble with Black Boys and Other Reflections on Race, Equity, and the Future of Public Education* (San Francisco: Jossey-Bass, 2008), 21; Tyre, *Trouble with Boys,* 43.

17. Dan Kindlon and Michael Thompson, *Raising Cain: Protecting the Emotional Life of Boys* (New York: Ballantine, 2000).

18. Susan K. Egan and David G. Perry, "Gender Identity: A Multidimensional Analysis with Implications for Psychosocial Adjustments," *Developmental Psychology* 37 (2001): 451–463. See also David G. Perry and Kay Bussey, *Social Development* (New Jersey: Prentice Hall, 1984).

19. Chu, "Relational Perspective."

20. For a detailed discussion of this argument, see Leonard Sax, *Why Gender Matters: What Parents and Teachers Need to Know about the Emerging Science of Sex Differences* (New York: Random House, 2006).

21. Michael Gurian, *A Fine Young Man: What Parents, Mentors, and Educators Can Do to Shape Adolescent Boys into Exceptional Men* (New York: Putnam, 1998), 5.

22. For critiques of the biologically based scholarship explaining the "boy crisis," see Tyre, *Trouble with Boys*; Eliot, *Pink Brain, Blue Brain*.

23. Eliot, *Pink Brain, Blue Brain*, 16.

24. Hrdy, *Mothers and Others*, 2009.

25. Ibid.; *Eliot, Pink Brain, Blue Brain*.

26. Lionel Trilling, *Freud and the Crisis of Our Culture* (Boston: Beacon Press, 1955), 58.

27. Tyre, *Trouble with Boys*.

28. Richard Whitmire, *Why Boys Fail: Saving our Sons from an Educational System That's Leaving Them Behind* (New York: AMACOM, 2010).

29. Nicholas Kristof, "The Boys Have Fallen Behind," *New York Times*, 28 March 2010: WK12.

30. Michelle Porshe, Stephanie Ross, and Catherine Snow, "From Preschool to Middle School: The Role of Masculinity in Low-income Urban Adolescent Boys' Literacy Skills and Academic Achievement. In ed. Niobe Way and Judy Chu *Adolescent Boys: Exploring Diverse Cultures of Boyhood*, (New York: New York University Press, 2004).

31. R. W. Connell, *Masculinities* (Berkeley: University of California Press, 2005), xiii.

32. C. J. Pascoe *Dude, You're a Fag* (Berkeley: University of California Press, 2007).

33. Saval, *Secret Lives of Boys*.

34. Noguera, *Trouble with Black Boys*.

35. Ann Ferguson, *Bad Boys: Public Schools in the Making of Black Masculinity* (Ann Arbor: University of Michigan Press, 2001).

36. This class takes place each year in the Little Red School House and Elisabeth Irwin High School.

37. Niobe Way and Yueming Jia, "Close friendships of Chinese Boys" Paper presented at the Society for Research on Child Development, March, 2009.

38. Kindlon and Thompson, *Raising Cain*, 90.

39. Gurian, *Fine Young Man*, 53.

40. William Pollack, *Real Boys' Voices* (New York, Penguin, 2000), 266

41. Michael Thompson, Catherine O'Neill-Grace, and Lawrence Cohen, *Best Friends, Worst Enemies: Understanding the Social Lives of Children* (New York: Ballantine Books, 2002).

42. Elizabeth Bergner Hurlock, *Adolescent Development* (New York: McGraw-Hill, 1949).

43. Frederick Bonser, "Chums: A Study in Youthful Friendships," *Pedagogical Seminary*, 9 (1902): 221.

44. Sullivan, *Interpersonal Theory of Psychiatry*, 246.

45. Ibid, 245.

46. Ibid., 245.

47. Duane Buhrmester and Wyndol Furman, "The Development of Companionship and Intimacy," *Child Development* 58 (1987): 1101–1113.

48. See Thomas Berndt, "Relations between Social Cognition, Nonsocial Cognition, and Social Behavior: The Case of Friendship," *Social Cognitive Development*, ed. John H. Flavell and Lee Ross (New York: Cambridge University Press: 1981) 176–189; Brian J. Bigelow and John J. La Gaipa, "The Development of Friendship, Values and Choice," *Friendship and Social Relations in Children*, ed. Hugh C. Foot, Anthony J. Chapman, and Jean R. Smith (Chichester, England: Wiley, 1980) 15–44; Wyndol Furman and Karen L. Bierman, "Children's Conceptions of Friendship: A Multimethod Study of Developmental Changes," *Developmental Psychology* 20 (1984): 925–933.

49. See Christopher M. Oldenburg and Kathryn A. Kerns, "Associations between Peer Relationships and Depressive Symptoms: Testing Moderator Effects of Gender and Age," *Journal of Early Adolescence* 17 (1997): 319–337; Eric M. Vernberg, "Experiences with Peers Following Relocation during Early Adolescence," *American Journal of Orthopsychiatry* 60 (1990): 466–472; Julia H. Bishop and Heidi M. Inderbitzen, "Peer Acceptance and Friendship: An Investigation of Their Relation to Self-Esteem," *Adolescence* 15 (1995): 476–489; Michael A. R. Townsend, Helen E. McCracken, and Keri M.Wilton, "Popularity and Intimacy as Determinants of Psychological Well-Being in Adolescent Friendships," *Journal of Early Adolescence* 8 (1988): 421–436; Douglas W. Nangle, Cynthia A. Erdley, Julie E. Newman, Craig A. Mason, and Erika M. Carpenter, "Popularity, Friendship Quantity, and Friendship Quality: Interactive Influences of Children's Loneliness and Depression," *Journal of Clinical Child and Adolescent Psychology* 32 (2003): 546–555; Michael Thompson et al., *Best Friends,*

Worst Enemies; Carlos Santos, Niobe Way and Diane Hughes, "Linking Masculinity and Education among Middle School Students," Paper presented at the Society of Research on Child Development, March, 2011.

50. Furman and Bierman, "Children's Conceptions of Friendship."

51. Ibid.

52. B. Bradford Brown and James Larson. "Peer Relationships in Adolescence." In *Handbook of Adolescent Psychology*. (Wiley & Sons, 2009). 74-104.

53. See Gary W. Ladd, *Children's Peer Relations and Social Competence: A Century of Progress* (New Haven: Yale University Press, 2005); Robert Selman and Keith Yeates, "The Social Regulation of Intimacy and Autonomy in Early Adolescence," in *Moral Development through Social Interaction,* ed. W. M. Kurtines and J. L. Gewirtz (New York: Wiley and Sons, 1987), 44–101; Ruth Sharabany, R. Gershoni, and J. E. Hoffman, "Girlfriend, boyfriend: Age and Sex Differences in Intimate Friendships," *Developmental Psychology* 17 (1981): 800–808.

54. Douglas W. Nangle and Cynthia A. Erdley, eds., *The Role of Friendship in Psychological Adjustment* (San Francisco: Jossey-Bass, 2001); Amanda Rose and Karen Rudolph, "A Review of Sex Differences in Peer Relationship Processes: Potential Trade-offs for the Emotional and Behavioral Development of Girls and Boys," *Psychological Bulletin* 132 (2006): 98–131.

55. Niobe Way and Lisa Chen, "Close and General Friendships among African American, Latino, and Asian American Adolescents from Low-Income Families," *Journal of Adolescent Research* 15 (2000): 274–301.

56. Rose and Rudolph, "Review of Sex Differences"; Denis Jarvinen and John Nicholls, "Adolescents' Social Goals, Beliefs about the Causes of Social Success, and Satisfaction in Peer Relations," *Developmental Psychology* 32 (1996): 435–441; Jacques Lempers and Dania Clark-Lempers, "A Functional Comparison of Same-Sex and Opposite Sex Friendships during Adolescence," *Journal of Adolescent Research* 8 (1993): 89–108; Jeffrey Parker and Steven Asher, "Friendship Quality in Middle Childhood: Links with Peer Groups Acceptance and Feeling of Loneliness and Social Dissatisfaction," *Developmental Psychology* 29 (1993): 611–621; Duane Buhrmester, "Need Fulfillment, Interpersonal Competence, and the Developmental Contexts of Early Adolescent Friendship," in *The Company They Keep: Friendship in Childhood and Adolescence, Cambridge Studies in Social and Emotional Development* ed. William Bukowski, Andrew Newcomb, and Willard Hartup (New York: Cambridge University Press, 1996), 158–185.

57. See Kimberley Radmacher and Margarita Azmitia, "Are There Gendered Pathways to Intimacy in Early Adolescents' and Emerging Adults' Friendships?" *Journal of Adolescent Research* 21 (2006): 415–448; P. M. Camarena, P. A. Sarigiani, and A. C. Petersen, "Gender-Specific Pathways to Intimacy in Early Adolescence," *Journal of Youth and Adolescence* 19 (1990) 19–32; Beverley Fehr, "Intimacy Expectations in Same-Sex Friendships: A Prototype Interaction Pattern Model," *Journal of Personality and Social Psychology,* 86 (2004): 265–284; L. R. McNelles and J. A. Connolly, "Intimacy between Adolescent Friends: Age and Gender Differences in Intimate Affect and Intimate Behaviors," *Journal of Research on Adolescence* 9 (1999): 143–159; Sharabany et al., "Girlfriend, Boyfriend."

58. Cynthia A. Erdley, Douglas W. Nangle, Julie E. Newman, and Erika M. Carpenter, "Children's Friendship Experiences and Psychological Adjustment: Theory and Research," in Nangle and Erdley, 5–24.

59. Virginia S. Burks, Kenneth A. Dodge, and Joseph M. Price, "Models of Internalizing Outcomes of Early Rejection," *Developmental and Psychopathology* 7 (1995): 683–696.

60. Duane Buhrmester, "Intimacy of Friendship, Interpersonal Competence, and Adjustment during Preadolescence and Adolescence," *Child Development* 61 (1990): 1101–1111.

61. See Valerie Hey, *The Company She Keeps: An Ethnography of Girls' Friendships* (England: Open University Press, 1997).

62. Margarita Azmitia, Kimberley Radmacher, and Moin Syed, eds. *The Intersections of Personal and Social Identities: New Directions for Child and Adolescent Development* (San Francisco: Jossey-Bass, 2008).

63. See Azmitia et al., *Intersections of Personal and Social Identities;* Way and Chu, *Adolescent Boys*; Thompson et al., *Best Friends, Worst Enemies.*

64. Stuart Miller, *Men and Friendship* (London: Gateway Books, 1983).

65. Ibid., xii.

66. Geoffrey L. Grief, *The Buddy System: Understanding Male Friendship* (New York: Oxford University Press, 2009).

67. David Levinson, *The Seasons of a Man's Life* (New York: Knopf, 1978), 335.

68. Geoffrey L. Greif, *The Buddy System,* 87.

69. John Bowlby, *Attachment and Loss: Vol. 1: Attachment* (New York: Basic Books, 1969).

70. Michael S. Kimmel and Michael A. Messner, *Men's Lives* (New York: Macmillan, 1989); Raewyn W. Connell, *Masculinities* (Cambridge: Polity, 1995); Joseph H. Pleck, Freya L. Sonenstein, and C. Ku Leighton, "Masculinity Ideology: Its Impact on Adolescent Male's Heterosexual Relationships," *Journal of Social Issues* 49 (1993): 11–29.

71. Pleck et al., "Masculinity Ideology: Its Impact on Adolescent Male's Heterosexual Relationships," 11–29.

72. Kimmel and Messner, *Men's Lives,* 1989. Edward H. Thompson, Jr., and Joseph H. Pleck, "Masculinity Ideologies: A Review of Research Instrumentation on Men and Masculinities," in *A New Psychology of Men,* ed. Ronald F. Levant and William S. Pollack (New York: Basic Books, 2003), 129–163.

73. Kimmel and Messner, *Men's Lives,* 10.

74. Carol Gilligan and David A. J. Richards, *The Deepening Darkness: Patriarchy, Resistance, and Democracy's Future* (New York: Cambridge University Press, 2009); Connell, *Masculinities.*

75. Michael Kimmel, *The Gendered Society* (Oxford: Oxford University Press, 2007); See also Aida Hurtado and Mrinal Sinha, "More Than Men: Latino Feminist Masculinities and Intersectionality," *Sex Roles* 59 (2008): 337–349; Aida Hurtado and Mrinal Sinha, "Restriction and Freedom in the Construction of Sexuality: Young Chicanas and Chicanes Speak Out," *Feminism & Psychology* 15 (2005), 33–38.

76. Deborah David and Robert Brannon, "The Male Sex Role: Our Culture's Blueprint of Manhood, and What It's Done for Us Lately," in *The Forty-Nine Percent Majority: The Male Sex Role,* ed. Deborah David and Robert Brannon (Reading, Mass.: Addison-Wesley, 1976), 1–45.

77. Michael V. Cicone and Diane N. Ruble, "Beliefs about Males," *Journal of Social Issues* 34 (1976): 5–16.

78. Caroline New, "Oppressed and Oppressors? The Systematic Mistreatment of Men," *Sociology* 35 (2001): 740.

79. Reed W. Larson and Joseph H. Pleck, "Hidden Feelings: Emotionality in Boys and Men," in *Gender and Motivation: Nebraska Symposium on Motivation,* ed. Dan Bernstein (Lincoln: University of Nebraska Press, 1999), 25–74; Guillermo Arciniega, Thomas Anderson, Zoila Tovar-Blank, and Terence Tracey, "Toward a Fuller Conception of Machismo: Development of a Traditional Machismo and Caballerismo Scale," *Journal of Counseling Psychology* 55 (2008): 19–33; Ramaswami Mahalingam and Sundari Balan, "Culture, Son

Preference and Beliefs about Masculity," *Journal of Research on Adolescents* 18 (2008): 541–545.

80. Arciniega et al., "Toward a Fuller Conception of Machismo."

81. Mahalingam and Balan, "Culture, Son Preference and Beliefs about Masculinity."

82. Richard F. Lazur and Richard Majors, "Men of Color: Ethnocultural Variations of Male Gender Role Strain," in Levant and Pollack, *A New Psychology of Men;* Rafael L. Ramirez, *What It Means to Be a Man: Reflections on Puerto Rican Masculinity,* (New Brunswick, N.J.: Rutgers University Press, 1999). Jose Abreu, Rodney Goodyear, Alvaro Campos, and Michael Newcomb, "Ethnic Belonging and Traditional Masculinity Ideology among African Americans, European Americans, and Latinos," *Psychology of Men & Masculinity* 1 (2000): 75–86; Wizdom Hammond and Jacqueline Mattis, "Being a Man about It: Manhood Meaning among African American Men," in *Psychology of Men & Masculinity* 6 (2005): 114–126; Andrea Hunter and James Davis, "Constructing Gender: An Exploration of Afro-American Men's Conceptualization of Manhood," *Gender & Society* 6 (1992): 464–479; Hurtado and Sinha, "More than Men"; Hurtado and Sinha, "Restriction and Freedom"

83. Abreu et al., "Ethnic Belonging and Traditional Masculinity Ideology"; Hammond and Mattis, "Being a Man about It"; Hunter and Davis, "Constructing Gender; Clyde Franklyn, "Hey, Home-Yo, Bro': Friendships among Black Men," in *Men's Friendships,* ed. Peter M. Nardi (Newbury Park, Calif.: Sage Publications, 1992). 201-215.

84. Hurtado and Sinha, "More Than Men."

85. Michael Kimmel, *Guyland: The Perilous World Where Boys Become Men,* (New York: Harper Collins, 2008), 44–45.

86. Ibid., 25–74, 531–543; Marianne LaFrance and Mahzarin Banaji, "Toward a Reconsideration of the Gender-Emotion Relationship," in *Emotion and Social Behavior,* ed. M. S. Clark (Newbury Park, Calif.: Sage, 1992), 178–201; Larson and Joseph, "Hidden Feelings," 25–74; Edward H. Thompson and Joseph H. Pleck, "The Structure of Male Role Norms," *American Behavioral Scientist* 29 (1986): 531–543.

87. Bambi B. Schieffelin, *The Give and Take of Everyday Life: Language Socialization of Kaluli Children* (Cambridge: Cambridge University Press, 1990), 249.

88. Lazur and Majors, "Men of Color," 337–358.

89. Ibid.; Arciniega et al., "Toward a Fuller Conception of Machismo," 19–33. Richard Majors and Janet M. Billson, *Cool Pose: The Dilemmas of Black Manhood in America* (New York: Touchstone, 1993).

90. A. H. Fischer and A. S. R. Manstead, "The Relation between Gender and Emotion in Different Cultures," in *Gender and Emotion: Social Psychological Perspectives,* ed. A. H. Fischer (Cambridge: Cambridge University Press, 2000), 71–94.

91. Larson and Pleck, "Hidden Feelings," 25–74.

92. Gigliana Melzi and Camila Fernández, "Talking about Past Emotions: Conversations between Peruvian Mothers and their Preschool Children," *Sex Roles* 50 (2004): 641–657.

93. Santos Carlos, Niobe Way, Dalia Levy, Taveeshi Gupta, Thiago Marques, and Lisa Silverman, "Beyond the Machismo Paradigm: Puerto Rican Boys' Narratives of Friendships," paper presented at the biennial meeting of the *Society for Research in Child Development,* Denver in March 27, 2009.

94. Taveeshi Gupta, Niobe Way, Carlos Santos, Preetika Mukherjee and Diane Hughes, "Male Gender Norms across India, China and the USA and Their Link to Psychological Well-Being—A Cross-Cultural Analysis," poster presented at the biennial conference of the Society for Research on Adolescence, Philadelphia, March 2010.

95. Kathleen Boykin McElhaney, Joseph Allen, Claire Stephenson, and Amanda Hare, "Attachment and Autonomy during Adolescence," in *Handbook of Adolescent Psychology: Individual Bases of Adolescent Development,* 3rd ed. (Hoboken: Wiley, 2009), 358–403.

96. Lyn Mikel Brown, Sharon Lamb, and Mark Tappan, *Packaging Boyhood: Saving Our Sons from Superheroes, Slackers and Other Media Stereotypes* (New York: St. Martin's Press, 2009), 8.

97. H. R. Markus and S. Kitayama, "Culture and the Self: Implications for Cognition, Emotion and Motivation," *Psychological Review* 38 (1991), 224–253; Melzi and Fernández, "Talking about Past Emotions" Robin Harwood, Joan Miller, and Nydia Lucca Irizarry, *Culture and Attachment: Perceptions of the Child in Context* (New York: Guilford Press, 1995); Hammond and Mattis, "Being a Man about It": Mary Brabeck, "The Moral Self, Values, and Circles of Belonging," in *Women's Ethnicities: Journeys through Psychology,* ed. Karen Fraser Wyche and Faye J. Crosby (Boulder, Colo.: Westview Press, 1996), 145–165; Mary Brabeck, "Models of Self among Young Men in the Guatemalan Highlands," in *Challenges of Cultural and Racial Diversity to Counseling,* ed. Gerardo Gonzalez, Isaura Alvarado, and Alberto Segrera (Alexandria, Va.: American Counseling Association, 1993), 12–19.

98. My studies in the U.S. are done in collaboration with Diane Hughes. In China, my collaborators are Yuemuy Jic, Hiro Yoshikawa, Xinyin Chen, Zuhong Lu, Dena He. In India, the project is led by Toweeshi Gupta and I serve as the Senior Advisor.

99. Gupta et al., "Male Gender Norms across China and the USA."

100. Ibid.

101. Connell, *Masculinities*.

102. Joseph H. Pleck, *The Myth of Masculinity* (Boston: The MIT Press, 1983); Pleck et al., "Masculinity Ideology," 11–29.

103. New, "Oppressed and Oppressors?"

104. Connell, *Masculinities*.

105. Pleck et al., *Masculinity Ideology*, 11–29.

106. Ibid.

107. Ibid.

108. Kristen Springer and Dawne Mouzon, "Masculinity and Healthcare Seeking among Midlife Men: Variation by Social Context," paper presented at the annual meeting of the American Sociological Association, Boston in July, 2008.

109. Ibid.

110. G. E. Good and P. K. Wood, "Male Gender Role Conflict, Depression, and Help Seeking: Do College Men Face Double Jeopardy?," *Journal of Counseling & Development* 74 (1995): 70–75; G. E. Good, P. P. Heppner, K. A. DeBord, and A. R. Fischer, "Understanding Men's Psychological Distress: Contributions of Problem-Solving Appraisal and Masculine Role Conflict," *Psychology of Men & Masculinity* 5 (2004): 168–177; J. R. Mahalik and A. B. Rochlen, "Men's Likely Responses to Clinical Depression: What Are They and Do Masculinity Norms Predict Them?," *Sex Roles* 55 (2006): 659–667.

111. Frosh et al., *Young Masculinities*.

112. Eugene D. Genovese, *Roll, Jordan, Roll: The World the Slaves Made* (London: Vintage, 1976), 658.

113. C. West and D. H. Zimmerman, "Doing Gender," *Gender and Society* 1 (1987): 125–151.

114. See Lyn Mikel Brown and Carol Gilligan, *Meeting at the Crossroads: Women's Psychology and Girls' Development* (Cambridge, Mass.: Boston University Press, 1992); Ward, "Raising Resisters."

115. Anyon, "Intersections of Gender and Class."

116. Ibid., 44.

117. Brown and Gilligan, *Meeting at the Crossroads*.

118. Ibid.

119. Gilligan, *Birth of Pleasure*.

120. Ibid., 133.

121. Ward, "Raising Resisters."

122. Ibid.; Lazur and Majors, "Men of Color," 341. Signithia Fordham and John Ogbu, "Black Students' School Success: Coping with the 'Burden of Acting White,'" *Urban Review* 18 (1986): 176–206.

123. Ward, "Raising Resisters," 85–99.

124. Lazur and Majors, "Men of Color," 337–358; Neff et al., "Machismo," 458–463.

125. Gilligan, *Birth of Pleasure*, 73.

126. Judy Chu, "A Relational Perspective on Adolescent Boys' Identity Development," in Niobe Way & Judy Chu *Adolescent Boys: Exploring Diverse Culture of Boyhood*, 78–106.

127. Ibid.,18.

128. Deborah Tolman, Renee Spencer, Tricia Harmon, Myra, Rosen-Reynoso, and Mge Striepe, "Getting Close, Staying Cool: Early Adolescent Boys' Experiences with Romantic Relationships," in Way and Chu *Adolescent Boys*, 235–255.

129. Frosh et al., *Young Masculinities*.

130. Nigel Edley and Margaret Wetherell, "Jockeying for Position: The Construction of Masculine Identities," *Discourse and Society* 8 (1997): 203–217; Brendan Gough, "'Biting Your Tongue': Negotiating Masculinities in Contemporary Britain," *Journal of Gender Studies* 1 (2001): 165–185.

131. Gilberto Conchas and Pedro Noguera, "Understanding the Exceptions: How Small Schools Support the Achievement of Academically Successful Black Boys." In Way and Chu *Adolescent Boys: Exploring Diverse Cultures* of Boyhood, 317-338.

132. Michael Reichert and Sharon Ravich, "Defying Normative Male Identities: The Transgressive Possibilities of Jewish Boyhood," *Youth and Society* 20 (2009): 1–26.

133. Gary Barker, *Dying to Be Men* (New York: Routledge, 2005).

134. Carlos Santos, *The Missing Story: Resistance to Ideals of Masculinity in the Friendships of Middle School Boys,* (Ph.D. diss.: New York University, 2010). Research for this study was conducted at the Center for Research on Culture, Development, and Education (CRCDE) under the direction of principle investigators Catherine Tamis-LeMonda, Niobe Way, Diane Hughes and Hiro Yoshikawa. It is funded by the National Science Foundation.

135. Santos et al., "Linking Masculinity and Education among Middle School Students".

136. Damasio, *Descartes' Error.*

137. De Waal, *Age of Empathy,* 7.

138. Ibid.

139. Ibid. 8.

140. Ibid., 43, 60.

141. Hrdy, *Mothers and Others.*

142. Ibid; For additional discussion of the decline in empathy, see Edward O'Brien, Courtney Hsing, and Sara Konrath, *Changes in Dispositional Empathy over Time in American College Students,* poster presented the annual meeting of the Association for Psychological Science, Boston, August 25th 2010.

143. Eliot, *Pink Brain, Blue Brain;* Tomasello, *Why We Cooperate.*

144. Eliot, *Pink Brain, Blue Brain,* 262.

145. Ibid., 74.

146. Ibid., 74.

147. O'Brien et al., *Changes in Dispositional Empathy.* Robert Putnam, *Bowling Alone: The Collapse and Revival of American Community* (New York: Simon & Schuster, 2001); John T. Cacioppo and William Patrick, *Loneliness: Human Nature and the Need for Social Connection* (New York: Norton, 2009).

148. I am drawing from data from my Relationships Among Peers (R.A.P.) study, my Connections Study, and my study of youth in Boston that was the basis of my doctoral dissertation.

149. U.S. Census, 2008

150. Han-Georg Gadamer, "The Problem of Historical Consciousness," in *Interpretive Social Science: A Second Look,* ed. Paul Rabinow and William M. Sullivan (Berkeley: University of California Press, 1979), 82–140.

151. Brown and Gilligan, *Meeting at the Crossroads.*

152. Ibid.

3. "SOMETIMES YOU NEED TO SPILL YOUR HEART OUT TO SOMEBODY"

1. These themes are also noted in Michael Thompson, Catherine O'Neill-Grace, and Lawrence Cohen, *Best Friends, Worst Enemies: Understanding the Social Lives of Children* (New York: Ballantine Books, 2002).

2. Jean Anyon, "Intersections of Gender and Class: Accommodation and Resistance by Working-Class and Affluent Females to Contradic-

tory Sex-Role Ideologies," in *Gender, Class and Education,* ed. Stephen Walker and Len Barton (London: Taylor and Francis, 1983).

3. See Lyn Mikel Brown, Sharon Lamb, and Mark Tappan, *Packaging Boyhood: Saving our Sons from Superheroes, Slackers, and Other Media Stereotypes* (New York: St. Martin's Press, 2009), 39.

4. See Niobe Way, *Everyday Courage: The Lives and Stories of Urban Teenagers* (New York University Press, 1998).

5. Brown et al., *Packaging Boyhood,* 29.

4. BOYS WITH FEELINGS

1. Judy Y. Chu, "Adolescent Boys' Friendships and Peer Group Culture," *New Directions for Child and Adolescent Development* 107 (2005): 7–22; Stephen Frosh, Ann Phoenix and Rob Pattman, *Young Masculinities: Understanding Boys in Contemporary Society* (Basingstoke, England: Palgrave, 2002); Margarita Azmitia, Kimberley Radmacher, and Moin Syed, eds. *The Intersections of Personal and Social Identities: New Directions for Child and Adolescent Development* (San Francisco: Jossey-Bass, 2008); Deborah Tolman, Renee Spencer, Tricia Harmon, Myra Rosen-Reynoso, and Meg Striepe, "Getting Close, Staying Cool: Early Adolescent Boys' Experiences with Romantic Relationships," in *Adolescent Boys: Exploring Diverse Cultures of Boyhood,* ed. Niobe Way and Judy Chu (New York: New York University Press, 2004), 235–255; William Pollack, *Real Boys' Voices* (New York, Penguin, 2000); Michael Thompson, Catherine O'Neill-Grace, and Lawrence Cohen, *Best Friends, Worst Enemies: Understanding the Social Lives of Children* (New York: Ballantine Books, 2002).

2. Carlos Santos, *"The Missing Story: Resistance to Ideals of Masculinity in the Friendships of Middle School Boys"* (Ph.D. dissertation: New York University, 2010); Taveeshi Gupta, Niobe Way, Rebecca McGill, Diane Hughes, Carlos Santos, "Masculinity norms in China and the U.S.A. and their link to psychological adjustment." Paper in progress. Judy Y. Chu, "A Relational Perspective on Adolescent Boy's Identity Development," in Way and Chu, *Adolescent Boys,* 78–106; Carlos Santos, Niobe Way, and Diane Hughes, "Linking Masculinity and Education among Middle School Students," paper presented at the Society of Research on Child Development, 2011.

3. Richard Majors and Janet M. Billson, *Cool Pose: The Dilemmas of Black Manhood in America* (New York: Touchstone, 1993).

4. Urie Bronfenbrenner, *The Ecology of Human Development: Experiments by Nature and Design* (Cambridge, Mass.: Harvard University Press, 1979).

5. Lise Eliot, *Pink Brain, Blue Brain: How Small Differences Grow into Troublesome Gaps—and What We Can Do about It* (New York: Mariner Books, 2010).

6. John Bowlby, *Attachment and Loss: Volume 1, Attachment* (New York: Basic Books, 1969); John Bowlby, *The Making and Breaking of Affectional Bonds* (London: Tavistock, 1979); Mary Ainsworth, "Patterns of Attachment Behavior Shown by the Infant with His Mother," *Merrill-Palmer Quarterly* 10 (1964): 51–58; Mary Ainsworth, Mary Blehar, Everett Waters, and Sally Wall, *Patterns of Attachment* (Hillsdale, NJ: Erlbaum, 1978).

7. Ibid.

8. Constance Flanagan, "Trust, Identity, and Civic Hope," *Applied Developmental Science* 7 (2003): 166–171.

9. Harry Stack Sullivan, *The Interpersonal Theory of Psychiatry* (New York: Norton, 1953).

10. Eliot, *Pink Brain, Blue Brain,* 262.

11. Santos, *Missing Story.* Research for this study was conducted at the Center for Research on Culture, Development, and Education (CRCDE) under the direction of principle investigators Diane Hughes and Niobe Way. The CRCDE is funded by National Science Foundation.

12. Ibid.

13. Kate Lombardi, April, 2010, personal communication.

14. Kate Lombardi, *Oedipus Wrecks: How Mothers Are Pushed away from Their Sons and Why They Should Push Back,* (New York: Avery, in press).

15. Catherine Tamis-LeMonda, and N. Cabrera, eds. *Handbook of Father Involvement: Multidisciplinary Perspectives* (Lawrence Erlbaum; 2002).

16. Ibid.

17. Carol Gilligan, *The Birth of Pleasure: A New Map of Love* (New York: Vintage, 2003).

18. See also Lyn Mikel Brown, Sharon Lamb and Michael Tappan, *Packaging Boyhood: Saving Our Sons from Superheroes, Slackers and Other Media Stereotypes* (New York: St. Martin's Press, 2009).

19. Ibid., 222.

20. Jamie Price, *Navigating Differences: Friendships Between Gay and Straight Men* (New York: Haworth Press, 1999).

21. Jean Anyon, "Intersections of Gender and Class: Accommodation and Resistance by Working-Class and Affluent Females to Contradictory Sex-Role Ideologies," in *Gender, Class and Education*, ed. Stephen Walker and Len Barton (London: Taylor and Francis, 1983).

22. Amy C. Wilkins, *Wannabes, Goths, and Christians: The Boundaries of Sex, Style, and Status* (Chicago: University of Chicago Press, 2008).

23. Niobe Way, Carlos Santos, Erika Niwa, and Constance Kim-Gervey, "To Be or Not to Be: An Exploration of Ethnic Identity Development in Context," in *The Intersections of Personal and Social Identities: New Directions for Child and Adolescent Development*, eds. Margarita Azmitia, Kimberly Radmacher and Moin Syed (San Francisco: Jossey-Bass, 2008), 61–79.

24. Ibid.

25. Ibid.

26. Santos, *The Missing Story*,

27. Way et al., "To be or not to be."

28. Ibid.

29. Ibid.

30. Ibid.

31. R. A. Ruiz, "Cultural and Historical Perspectives in Counseling Hispanics," in *Counseling the Culturally Different*, ed. D. W. Sue (New York: Wiley, 1981), 191; see also G. Miguel Arciniega, Thomas Anderson, Zoila G. Tovar-Blank, and Terence J. G. Tracey, "Toward a Fuller Conception of Machismo: Development of a Traditional Machismo and Caballerismo Scale," *Journal of Counseling Psychology* 55 (2008): 19–33; George J. Sanchez, *Becoming Mexican American: Ethnicity, Culture, and Identity in Chicano Los Angeles, 1900–1945* (New York: Oxford University Press, 1993).

32. Luis F. Valdez, Augustine Baron, Jr., and Francisco Q. Ponce, "Counseling Hispanic Men," in *Handbook of Counseling and Psychotherapy with Men*, ed. M. Scher and M. Stevens (Thousand Oaks, Calif.: Sage, 1987), 210.

33. Janie V. Ward, "Raising Resisters: The Role of Truth Telling in the Psychological Development of African American Girls," in *Urban Girls: Resisting Stereotypes, Creating Identities*, ed. Bonnie J. Ross Leadbeater and Niobe Way (New York: New York University Press, 1996).

34. Richard F. Lazur and Richard Majors, "Men of Color: Ethnocultural Variations of Male Gender Role Strain," in *A New Psychology of*

Men, ed. Ronald F. Levant & William S. Pollack (New York: Basic Books, 1995); O. Ramirez, "Mexican-American Children and Adolescents," in *Children of Color: Psychological Interventions with Minority Youth*, ed. J. T. Gibbs and L. N. Huang (San Francisco: Jossey-Bass, 1989), 224–250.

35. 2007 *American Community Survey, Socioeconomic Characteristics by Race/Hispanic Origin and Ancestry Group*, New York City Department of City Planning, www.nyc.gov/html/dcp/pdf/census/acs_socio_07_nyc.pdf, 2007; Edward Telles and Vilma Ortiz, *Generations of Exclusion: Mexican Americans, Assimilation, and Race* (New York: Sage, 2009).

36. Pew Hispanic Center, "Statistical portrait of Hispanics in the United States," 2007.

37. Way et al., *To Be or Not to Be.*

38. Santos, "Missing Story."

39. Clyde Franklyn, "'Hey, Home—Yo, Bro': Friendship Among Black Men," in *Men's Friendships*, ed. Peter M. Nardi (Newbury Park Calif.: Sage Publications, 1992) 205–215.

40. Thomas Kochman, *Black and White Styles in Conflict* (Chicago: University of Chicago Press, 1981); Majors and Billson, *Cool Pose*; Lazur and Majors, *Men of Color.*

41. Lazur and Majors, *Men of Color.*

42. "Lil Wayne and Baby Kissing Photo . . . Rapper Admits Is Real," www.associatedcontent.com/article/81432/lil_wayne_and_baby_kissing_photo_rapper.html?cat=49 (accessed 19 April 2009).

43. See Michael Cunningham, "African-American Adolescent Males' Perceptions of Their Community Resources and Constraints: A Longitudinal Analysis," *Journal of Community Psychology* 25 (1999): 569–588; Stevenson, "Missed, Dissed, and Pissed"; M. B. Spencer, D. Dupree and T. Hartmann, "A Phenomenological Variant of Ecological Systems Theory (PVEST): A Self-Organization Perspective in Context," *Development and Psychopathology* 9 (1997): 817–833; Michael Cunningham and Leah Newkirk Meunier, "The Influence of Peer Experiences on Bravado Attitudes among African American Males," in Way and Chu, *Adolescent Boys*, 219–232.

44. C. J. Pascoe, *Dude, You're a Fag: Masculinity and Sexuality in High School* (Berkeley: University of California Press, 2007).

45. See Todd Edward Boyd, *Am I Black Enough for You?: Popular Culture from the 'Hood and Beyond* (Bloomington University, Indiana Press, 1997). See also Beverly Tatum, *Why Are All the Black Kids Sitting Together in the Cafeteria* (Random House, 1998).

46. Franklyn, "'Hey, Home—Yo, Bro,'" 203.

47. Q. Kong, *Lunyu* (Shanghai: Zhonghua, 2006).

48. B. Li, "Wen wangchangling zuo qian long biao, yao you ci ji," in *An Anthology of Tang Dynasty's Poems,* ed. D. Q. Shen (Shanghai: ZhongHua, 1975), 266; B. Li, *To My Friends,* ed. D. Q. Peng et al (Yangzhou, China: Yangzhou Book Company, 1976); L. Li, "Da Suwu Shu," in *A Collection of Literacy,* ed. T. Xiao (Shanghai: Zhonghua, 1977).

49. Niobe Way and Yueming Jia, "Friendships among Chinese Adolescents," paper presented at the Society For Research on Child Development, March 2009. Research was conducted in Nanjing, China as part of the Metroteen Project in affiliation with SouthEast University. Principle investigators are Niobe Way, Hiro Yoshikawa, Xinyin Chen, Zuhong Lu, and Deng He.

50. David L. Eng, *Racial Castration: Managing Masculinity in Asian America* (Durham, N.C.: Duke University Press, 2005); Joy Lei, "(Un)Necessary Toughness?: Those 'Loud Black Girls' and Those 'Quiet Asian Boys,'" *Anthropology & Education Quarterly* 34 (2003), 158–181; Stacey Lee, *Beyond Silenced Voices: Class, Race, and Gender in United States schools,* ed. Lois Weis and Michelle Fine (Albany: State University of New York, 2005).

51. Stuart Miller, *Men and Friendship* (Los Angeles: Houghton Mifflin, 1983).

52. Aida Hurtado and Mrinal Sinha, "More Than Men: Latino Feminist Masculinities and Intersectionality," *Sex Roles* 59 (2008): 337–349.

53. Niobe Way, María Hernández, Leoandra Rogers, and Diane Hughes, "Stereotypes As a Context of Identity Development: An Investigation of Ethnic Identities among Chinese American, Dominican, and European American Adolescents," manuscript in progress, 2010.

54. Franklyn, "'Hey, Home—Yo, Bro'"; Frosh et al, *Young Masculinities.*

55. Robert Roeser, Jacquelynne Eccles, and Arnold Sameroff, "School as a Context of Early Adolescents' Academic and Social-Emotional Development: A Summary of Research Findings," *Elementary School Journal* 100 (2000): 443–471.

56. Niobe Way and Leondra Rogers, *The Ghost in the House: Stereotypes and Their Impact on Adolescent Development,* manuscript in progress.

5. NICK AND GEORGE

1. See Niobe Way, *Everyday Courage: The Lives and Stories of Urban Teenagers* (New York: New York University Press, 1998).

2. Ibid.

3. Robert Selman, *The Growth of Interpersonal Understanding: Developmental and Clinical Analyses* (New York: Academic Press, 1980).

4. Harry Stack Sullivan, *The Interpersonal Theory of Psychiatry* (New York: Norton, 1953).

5. See Judy Chu's work for more discussion on the importance of being known: Chu, "Relational Perspective."

6. William Pollack, *Real Boys: Rescuing Our Sons from the Myths of Boyhood* (New York: Holt, 1998).

7. Antonio Damasio, *Descartes' Error: Emotion, Reason, and the Human Brain* (New York: Harper Perennial, 1995); Frans de Waal, *The Age of Empathy: Nature's Lessons for a Kinder Society* (New York: Three Rivers Press, 2010); Sarah B. Hrdy, *Mothers and Others: Maternal Instincts and How They Shape the Human Species* (Cambridge, Mass: Harvard University Press, 2009).

6. "WHEN YOU GROW UP, YOUR HEART DIES"

1. The title of this chapter is a quote from Allison, a character in the movie *The Breakfast Club*, a movie directed by John Hughes.

2. "Suicide Rates," *World Health Organization*, www.who.int/mental_health/prevention/suicide/suiciderates/en (accessed May/2003).

3. Richard F. Lazur and Richard Majors, "Men of Color: Ethnocultural Variations of Male Gender Role Strain," in *A New Psychology of Men*, ed. Ronald F. Levant and William S. Pollack (New York: Basic Books, 1995), 337–358.

4. Maurice Sendak, *Pierre* (Weston Books, 1976).

5. Stuart Miller, *Men and Friendship.* (London: Gateway Books, 1983); Peter Nardi, *Men's Friendships* (Newbury Park, Calif.: Sage Publications, 1992).

7. AS BOYS BECOME MEN

1. Victor Seidler, "Rejection, Vulnerability, and Friendship," in *Men's Friendships,* ed. Peter Nardi (Newbury Park: Sage, 1992), 15–17.

2. Michael Thompson, Catherine O'Neill-Grace and Lawrence Cohen, *Best Friends, Worst Enemies: Understanding the Social Lives of Children* (New York: Ballantine Books, 2002); Stuart Miller, *Men and Friendship*. London: Gateway Books.

3. See Richard Wilkinson and Kate Pickett, *The Spirit Level: Why Greater Equality Makes Societies Stronger* (London: Bloomsbury Press, 2009); Tara Parker-Pope, "Well, What Are Friends For? A Longer Life," *New York Times*, 20 April 2009;

4. Urie Bronfenbrenner, Peter D McClelland, Elaine Wethington, Phyllis Moen and Stephen Ceci, *The State of Americans: This Generation and The Next* (New York: Simon and Schuster, 2007); John T. Cacioppo and William Patrick, *Loneliness: Human Nature and the Need for Social Connection* (New York: Norton, 2009); Miller McPherson, Lynn Smith-Lovin, and Mathew E. Brashears, "Social Isolation in America: Changes in Core Discussion Networks over Two Decades," *American Sociological Review* 71 (2008): 353–375; Constance Flanagan, "Trust, Identity, and Civic Hope," *Applied Developmental Science* 7 (2003): 166–171.

5. McPherson et al., "Social Isolation in America."

6. Eric Uslaner, *The Moral Foundations of Trust* (Cambridge: Cambridge University Press, 2002).

7. Bronfenbrenner et al., *State of Americans*.

8. T. Smith, *Transition to Adulthood and the Generation Gap from the 1970's to the 1990's*, report prepared for the MacArthur Planning Network on Transitions to Adulthood and Public Policy (Chicago: National Opinion Research Center, University of Chicago, 2000).

9. See Wilkinson and Pickett, *The Spirit Level*.

10. For a discussion of a similar pattern with girls, see Lyn Mikel Brown and Carol Gilligan, *Meeting at the Crossroads: Women's Psychology and Girls' Development* (Cambridge, Mass: Harvard University Press, 1992).

11. Robert D. Putnam, *Bowling Alone: The Collapse and Revival of American Community* (New York: Simon and Schuster, 2000).

12. Emile Durkheim, *Suicide: A Study in Sociology* (New York: Free Press, 1951).

13. Sarah Blaffer Hrdy, *Mothers and Others: The Evolutionary Origins of Mutual Understanding* (Cambridge, Mass: Harvard University Press, 2009), 286.

14. Putnam, *Bowling Alone*.

15. Hrdy, *Mothers and Others*.

16. Wilkinson and Pickett, *The Spirit Level*, 213.

17. Stephanie Coontz, "Too Close for Comfort," *New York Times,* 7 November 2006.

18. Gregory Lehne, "Homophobia among men: Supporting and Defining the Male Role." In *Men's Lives* ed. Michael Kimmel and Michael Messner. New York: Macmillan Press, 1989, p. 422.

19. "No Homo," www.urbandictionary.com/define.php?term= no percent20homo (accessed March, 2008).

20. Christina Hoff Sommers, *The War against Boys: How Misguided Feminism Is Harming Our Young Men* (New York: Simon and Schuster, 2001). Joanne Lipman, "The Mismeasure of Woman," *New York Times,* 23 October 2009.

21. "Fatal Shooting at US Amish School," *BBC World News,* 3 October, 2009, 1.

22. Michael Rowe, "What It Says about Us When a 17 Month Old Boy Is Beaten to Death for 'Acting Like a Girl,'" *Huffington Post,* 5 August 2010.

23. Ferguson, *Bad Boys;* Howard C. Stevenson, "Boys in Men's Clothing: Racial Socialization and Neighborhood Safety as Buffers to Hypervulnerability in African American Males," in *Adolescent Boys: Exploring Diverse Cultures of Boyhood,* ed. Niobe Way and Judy Y. Chu (New York: New York University Press, 2004), 59–77.

24. Pedro Noguera, *The Trouble with Black Boys: And Other Reflections on Race, Equity, and the Future of Public Education* (San Francisco: Jossey-Bass, 2008).

25. Joy Lei, "(Un)Necessary Toughness?: Those 'Loud Black Girls' and Those 'Quiet Asian Boys,'" *Anthropology & Education Quarterly* 34 (2003): 158–181; Stacey Lee, *Beyond Silenced Voices: Class, Race, and Gender in United States schools,* ed. Lois Weis and Michelle Fine (Albany: State University of New York Press, 2005).

26. Jacqueline Nguyen, personal communication.

27. For additional examples, see C. J. Pascoe, *Dude, You're a Fag: Masculinity and Sexuality in High School* (Berkeley: University of California Press, 2007).

28. Gail Dines and Jean Humez, *Gender, Race and Class in Media* (Calif.: Sage, 2002); Brown et al., *Packaging Boyhood.*

29. "Find Your Inner Bro, Bro!" GQ, July 2009.

30. Ibid

31. See Michael Kimmel, *Guyland: The Perilous World Where Boys Become Men* (New York: Harper Collins, 2008).

32. Mathew Oransky and Jeanna Marecek, " 'I'm Not Going To Be a Girl': Masculinity and Emotions in Boys' Friendships and Peer Groups," *Journal of Adolescent Research* 24 (2009): 218.

33. See Michael Tomasello, *Why We Cooperate* (Cambridge: MIT Press, 2009). Sarah B. Hrdy, *Mothers and Others: Maternal Instincts and How They Shape the Human Species* (Cambridge, Mass: Harvard University Press, 2009); Frans de Waal, *The Age of Empathy: Nature's lessons for a Kinder Society* (New York: Three Rivers Press, 2010).

8. FERNANDO AND DANNY

1. Janie V. Ward, "Raising Resisters: The Role of Truth Telling in the Psychological Development of African American Girls," in *Urban Girls: Resisting Stereotypes, Creating Identities,* ed. Bonnie J. Ross Leadbeater and Niobe Way (New York: New York University Press, 1996).

2. For a discussion of the long working hours of immigrants, see Hiro Yoshikawa, *Immigrants Raising Citizens: Undocumented Parents of the Second Generation* (New York: Sage, forthcoming).

3. A quote from one of the boys in my studies.

4. For similar patterns, see Judy Y. Chu, "A Relational Perspective on Adolescent Boys' Identity Development," in *Adolescent Boys: Exploring Diverse Cultures of Boyhood,* ed. Niobe Way and Judy Y. Chu (New York: New York University Press, 2004), 78–106.

5. A similar pattern among girls was noted by Lyn Mikel Brown and Carol Gilligan, *Meeting at the Crossroads: Women's Psychology and Girls' Development* (Cambridge, Mass: Harvard University Press, 1992).

6. Brown and Gilligan, *Meeting at the Crossroads;* Carol Gilligan, *Joining the Resistance:* (Polity Press, In press).

7. Susan R. Rosenbloom and Niobe Way, "Experience of Discrimination among African American, Asian American, and Latino Adolescents in an Urban High School," *Youth and Society* 35 (2004): 420–451; Melissa Greene, Niobe Way, and Kerstin Pahl, "Trajectories of Perceived Adult and Peer Discrimination among Black, Latino, and Asian American Adolescents: Patterns and Psychological Correlates, *Developmental Psychology* 42 (2006): 218–238; Desiree Qin, Niobe Way, and Preetika Mukherjee, "The Other Side of the Model Minority Story: The Familial and Peer Challenges Faced by Chinese American Adolescents," *Youth and Society* 39 (2008): 480–506.

8. Brown and Gilligan, *Meeting at the Crossroads,* 162.

9. THE CRISIS OF CONNECTION

1. David G. Myers, *Social Psychology, 9th ed.* (Boston: McGraw Hill, 2008). Gilligan, *In a Different Voice: Psychological Theory and Women's Development* (Cambridge: Harvard University Press, 1982); Gilligan, *Birth of Pleasure: A New Map of Love* (New York: Vintage, 2003).

2. Dana Edell, "'Say It How It Is:' Urban Teenage Girls Challenge and Perpetuate Cultural Narratives Through Writing and Performing Theater," (Ph.D. Diss: New York University, 2010).

3. See Lyn Mikel Brown and Carol Gilligan, *Meeting at the Crossroads: Women's Psychology and Girls' Development* (Cambridge, Mass.: Harvard University Press, 1992).

4. Carol Gilligan, *Joining the Resistance* (Cambridge: Polity Press, in press).

5. Ibid.

6. Harry Brod and Michael Kaufman, *Theorizing Masculinities: Men and Masculinity* (New York: Sage, 1994).

7. Maureen Dowd, "Blue Is the New Black," *The New York Times,* 20 September 2009: WK9.

8. David Von Drehle, "The Myth about Boys," *Time,* 26 July, 2007.

9. Karen Hansen, "Our Eyes Behold Each Others: Masculinity and Intimate Friendship in Antebellum New England," in *Men's Friendships,* ed. Peter Nardi (Newbury Park, Calif.: Sage, 1992).

10. Harry Stack Sullivan, *The Interpersonal Theory of Psychiatry* (New York: Norton, 1953); Judy Chu, "A Relational Perspective on Adolescent Boys' Identity Development," in Niobe Way and Judy Chu (ed) *Adolescent Boys: Exploring Diverse Cultures of Boyhood,* 78–106.

11. Antonio Damasio, *Descartes' Error: Emotion, Reason, and the Human Brain* (New York: Harper Perennial, 1995).

12. Lise Eliot, *Pink Brain, Blue Brain: How Small Differences Grow into Troublesome Gaps—and What We Can Do about It* (New York: Mariner Books, 2010).

13. Sarah B. Hrdy, *Mothers and Others: Maternal Instincts and How They Shape the Human Species* (Cambridge, Mass: Harvard University Press, 2009); Frans de Waal, *The Age of Empathy: Nature's Lessons for a Kinder Society* (New York: Three Rivers Press, 2010).

14. Nicholas Kristof, "The Boys Have Fallen Behind," *New York Times,* 28 March, 2010: WK12.

15. Hrdy, *Mothers and Others;* De Waal, *The Age of Empathy;* Michael Tomasello, *Why We Cooperate* (Cambridge, Mass: MIT Press, 2009); Damasio, *Descartes' Error.*

16. Eliot, *Pink Brain, Blue Brain.*

17. Richard Alleyne, "Generation Me Students Have Less Empathy Than 20 Years Ago," *Telegraph,* 28 May 2010.

18. Sara Konrath, "Empathy: College Students Don't Have as Much as They Used To," Presented at the annual meeting of the Association for Psychological Science, August, 20, 2010.

19. Tara Parker-Pope, "What are Friends for? A Longer Life," *New York Times,* 20 April 2009, 1; Robert Putnam, *Bowling Alone: The Collapse and Revival of American Community* (New York: Simon and Schuster, 2001); Richard Wilkinson and Kate Pickett, *The Spirit Level: Why Greater Equality Makes Societies Stronger* (London: Bloomsbury Press, 2009); Eric Klinenberg, *Heatwave: A Social Autopsy of Disaster in Chicago* (Chicago: University of Chicago Press, 2003).

20. Hilary Stout, "A Best Friend? You Must Be Kidding," *New York Times,* 16 June, 2010.

21. Carol Gilligan has used this phrase throughout her work. See, for example, Carol Gilligan, "Teaching Shakespeare's Sister: Notes from the Underground of Female Adolescence," in *Making Connections: The Relational Worlds of Adolescent Girls at Emma Willard School,* ed. Carol Gilligan, N. Lyons, and T. Hanmer (Cambridge: Harvard University Press, 1990), 6–29; Gilligan, *Birth of Pleasure.*

22. Niobe Way, Ranjini Reddy, and Jean Rhodes, "Students' Perceptions of School Climate During the Middle School Years: Association with Trajectories of Psychological and Behavioral Adjustment," *Community Psychology* 40 (2007): 194–213; see also Maria Hernandez, Diane Hughes, Niobe Way and Rebecca McGill. Relationships in school as a predictor of Academic Engagement, paper in progress. Robert Roeser, Jacquelynne Eccles and Arnold Sameroff, "School As a Context of Early Adolescents' Academic and Social-Emotional Development: A Summary of Research Findings," *The Elementary School Journal* 100 (2000): 443–471.

23. Simone Schnall, Kent D. Harber, Jeanine K. Stefanucci, and Dennis R. Proffitt, "Social Support and the Perception of Geographical Slant," *Journal of Experimental Social Psychology* 44 (2008): 1246–1255.

24. Gilligan, *In a Different Voice.*

25. De Waal, *Age of Empathy,* 7.

26. Michael Kimmel, *Guyland* (New York City: Harper Collins, 2008); Brod and Kaufman, *Theorizing Masculinities;* Gary Barker, *Dying to Be Men: Youth, Masculinity and Social Exclusion* (New York: Routledge, 2005).

27. See Gilligan, *In a Different Voice;* Gilligan, *Birth of Pleasure.* Gilligan, *Joining the Resistance* (Cambridge: Polity Press, in press).

28. Ibid.; Kimmel, *Guyland;* Jean Miller, *Toward a New Psychology of Women* (New York: Beacon Press, 1987); Wilkernson and Pickett, *The Spirit Level;* Putnam, *Bowling Alone;* Constance Flanagan, "Trust, Identity, and Civic Hope," *Applied Developmental Science* 7 (2003): 166–171; Brod and Kaufman, *Theorizing Masculinities;* Michael Reichert and Sharon Ravich, "Defying Normative Male Identities: The Transgressive Possibilities of Jewish Boyhood," *Youth and Society* 20 (2009):1–26; John T. Cacioppo and William Patrick, *Loneliness: Human Nature and the Need for Social Connection* (New York: W.W. Norton & Company, 2009). Brown and Gilligan, *Meeting at the Crossroads;* Carol Gilligan, *Joining the Resistance.*

29. Carlos Santos, *The Missing Story: Resistance to Ideals of Masculinity in the Friendships of Middle School Boys,* (Ph.D. disser.: New York University, 2010).

30. Brod and Kaufman, *Theorizing Masculinities.*

31. Leondra Rogers, *The Intersections of Ethnic and Gender Identities among African American Boys,* (Ph.D. Disser.: New York University).

32. Lyn Mikel Brown, Sharon Lamb, and Mark Tappan, *Packaging Boyhood: Saving Our Sons from Superheroes, Slackers, and Other Media Stereotypes* (New York: St. Martin's Press, 2009).

33. Orlando Patterson, "The Last Sociologist," *New York Times,* May 2002.

34. Lionel Trilling, *Freud and the Crisis of Our Culture* (Boston: Beacon Press, 1955), 58.

35. David Richards and Carol Gilligan, *The Deepening Darkness: Patriarchy, Resistance, and Democracy's Future* (New York: Cambridge University Press, 2009).

36. Hrdy, *Mothers and Others,* 4.

37. de Waal, *Age of Empathy;* Tomasello, *Why We Cooperate.*

38. Cacioppo and Patrick, *Loneliness.*

39. Brown and Gilligan, *Meeting at the Crossroads,* 11–35.

40. D. Olweus, "Bully/Victim Problems among Schoolchildren: Basic Facts and Effects of a School Based Intervention Program," in *The Development and Treatment of Childhood Aggression,* ed. D. J. Pepler and K. H. Rubin (Hillsdale, NJ: Erlbaum, 1991), 411–448; D. Olweus, *Bullying at School: What We Know and What We Can Do* (Cambridge: Blackwell, 1993); D. Olweus, "The Olweus Bullying Prevention Pro-

gramme: Design and Implementation Issues and a New National Initiative in Norway," in *Bullying In Schools: How Successful Can Interventions Be?* ed. P. K. Smith, D. Pepler, and K. Rigby (Cambridge: Cambridge University Press, 2004), 13–36; D. Olweus, S. P. Limber, and S. Mihalic, *The Bullying Prevention Program: Blueprints for Violence Prevention, vol. 10* (Boulder: Center for the Study and Prevention of Violence, 1999).

41. S. Black, "An Ongoing Evaluation of the Bullying Prevention Program in Philadelphia Schools: Student Survey and Student Observation Data," paper presented at Centers for Disease Control's Safety in Numbers Conference, Atlanta, 2003; S. P. Limber, "Implementation of the Olweus Bullying Prevention Program: Lessons Learned from the Field," in *Bullying in American Schools: A Social-Ecological Perspective on Prevention and Intervention,* ed. D. Espelage and S. Swearer (Mahwah, N.J.: Erlbaum, 2004b): 351–363.

42. Susan Engel and Marlene Sandstrom, "There's Only One Way to Stop a Bully," *New York Times,* 22 July 2010

43. Damasio, *Descartes' Error*

44. See Wilkinson and Pickett, *The Spirit Level.*

45. Joseph T. Cox is headmaster of The Haverford School in Haverford, Pennsylvania. Prior to assuming his position at Haverford, he served 30 years in the U. S. Army, 14 of which he spent teaching literature at the U. S. Military Academy at West Point. He is a Vietnam veteran and retired from the military at the rank of colonel. He has a B.A. from Lafayette College, and a Ph.D. from the University of North Carolina at Chapel Hill. His publications include a collection of poems, *Garden's Close,* an anthology of early American war prose, *The Written Wars,* and numerous prose and poetry publications.

ACKNOWLEDGMENTS

Just as it takes a village to raise a child, it took a village to conduct the research for and write this book. My village included the teenage boys themselves, of course, who courageously told it like it is, year after year. Thank you, boys, for allowing me to see the hand in front of my face. My village also included the undergraduate and graduate students who helped me collect and analyze the data; my editor at Harvard University Press, who understood the importance of the book immediately; my "deep depth" friends, with whom I share *my* deepest secrets and without whom I would feel lost; and my family who provide ongoing emotional *and* editorial support. Now let me put names to some of these people.

Apropos the theme of this book, I will start with my friends who made this book happen. Carol Gilligan, my mentor in graduate school and now a best friend, changed the world by making the radical insight that girls and women are human too. She has shaped every step of my research, from the theoretical framework to the way in which I collected and analyzed the data. Our conversations during our weekly breakfasts have been the source of profound inspiration and have greatly fostered my resistance to thin culture interpretations of the world. Carol has made it possible for me to stay in the thick of it. This book would not have happened without her empirically grounded and brilliant insights over the past three decades and her support, guidance, and love.

Other friends who have assisted in the production of this book and to whom I am "thickly" indebted are Hiro Yoshikawa and Pedro Noguera. Hiro, who was willing to travel to the other side of the world with me to conduct research, and Pedro have provided inspiration, guidance, and emotional support from the beginning of the writing process to the end. Both of these men have been able to stay true to what they know, and for that I am deeply grateful. I also want to thank Gary Barker and Michael Reichert for their critical insights. And then there is Adrian Staub, who contributed a paragraph in the book, offered superb editorial guidance, and has proven to me that a man can stay connected to his heart and remain a man in the best sense of the word.

My gratitude also extends to my editor at Harvard University Press, Elizabeth Knoll, who has been the supportive voice urging me, with an occasional threat, to complete the book. Her guidance and humor in the midst of hard times have been essential.

While these friends and colleagues have provided me the support to write the book, the project would not have happened if the data hadn't been collected and analyzed. Thus, right up there with the boys in my studies, who unfortunately can't be individually named, are the dozens of research assistants who helped me collect and analyze the data over the past twenty years. While there are more than I can enumerate, the ones who have been most involved in the collection and/or analysis of the data include: Will Folberth, Rachel Gingold, Taveeshi Gupta, Robbie Harris, Geena Kuriakose, Dalia Levy, Thiago Marques, Tine Pahl, Susan Rosenbloom, Mariana Rotenberg, Carlos Santos, and Mara Washburn. Their dedication to the project and to the boys themselves has been remarkable and is *the reason* why the data are so rich and the analysis so deep. The project wouldn't have been what it is without their incredible minds and hearts. I want also to extend a note of gratitude to my students Dana Edell and Onnie Rogers who didn't collect or analyze the data but who carefully read the manuscript, provided helpful feedback, and have been enthusiastic supporters throughout the process. The students in my Youth and Masculinity (Y.A.M.) research group at N.Y.U. have also been extremely helpful and supportive. And I must also thank my assistant, Lucy Zhang, who worked on the book with a zen-like calmness in the midst of my hurricane.

A book about friendships would not be complete if I did not also thank my BFFs, who have not been directly involved in the project but who have supported me throughout the process: Dana Burdy, Dalton Conley, Alessandra Durstine, Femke Galle, Jennifer Hill, Joan Malczewski, Mo Ogrodnick, Cybele Raver, Jean Rhodes, and Ruth Wyatt. They are the ones to whom I turn so that I won't go "wacko." Thank you for tolerating my peaks and valleys over the years. My gratitude also extends to my colleague, friend, and intellectual sister Diane Hughes for giving me time to write the book even when she and I were supposed to be writing journal articles based on our middle school data. Her patience has been remarkable. (Yes, Diane, I will now turn to those articles.)

Another form of support from which I have benefited is that provided by those who have literally given me space in which to write. Thank you to the staff, particularly Iya Salhab and Juan Figueroa, at the café Pain Quotidian for letting me use the café as my office and who sacrificed months' worth of tips so I could sit in my corner table throughout the day with my computer and coffee and talk to myself as I wrote and rewrote passage after passage.

Finally, I turn to my glorious family. My god, my mother, Brenda Way, who has been there each step of the way, correcting each grammatical error from the time I began to talk and throughout my career, and providing me with a constant dose of inspiration and love. She has edited every page of this book and has been a best friend to boot. I owe her everything. I also thank my adoring stepfather Henry Erlich, and my father, Peter Way, for their love and support; my brothers, Justin and Lucan, who taught me early on about the importance of friendships; my brilliant sister, Thaisa, who helps me stayed connected to what I know; Uli Baer with whom and through whom I have learned so much; and my awesome children, Raphael and Chiara, whose love makes me stay in the thick of it and who remind me, with their humor and their sharp insights about the world, why I do the work that I do and what it means to be human in the best sense of the word. I am a lucky soul.

INDEX

Abandonment, 94, 102, 111, 254. *See also* Loss

Academic achievement and engagement, 8, 43, 279–280; feminization of, 26–27, 47–50; literature on, 43, 47–50; resistance and, 72–73; school social dynamics and, 118, 123–140; sports and, 123–124

Accommodation, 86–88, 261; by African Americans, 67, 134; as human nature, 68–69; by Latinos, 129–130; literature on, 42; parents in, 272; resistance and, 116, 124, 226; social dynamics and, 124–125. *See also* Resistance

Achievement orientation, 59

Active orientation, 59

African Americans: disconnection and, 224–225; emotional expressivity and, 131–134; hypermasculinity and, 6, 131–134, 224–227; Puerto Ricans and, 128–129; resistance by, 67–68, 70, 72, 132–134; socioeconomic status and, 139. *See also* Ethnicity

The Age of Empathy (de Waal), 28–29, 74–75

Aggression and violence, 5, 43, 268; cultural emphasis on, 74–75; disconnection and, 222–223; ethnicity and, 6; homophobia and, 222–223

Ainsworth, Mary, 120

Alienation, 36, 216–217, 250–251, 256. *See also* Disconnection

Anger, 22, 96, 197; as cover-up for sadness, 113; ethnicity and, 149–150; Fernando on, 240, 241; girlfriends and, 234, 241; indifference and, 197–199; loss and, 185, 189–194, 213; masculinity and, 59; trust and, 106–107, 244

Anomie, 216–217

Anti-intellectualism, 26–27, 49–50, 114–115

Anyon, Jean, 68, 105, 124–125

Appearance, of masculinity, 125–130

Arciniega, Miguel, 60

Asian Americans, 260–261; Danny, 242–261; disconnection and, 225–226; emotional expressivity and, 6; on Puerto Ricans, 128; resistance by, 134–137; stereotypes of, 136–137. *See also* Ethnicity

Assertiveness, 64–65

Attachment theory, 57–58, 120

Attention deficit hyperactivity disorder, 43

Autonomy, 36, 38; betrayal and, 204; Danny on, 245–247, 255–259; disconnection and, 217–218, 223; George on, 176–177; indifference and, 195–204; loss of friendships and, 212–216; as masculinity, 63–64

Azmitia, Margarita, 16, 56, 87

Baby, 132–133

The Backlash against American Women (Faludi), 221

Bad Boys (Ferguson), 50–51

Balan, Sundari, 60

Barker, Gary, 72

Best Friends, Worst Enemies (Thompson), 23

"A Best Friend? You Must Be Kidding," 266

Betrayal, 12, 38; autonomy and, 204; Danny on, 247, 251, 257–258; disrespect and, 190–191; emotions over, 101–102; fear of, 157–162, 159–160, 193–194; Fernando on, 234–235, 237–238; George on, 169–171; girlfriends and, 234–235, 237; indifference to, 197–198; justice and, 105–106; rumors and, 170; secrets and, 94, 99–100; stoicism and, 204. *See also* Loss

Biological differences, 44, 46–47, 58–67

Bonser, F. G., 3

Bowlby, John, 120

Bowling Alone (Putnam), 210–220

Boy code, 4–5; code switching and, 105–106; Fernando on, 233; indifference and, 202–203; literature on, 44–45; resistance to, 112–116

Boy crisis, 25, 43–53; human crisis vs., 27; masculinity and, 44–45; responses to, 264–265

Boys Adrift (Sax), 46

"Boys Don't Cry" (Cox), 281

Brannon, Robert, 59

Bromance (TV show), 138

Bronfenbrenner, Urie, 118, 211

Brown, Chris, 275

Brown, Lyn Mikel, 22, 63; Listening Guide by, 84–86; on loss, 254, 261; on marketing, 114–115; on resistance, 68–69; on sports, 124

Buhrmester, Duana, 55

Bukowski, William, 3

Bullying, 266, 279–280; in England, 139–140; ethnicity and, 131

Cacioppo, John T., 277–278

Cameroon, 7

Case studies: Danny, 242–261; Fernando, 229, 230–242; George, 143–144, 162–179; Nick, 143–162

Center for the Study of Boys' and Girls' Lives, 269–270

China, 7. *See also* Asian Americans

Chu, Judy, 71–72

Chums, 14, 33, 38–39, 53–54, 64

Cicone, Michael, 59

Code switching, 105–106

Cognitive development, 22

Competition, 220–223, 268

Conchas, Gil, 72

Conflict, 32, 166, 174, 279; Fernando on, 232, 234; secrets and, 98, 114, 119–120

Confucius, 135

Connection. *See* Social connectedness

Connell, Raewyn, 65–66, 87–88

Context, 41–43; change and, 278–279; ecological, 118; interview interpretation and, 85; loss and, 155; research and, 55, 57–58; resistance and, 139–140; social dynamics and, 124–125; toughness and, 65

Coontz, Stephanie, 219–220

Cott, Nancy F., 30

Cox, Joseph T., 281

Cultures: disconnection and, 216–217; emotions shaped by, 28–29, 33–34; friendships in different, 6–7; interdependent vs. independent, 62; interview interpretation and, 85; literature on, 50–51; masculinity and, 58–67; neuroscience and, 24; resistance against, 10, 45; self apart from, 47; social disconnection in, 210–220; thick vs. thin, 23–24; value placed on friendship in, 27–28

Cunningham, Michael, 133

Damasio, Antonio, 74

David, Deborah, 59

Democracy, 276–277

Demographics, 35, 78–79, 131, 137

Depression, 8, 9, 54; loss of friendship and, 12, 20, 21, 196–197; masculinity and, 66, 217, 223; resistance and, 69, 73

Descartes' Error (Damasio), 74

Desire for friendship, 11, 18–24, 163–165; Danny on, 252; disconnection from, 209–228; early and middle adolescence, 163–165; Fernando on, 237; indifference and, 191–194; late adolescence, 184–185, 204–208; memory and, 262–263

Developmental research, 38–39; ecological theories in, 41–43; resistance and, 73; on resistance and accommodation, 68–69

Diaz, Junot, 129

Diesel Jeans, 49, 115

Difficulty, perceptions of task, 8–9

Disconnection, 160–161, 179, 183–184, 209–228; antifeminism and, 221–223; competition and hierarchy in, 220–223; consequences of, 266–268; empathy and, 265–266; ethnic stereotypes and, 224–227; global increase in, 210–220; homophobia and, 218, 219–223; human nature vs., 227–228; income inequality and, 218–219; maturity and, 223–225, 268–269; thick cultural explanation of, 216–227; thin cultural explanation of, 212–216

Dominance, 59

Dominican Americans, 128, 130–131, 260–261

Dude, You're a Fag (Pascoe), 50

Durkheim, Emile, 216–217

Ecological theories, 41–43, 118

Edell, Dana, 262

Eliot, Lise, 28, 46, 264–265; on cultural influences, 76–77; on parents, 121

"Emo" teenagers, 137–138

Emotion: assumptions about, 52–53; awareness of, 92–93, 100–101; biological differences in, 44, 46–47; capacity of men for, 5–6; cognition and, 74; ethnicity and, 6, 61–62, 128–131; evolution and, 42; expressivity and, 6, 15–17, 127, 147–148, 169–170; George on, 164; homosexuality equated with, 29–33; indifference and, 194–204; maturity

and, 21–23, 183–208; neuroscience on, 23–24; parents and, 118–123; stoicism and (*see* Stoicism, emotional); White boys and, 137–139

Empathy, 27; decline in, 265–266; desire for, 205; George on, 164, 166–167; as human quality, 28–29, 34; Nick on, 153, 156

Eng, David, 6

Engel, Susan, 279–280

Erdley, Cynthia, 8, 55

Erikson, Erik, 38

Escape, 175

Ethnicity, 34; demographics of, 35; disconnection and, 224–227; discrimination and, 260–261; emotional expressiveness and, 6, 61–62, 128–131; fighting and, 149–150; literature on, 43, 50–52; "look" of masculinity and, 125–140; resistance and, 67–68, 70; similarity of friendships and, 15; social dynamics and, 125–140

Faludi, Susan, 221

Family. *See* Parents and family

Fathers. *See* Parents and family

The Feeling of What Happens (Damasio), 74

Feminization, 26–27; of academics, 47–50; of Asian Americans, 136–137; of emotion vs. rationality, 75; ethnicity and, 6

Ferguson, Ann, 50–51

A Fine Young Man (Gurian), 46

Fischer, Agneta, 61–62

Flanagan, Constance, 121

Franklin, Clyde, 139

Freudianism, 27, 31–32, 219–220

Friendships: assumptions about, 52–53; close vs. best, 171, 246, 249; Confucian view of, 135; cultural differences in, 6–7; decline in, 265–268; desire for, 11, 18–24, 163–165, 184–185, 191–194, 204–208; discouraging, 266; effort in, 158–159; evolution and, 42; with girls, 165; girls as impediments to, 111–112; ideal vs. real, 92, 106, 152, 201, 206, 242, 244, 252, 254–255, 259, 280; importance of,

Friendships *(continued)*
106–107, 255; loss of, in America, 27–28; with parents, 118–120; risk in, 171–172; as sanctuary, 175–176; studies on, 53–58; viewed as superficial, 3–7; well-being and, 2, 8–10; Western tradition of, 29, 30, 137
Frosh, Stephen, 5, 14, 67, 72
Furman, William, 54

Gadamer, Hans-George, 83
Gangs, 8
Garcia Marquez, Gabriel, 129
Geertz, Clifford, 24–25
Gender role strain, 66
Gender stereotypes. *See* Stereotypes
Genovese, Eugene D., 67–68
Ghana, 7
Gilligan, Carol, 22; on democracy vs. patriarchy, 276–277; Listening Guide by, 84–86; on loss, 254, 261; on resistance, 68–69, 71
Girls and girlfriends: Fernando on, 241; as impediments to friendship, 111–112, 148; isolation vs., 223; loss of friendship due to, 158–159, 177–178, 187, 213–214, 241; masculinity conventions reinforced by, 272–276; as reason for loss of friendships, 25–26; resistance to stereotypes about, 72; sharing with boys vs., 108–112; trust tests and, 100; value placed on, 3
Gray, John, 61
Greif, Geoffrey, 57
Gurian, Michael, 46, 52–53
Guy code. *See* Boy code
Guyland (Kimmel), 5, 44, 227

Hall, G. Stanley, 13
Hansen, Karen, 30, 31–32
Harris, Judith, 27–28
Health, 3, 9–10, 185, 210; gender stereotypes and, 50, 55, 65–67, 223, 280; parental attachment and, 120; social connection and, 214, 218–219. *See also* Well-being
Hierarchy, 220–223
Homicide rates, 43
Homophobia and homosexuality, 26–27, 29–33, 81; African Ameri-
cans and, 133–134; desire for intimacy and, 208, 209; disconnection and, 218, 219–220; "emo" teens and, 137–138; emotional expressivity and, 63, 112, 118; ethnic stereotypes and, 6; fear of misinterpretation and, 172, 254; Fernando and, 235–236; immigrant status and, 260, 261; indifference vs., 196–197; loss of friendships and, 18, 19, 212–216; masculinity defined by, 59–60; self-definition by omission and, 184; social dynamics and, 124; sports and, 123–124; White boys and, 138–139, 226–227
Honeymoons, 6–7, 25
Hrdy, Sarah, 47, 76, 217, 218, 277
Human nature, 74–77; empathy in, 28–29, 34, 76; false constructs of, 227–228; social nature of, 277–278
Humor, 114–115, 242
Hutado, Aida, 60

Identity, social, 118; homophobia and, 184; secrets and, 231–232
Iglesias, Enrique, 129
I Love You, Man (movie), 138
Immigrant status, 34, 128–129, 133–134, 137, 260–261
Independence, 36, 38; cultural differences in, 62; disconnection and, 217–218, 223; as masculinity, 63–64
Individualism, 217–218
Insula activation, 23–24
Interdependence, 62, 64
Interview method research, 39, 56–57, 77–87
Intimacy: boy code and, 4–5; Danny on, 243–245; descriptions of, 107–108; desire for, 179–180, 205–208; Fernando on, 233–234; gender and, 54–55; groups and, 95; homosexuality equated with, 29–33; loss of, 177, 178–179; physical, 95, 264; value placed on, 92–93
Isolation, 36, 223–225, 253–254, 266; increased, 27; well-being and, 8–10. *See also* Disconnection
"I" statements, 86; Danny's, 250; fear of betrayal and, 102; George's, 176;

of indifference, 201–202; Justin's, 201–202; Nick's, 152, 159–160; stoic, 250; tension between real and ideal in, 152

Jewish boys, 72
Justice, 105–106

Kagan, Celine, 51–52, 272–275
Kimmel, Michael, 5, 7–8, 44, 87; on homophobia, 59, 227; on masculinity, 58, 61
Kindlon, Dan, 5, 44, 52
Kindness, 103
Klinenberg, Eric, 10
Konrath, Sara, 265
Kristof, Nicolas, 48

Lakotas, 7
Larson, Reed, 62
Latinos: disconnection and, 224–225; emotional expressivity and, 6, 129–131; Fernando, 229, 230–242; hypermasculinity and, 224–225; "look" of masculinity in, 125–130; macho and, 149–150. *See also* Ethnicity
Lehne, Gregory, 220
Levinson, Daniel, 57
Li Bai, 135
Lil' Wayne, 132–133
The Little Mermaid (movie), 262–263
Lombardi, Kate, 122, 123
Loneliness, 12, 183–184, 266
Loneliness: Human Nature and the Need for Social Connection (Cacioppo and Patrick), 277–278
Loss, 18–24; agency in, 161–162; changing priorities and, 151; desire and, 191–194; disrespect and, 190; fear of, 159–160; Fernando on, 230–242; George on, 169–171, 175–179; girlfriends as cause of, 25–26, 177–178, 187; indifference toward, 194–204; as inevitable, 188–189, 232; as maturity, 183–208; mobility and, 187–188, 213–214, 215–216; Nick on, 149–157; patterns of, 180; psychological cost of, 36; research on, 57; thick cultural interpretation of,

216–227; thin cultural interpretation of, 212–216; vulnerability and, 186–194; work as cause of, 214–216

Machismo, 60, 129–130, 149–150
Mahalingam, Ramaswami, 60
Majors, Richard, 61
Manstead, Anthony, 61–62
Maracek, Jeanne, 227
Marriage: friendships recognized in, 6–7, 25; as only intimate relationship, 210, 219–220
Masculinity: anger and, 189–190; assertiveness in, 64–65; boy code and, 4–5, 44–45; Danny on, 253; defined as not female, 59–60; disconnection and, 222–223; emotional stoicism as, 61–63, 113–114; ethnicity and, 125–140, 224–227; Fernando on, 235–236; flexibility in, 216–217; friendship discouraged in, 26–27; hyper-, 5, 6, 60, 131–134, 224–227; indifference and, 194–204; literature on, 42, 43; looking the part in, 125–140; loss of friendship and, 183–184; mask of, 4, 171, 253; oppressiveness of stereotypical, 65–67; research on, 58–67; resistance to, 172–173; school social dynamics and, 123–140; toughness in, 64–65; vulnerability and, 104–105, 147–148. *See also* Homophobia and homosexuality
Maturity, 12, 36; Danny on, 255–259; disconnection and, 209–228, 223–225, 268–269; emotional "hardness" in, 21–23; Fernando on, 236–238; George on, 176–177; loss of friendships in, 18–24, 155, 183–208; sacrifices in, 228
McPherson, Miller, 210
Mean girls, 110–111
Media, 263–264, 270; on independence, 63–64; on male friendships, 3–7; resistance in, 138
Melzi, Gigliana, 62
Men Are from Mars and Women Are from Venus (Gray), 61
Men of a Certain Age (TV show), 138

Messner, Michael, 58
Miguel, Luis, 129
Miller, Stuart, 23, 29, 56
Mothers. *See* Parents and family
Mothers and Others (Hrdy), 76

National Institute of Mental Health,
  23–24
Neruda, Pablo, 129
Neuroscience, 23–24, 264; biological
  difference theory and, 46; on cul-
  ture and emotion, 28–29, 76–77; on
  human nature, 74
New, Carolyn, 59, 65
Nguyen, Jacqueline, 225
Noguera, Pedro, 50, 87
"No homo," 220, 235–236
Norway, social skills programs in,
  279
The Nurture Assumption (Harris),
  27–28

Oedipus Wrecks (Lombardi), 122
"Oh Boy: Masculinity in Twentieth-
  Century Literature" (Kagan), 51–52
Oransky, Matthew, 227

Packaging Boyhood (Brown), 63, 124
Parents and family, 27–28, 260;
  accommodation and, 272; attachment theory on, 57–58, 120; blending of friends', 146–147; Danny on,
  242–243, 245, 246–247, 248;
  disconnection and nuclear, 218;
  emotional skill and, 118–123,
  140–141; empathy and, 76; Fernando on, 230–231, 232–233, 236,
  239; George on, 162–163, 166,
  168–169, 174–175; Nick on, 145,
  154, 156; resistance and, 122–123
Pascoe, C. J., 50
Passionate language, 1–3, 8, 62, 117,
  198; desire for friendships and,
  20–21, 38; ethnicity and, 127, 132
Patriarchy, 24, 44–46, 66, 87, 144,
  276–277
Patrick, William, 277–278
Pickett, Kate, 9–10, 218
Pink Brain, Blue Brain (Eliot), 28, 46,
  76–77, 265
Pleck, Joseph, 58, 66, 87–88

Pollack, William, 7–8, 14, 44, 53, 87,
  171, 263
Potter, Harry, 138, 270
Price, Jamie, 124
Problem-solving skills, 97–99,
  163–164, 251–252
Psychological well-being, 2, 8–10;
  gender and, 55; resistance and,
  72–73; sharing and, 12–18
Puerto Ricans: "look" of masculinity
  of, 125–130; Nick and George,
  143–180
Putnam, Robert, 210

*Raising Cain: Protecting the Emo-
  tional Life of Boys* (Kindlon and
  Thompson), 5, 44, 52
Rappers, hypermasculinity and, 6, 61,
  63–64, 132–133
Rationality, 59, 74, 173, 178, 264
Ravitch, Sharon, 72
Raymond, Diane, 220
Real Boys (Pollack), 44, 171, 263
"Real Guy's Top Ten List" (Kimmel),
  61
Reichert, Michael, 72, 269–270
Research: on capacity for emotional
  satisfaction, 5–6; context and, 55,
  57–58; ecological theories in,
  41–43; on friendship in well-being,
  8–10; on friendships, 53–58; on
  human nature, 74–77; incentives in,
  81–82; interviewers for, 79–81;
  literatures, 42–43; of male friendships, 38–39; on male friendships,
  3–7; on masculinity, 58–67;
  methodologies in, 39, 55–57; qualitative, 56–57; recruitment and
  retention for, 78–79; on resistance,
  67–74; thick vs. thin culture explanations in, 24–33; Way's methodology for, 77–87
Resistance, 10, 269–270; by African
  Americans, 67–68, 70, 72,
  132–134; by Asian Americans,
  134–137; code switching and,
  105–106; context and, 139–140;
  developmental change and, 73;
  against ethnic stereotypes, 50–52;
  Fernando and, 235–236; interview
  analysis and, 86–87; literature on,

42, 45, 51–52; to masculinity
conventions, 105–106; Nick on,
149–151; parents and, 122–123;
psychological vs. political, 69–70;
by Puerto Ricans, 127–128; repetition of stereotypes and, 93,
112–116; research on, 67–74;
school social dynamics and,
123–140; social dynamics and,
123–125; stories of, 143–180;
well-being and, 72–73, 117; by
White boys, 137–139
Richards, David, 276–277
Rihanna, 275
Rogers, Onnie, 224–225
Role models, 26–27, 48, 260, 272
Roll, Jordan, Roll (Genovese), 67–68
Romantic language, 1–3, 8, 153,
191–194
Romantic relationships, 3
Rotundo, E. A., 31
Rubin, Kenneth, 4
Ruble, Diane, 59

Safety, 103, 104, 197
Sandstrom, Marlene, 279–280
Santos, Carlos, 72–73, 121–122,
122–123, 140–141, 272
Saval, Malina, 15, 50
Sax, Leonard, 46
Schieffelin, Bambi, 61
Schnayer, Ellie, 273–275
Schools and schooling: social dynam-
ics in, 118, 123–140; thick/thin
culture interpretations of, 47–49.
See also Academic achievement and
engagement
The Secret Lives of Boys (Saval), 15,
50
Secrets, 12–18, 93–100; betrayal and,
94, 99–100; with boys vs. girls,
108–112; Danny on, 243–244,
246–247, 258; Fernando on, 231;
George on, 167–168; regular vs.
deep, 98–99
Seidler, Victor, 209–210
Self-worth, 8, 14, 164–165
Sendak, Maurice, 198
Sharing of thoughts and feelings, 2,
12–18, 91–116, 280; with boys vs.
girls, 108–112; Danny on, 243–244,

246–247, 248, 257; desire for,
205–208; disconnection and, 210;
feeling known and, 169, 179–180;
Fernando on, 231; frequency of,
16–17; George on, 164–165,
167–168, 174; in groups, 95; indifference toward, 194–204; loss of
friendship and, 186–187; problem-
solving and, 97–99, 163–164;
well-being and, 12–18, 96–97.
See also Secrets
Sinha, Mrinal, 60
Slavery, resistance to, 67–68
Social connectedness: crisis in, 27,
262–281; decrease in, 210–220; as
human nature, 277–278; process of
losing, 160–161, 179; thick cultural
explanation of loss of, 216–227;
thin cultural explanation of loss of,
212–216. *See also* Disconnection
Socialization: emotional stoicism in, 5,
62; participation in, 10; resistance
to, 10, 67–74
Social power, 123–140, 139, 141–142
Social science perspective, 8–10,
216–217
Social status, 9–10, 118, 123–140
Socioeconomic background, 15, 34;
African Americans and, 133; auton-
omy/independence and, 64; disconnection and, 217, 218–219;
resistance and, 72; trust and, 151;
White boys and, 137–139
The Spirit Level (Wilkernson and
Pickett), 9–10, 218
Sports, 123–124, 144, 163
Springer, Kristen, 66
The State of Americans (Bronfenbrenner), 211
Stereotypes, 2, 263–264; boys' lived
experiences vs., 10–11, 117–118,
145–146; changing, 278–279;
confusion over facts vs., 224–225;
disconnection and, 224–227; of
emotional acuity, 16–17; of empathy, 28–29; ethnicity and, 6, 51–52;
exposing, 270–272; girls reinforcing, 272–276; health and, 50, 55,
65–67, 223, 280; hypermasculine,
6; intensification theories on,
44–45; "look" of masculinity and,

Stereotypes *(continued)*
   125–140; loss of friendships and,
   18–24, 183–208; naturalization of,
   19, 29, 73–74, 140, 261; neuroscience and, 23–24, 28–29, 46, 74,
   76–77, 264; Nick on, 149–151;
   oppressiveness of, 65–67; parents
   and, 122–123; perpetuation of, 117,
   142, 269–270, 272–278; resistance against, 10, 45, 67–74, 93,
   112–116, 172–173; social dynamics
   and, 123–125; superficial friendships as, 3–7; thick vs. thin culture
   views of, 25–33. *See also* Homophobia and homosexuality; Masculinity
Stevenson, Howard, 32, 133
Stoicism, emotional, 5, 6, 10; betrayal
   and, 204; Danny on, 247–258;
   disconnection and, 223; Fernando
   on, 237; indifference and, 194–204;
   loss and, 185; as masculinity, 36,
   44, 61–65, 86–87, 125, 223, 249;
   Nick and, 152; process of acquiring,
   160–161
Suicide, 8, 11, 18, 43
Sullivan, Harry Stack, 13–14, 33, 38,
   39, 53–54
Support, 103
Survey method research, 39

Talking. *See* Passionate language;
   Secrets; Sharing of thoughts and
   feelings
Thick/thin culture interpretations,
   24–33, 36, 42–43, 142; on biological differences, 44, 46–47; of
   democracy, 276–277; on ethnicity,
   50–51; of loss of friendships,
   212–227; on schools and schooling,
   47–49; of social distrust, 211–212
Thompson, Michael, 5, 15–16, 23, 44,
   52, 53, 56
Tolman, Deborah, 72
Toughness, 64–65, 146, 147–148
Trilling, Lionel, 47
The Trouble with Black Boys
   (Noguera), 50
The Trouble with Boys (Tyre),
   47–48

Trust, 92–93; anger and, 106–107; in
   boys vs. girls, 108–112; Danny on,
   244, 246–247, 248–249, 252; desire
   for, 191–194; disconnection and,
   265–268; disrespect and, 190; fear
   of hurt and, 159–160; Fernando on,
   230–242; George on, 165–166,
   167; loss of, 12, 18–24, 189–194;
   protection and, 115–116; secrets
   and, 93–100; societal loss of,
   210–220; socioeconomic status and,
   151; tests of, 99–100, 170–171. *See
   also* Betrayal; Vulnerability
Tyre, Peg, 47–48

University of Virginia, 8–9
Urban Dictionary, 220

Values, 167, 231
Violence. *See* Aggression and violence
Vulnerability, 12–18; betrayal and,
   101–102; with boys vs. girls,
   108–112; expression of, 71–72,
   92–93, 100–108; Fernando and,
   241–242; George on, 163–164;
   homophobia and, 29; loss and,
   186–194; masculine clichés and,
   147–148; parents and, 118–123;
   socialization and, 5

Waal, Frans de, 28–29, 74–75, 268
Webster, Daniel, 31
Well-being, 2, 8–10, 210; Danny on,
   243–244; disconnection and,
   266–268; gender stereotypes and,
   65–67; George on, 167–168, 174;
   loss and, 36; resistance and, 72–73,
   117; sharing and, 12–18, 96–97,
   167–168
White boys, 137–139, 226–227
Wilkernson, Richard, 9–10, 218
Wilkins, Amy C., 125–126
Williams, Walter, 32
Women's movement, backlash against,
   26, 221–223
The Wonder of Boys (Gurian), 46

Young Masculinities (Frosh), 67
YouTube, 270
Yueming Jia, 135–136